Marketing in the 21st Century and Beyond

MARKETING IN THE 21ST CENTURY AND BEYOND

Timeless Strategies for Success, Condensed Edition

Bruce D. Keillor, Editor

 PRAEGER

AN IMPRINT OF ABC-CLIO, LLC
Santa Barbara, California • Denver, Colorado • Oxford, England

Copyright 2013 by ABC-CLIO, LLC

Library of Congress Cataloging-in-Publication Data

Marketing in the 21st century and beyond : timeless strategies for success / [edited by] Bruce D. Keillor. — Condensed ed.
    p. cm.
Rev. ed. of: Marketing in the 21st century. c2007.
Includes bibliographical references and index.
ISBN 978–1–4408–2852–2 (hbk. : alk. paper) — ISBN 978–1–4408–2853–9 (ebook)
1. Marketing. I. Keillor, Bruce David. II. Marketing in the 21st century.
HF5415.M2194 2013
658.8—dc23   2012029549

ISBN: 978–1–4408–2852–2
EISBN: 978–1–4408–2853–9

17 16 15 14 13   1 2 3 4 5

This book is also available on the World Wide Web as an eBook.
Visit www.abc-clio.com for details.

Praeger
An Imprint of ABC-CLIO, LLC

ABC-CLIO, LLC
130 Cremona Drive, P.O. Box 1911
Santa Barbara, California 93116-1911

This book is printed on acid-free paper ∞

Manufactured in the United States of America

Dedicated to
Tobias Conor Jasper III
Scholar Extraordinaire

CONTENTS

INTRODUCTION

A few years ago we published the highly successful four-volume set *Marketing in the 21st Century*. Drawing on insights from both the academic and practitioner worlds, the set covered important issues related to global marketing, interactive and multichannel marketing, company and customer relations, and integrated marketing communications. Our goal was to provide a comprehensive reference resource for business decision makers and anyone who was a student of marketing. The market, and the marketing environment, has undergone significant changes since the publication of the original set but, as the saying goes, "the more things change, the more they stay the same." This new volume, *Marketing in the 21st Century and Beyond: Timeless Strategies for Success*, has taken, and updated, the key chapters from that original set—and also included some emerging topics such as social media marketing—to create a single source for marketing success as we move into the second decade of the 21st century.

Like the four-volume set, this edition is organized into four parts. The first—Company and Customer Relationship Marketing—begins by addressing the timeless question: "What does 'relationship marketing' really mean?" Exploring the different facets of how companies can effectively establish an ongoing relationship with its best customers, this chapter sets the stage for the entire book. In this first part we also delve into company-customer interaction in the form of sales force strategy, market feedback and innovation, and finally the fundamental challenges related to negotiating from the perspective of both the customer and the firm itself.

In the second part—Integrated Marketing: The Product-Customer Connection—this theme of relationship marketing is expanded. Using cutting-edge thinking from experts working in the field, we begin with the notion of identifying the firm's core competency and matching that competency with the value proposition targeted at the customer. This then segues into the topic of anticipating how the customer's view of that value proposition might change—and how businesses can proactively anticipate those changes. There is also a chapter on how newly emerging companies, and entrepreneurial individuals, can be successful in a dynamic marketplace. The part concludes with a straightforward, practical guide for using social media to create an effective long-term relationship with your target markets.

However, understanding the importance of relationship marketing, and establishing a connection between your firm, its products, and the customers in the marketplace is not enough. In the third part—Marketing Channels: The New Realities—the issue of creating and maintaining the channel to the customer is addressed. Built around an interactive, multichannel perspective, the three chapters address the various aspects of multichannel marketing, the unique challenges presented by business-to-business marketing, and also the ever-changing area of direct marketing.

The book concludes with the recognition that no matter the size of a company, the 21st-century marketplace is global in nature. In this part, titled Global Marketing: New Challenges and Opportunities, we start off by developing an understanding of what these new global-marketing realities really mean. There is a comprehensive discussion of one of the most difficult areas of international and global marketing—dealing with culture and cultural differences. Building on this we also consider how to create and maintain value-added strategies across different markets. The part then concludes—coming full circle from the first chapter dealing with relationship marketing—by looking closely at customer service in the global market.

Each of the chapters in this volume represents strategies that will help business succeed in the ever-changing 21st-century market environment. They also provide thought-provoking perspectives for students of marketing designed to help create a foundation for further study and research. It is my sincere belief that this book represents one of the best, most comprehensive sources of cutting-edge marketing thought. I trust you will find these chapters valuable in navigating your way through the realities of the 21st-century marketplace.

Bruce D. Keillor

Part I

COMPANY AND CUSTOMER RELATIONSHIP MARKETING

CHAPTER 1

What Does "Relationship Marketing" Really Mean?

Linda M. Orr

INTRODUCTION

We know that it costs, on average, anywhere from 6 to 10 times more to get a new customer than to keep an old customer. Yet most Fortune 500 companies lose 50 percent of their customers in five years. Furthermore, the average company communicates only four times per year with current customers and six times per year with prospects. That translates into the fact that customer loyalty is worth more than 10 times a single purchase. Some statistics even show that a 5 percent increase in customer retention can increase profits 25 to 125 percent! Selling in the 21st century is light-years different from what it was in the 20th century. Let's face it, in the 21st century selling is not about manipulation and it is not about each individual sale. Competition is too fierce, markets are saturated, and customers are too smart.

Great sales pitches, well-crafted marketing strategies, and creative advertising can be very persuasive, and they can even get people to buy your product. But to keep customers in the long run, you must treat them right and build a relationship with them. Even if you have a very expensive product that people buy only once in their lifetime, you will be rewarded through positive word of mouth if you treat your customers the right way. You have to make every moment not just about that individual sale, but about the long term.

To bring in new customers and to keep old ones, you have to realize that the externalizing of failures and internalizing of successes holds true for the customers as well. Remember the old adage: "Nobody likes to be sold, but everyone likes to buy." That means that if a customer has a problem or feels manipulated, it becomes your fault. If a customer makes a great choice or hunts down the perfect "bargain," they will give themselves the credit. Where does that leave you? It means you have to leave your ego at the door and realize it is not really all that simple. You have got to focus on keeping customers happy, and the only way to do that is by building and maintaining a relationship. You have to get past the 1950s pushy marketing in which the answer is to "persuade" new customers. You have to realize that you must go beyond the basic psychological processes and work to maintain a relationship. When relationships are formed, single failures and even successes can be overlooked. Customers really want convenience too, and they know just as well as you should that it is expensive to find new providers. In today's service-oriented economy, relationship building and excellent service are more than competitive weapons. They are survival skills.

WHAT IS RELATIONSHIP MARKETING?

Relationship marketing is a total strategy that involves all the marketing mix variables to create and keep loyal customers. Remember back to Marketing 101 and keep in mind the four Ps, which are the "elements" of a marketing strategy that a firm has at its disposal to utilize to reach the target customer. Product, place, price, and promotion: these are all key factors, even today in the 21st century—and it is all about strategy. You have got to have a clear strategy first and make this well defined in your mission statement. Without a clear, well-defined strategic direction that is translated to everyone (all stakeholders) and filtered down throughout every part of the organization, you have nothing.

Within your strategy you must figure out what your unique selling and value proposition is. What do you have to offer the consumer? How are you different? How will you stand out in the marketplace? Why is the consumer buying your product? To determine this, you will need to go back and revisit every element of the marketing mix and decide which direction to take, keeping in mind that whatever path you choose, you must be consistent and have all your elements integrated together to send one clear, dependable message. The importance of this consistency of strategy cannot be understated.

Think back to your strategy or marketing mix variables and your value proposition. A critical component of your value proposition must include how you plan to satisfy your customers, which will then create beneficial and long-lasting relationships. These relationships must become the heart of any business's strategy that is operating in the 21st century. We spend too much time and effort formulating our strategies and learning about our customers to not follow through and assess satisfaction and then work to maintain relationships. In the 21st century, strategies have to be a two-way street and have to include the long term. A focus on onetime transactions cannot succeed anymore. Remember, relationship marketing is a total strategy focused on creating and maintaining long-term, mutually beneficial relationships.

THE ORIGINS OF RELATIONSHIP MARKETING

Much of what we know about relationship marketing came from earlier research in sociology, psychology, and anthropology about dating, relationships, and marriage. After all, we are working to create bonds that will last forever; the only difference is that we want to create these bonds with multiple consumers. Relationship selling is like a marriage. To make it work, you must work at it. It is not easy, and at times the costs to you will outweigh the profits that you are receiving in turn. Much like in marriage, awareness, credibility, trust, and chemistry govern the relationship. The importance of each must be emphasized continuously. You must be prepared to deliver on every promise. If you do not deliver, you must be prepared for a fight or struggle. If you have enough negativity, be prepared for divorce.

The stages of the formation of a business relationship follow that of the dating/marital relationship. It is important to think about how much time and effort must go into each stage, which, just like in dating relationships, will determine the value of the relationship and the potential for that relationship to continue. Initially, young single people must search for mates. In selling, this stage is called prospecting. Prospecting is hard work and nobody likes it. You have to get shot down numerous times to hear just one yes. People do not want to give out their phone number. You have no trust, no awareness, and no credibility at this stage. It is really hard work.

Then you get a phone number, and in social relationships, you begin the process of dating. In selling, you begin to establish rapport. No matter which situation you are referring to, the same thing is happening: you are searching for some mutual attraction and chemistry. Does this person have something to offer that I want? Then, as the sales process continues, astute salespeople will probe for needs. In social relationships, this is when the courtship begins. In a selling situation, salespeople who have listened to needs can then appropriately respond to those needs. They can present a product or service that most likely fulfills all the customer's needs and provides a satisfying solution. In social situations, this is when a couple begins to fall in love, if and only if appropriate needs are met.

Next, if all has gone well, is either the closing of the sale or wedding bells. As we know from both sales knowledge and relationship knowledge, this step in no way ensures commitment. Buying a product (or entering a marriage) requires some degree of a leap of faith. Just as you never truly know a person until you actually live with that person and begin to build a life with him or her, you do not know if you will be satisfied with a product until you actually use it. Will the quality hold up?

If not, will the company be there to fix it? Will they honor all warranties? This part of the process, the after the sale/commitment, is when trust is truly built. So many marketers (and daters for that matter) assume that trust has been created because the sale was made, when in actuality the most critical component of the relationship—trust—does not form until the after-the-fact use of the product and the follow-up. Customer satisfaction can come from a onetime successful sale. Customer loyalty, which is the Holy Grail to all marketers, can come only from repeated transactions and the formation of a relationship.

So, are your customers satisfied or loyal? A satisfied customer is a buyer who has a good purchasing experience with a particular supplier, but plans to buy from whichever vendor offers the best opportunity in the future. Meanwhile, a loyal customer is a buyer who has selected a particular supplier over time and intends to buy from that same supplier in the future. Customer loyalty is the ultimate goal of relationship marketing. It takes a solid, consistent, well-thought strategy directed at satisfying customer needs to achieve this over a long period of time.

HOW RELATIONSHIP SELLING IS DIFFERENT

Traditional 20th-century transaction selling was synonymous with terms like the "hard sell," "my way or the highway selling," or "manipulative selling." Many mind-sets existed about selling in the 20th century. Selling was thought to be a contest. Selling was persuasive. Customers must be talked into buying certain products; they must be sold. Great salespeople are great manipulators. Buyers and sellers alike might be lying. There was even a key acronym in older selling textbooks, as late as the late 1990s: ABC. ABC stood for "Always be closing," because, of course, the close is everything. Who cares about the future? You got your sale, right?

The 20th-century sales process many times included a canned presentation, which was very much one-sided. In this presentation, the salesperson did all the talking and barely let the customer get a word in. If they cannot talk, they cannot say no, right? The salesperson was focused on persuading and overcoming objections. It always goes back to convincing the customer that they are wrong and you are right. Salespeople were seen as an annoyance at a minimum and even something to fear at the maximum level. They could not be trusted. Salespeople out on the road were considered very lonely people, and they probably were.

Contrast all of this to relationship selling. Even the terminology is different. We use terms like "collaborative selling," "partnering," "nonmanipulative selling," "consultative selling," "problem-solving selling," and the "soft sell." Relationship selling in the 21st century has a completely different mind-set.

Selling is thought of as a service in which salespeople help customers find solutions to problems. Customers love to buy because they have needs and want to find solutions to satisfy those needs. In relationship selling, buyers want to trust the salesperson. They know that this trust will be mutually beneficial because there will be reduced search costs on both sides of the equation. In relationship selling, customer service comes first. Great sellers truly care. And most importantly, it is not a onetime event; it works—again and again and again.

The 21st-century relationship selling process is completely different from the 20th-century process. The sales process is a two-sided, flexible interaction. In fact, many great salespeople realize that it is better to let the customers do most of the talking. The salesperson takes on the role of a person probing for needs by asking questions. It is talking *with* the customer and not talking *to* the customer. Salespeople in the 21st century seek to be helpers who can resolve concerns. They are not feared. They are thought of as partners and sometimes even friends. These are the keys to relationship selling in the 21st century. It is a very different process, strategy, and mind-set.

RELATIONSHIP MARKETING AND CUSTOMER SERVICE = SATISFACTION AND LOYALTY

As the research shows, building relationships is almost always more successful and profitable than creating onetime transactions. Over the long run, nothing is more cost-effective than establishing a base of satisfied customers. In some industries, over 80 percent of all future sales come from the existing customer base. This is done through the provision of exceptional service, especially after the sale has been made. Customers make initial purchases because of the *promise* of great service. Repeat sales are made because of *provision* of great service. Firms that can achieve a very lofty goal and be rated *high* by customers in their *provision* of customer service grow twice as fast as companies rated poorly and charge an average of 9 percent more than those companies. Imagine that—treat customers well, let the word get out there, and you can charge more. That increase in profits is in addition to the added revenues and decreased expenditures created by having loyal customers.

Thus even though we have discussed service, satisfaction, and loyalty, it is equally important to understand customer dissatisfaction. Unfortunately, only 1 customer in 27 will volunteer his or her feelings to the seller when dissatisfied; others just buy elsewhere next time. Therefore it is critical to provide proper service and follow-up to continually gauge and track customer experiences. When customers are dissatisfied, managers often wonder whether or not they should placate those complaining customers. There is an often asked question: what can a firm afford to spend to convert a complaining customer into a satisfied customer?

Remember the figure just mentioned: most sales (perhaps 80%) come from prior customers. In the business-to-business sector, the average cost of securing an order from a *new* prospect is $1,673. Meanwhile, the average cost of securing an order from an *existing* industrial account is only $717. That is a difference of $956. Additionally, existing firms are more likely than new firms to place large orders and orders with higher margins. Thus relationship marketing equals satisfaction, loyalty, and increased profits.

THE UTMOST IMPORTANCE OF TRUST

The first research into relationship marketing evolved from the marriage literature. Thus courtship and dating are always good examples to use when describing the characteristics of relationships and why they are so important. We enter into relationships, personal or business, to minimize effort and risk. Just as it becomes tiresome and burdensome to continually find new people to date, it is extremely expensive for new businesses to constantly gain new customers. Plus, as a consumer enters into a relationship with a business, the business gains because they better understand the customer's needs and they know how to better serve that customer. Likewise, the customer gains because they do not have to continually seek alternative suppliers. Just think about when you move to a new city. It is stressful just to figure out which local grocery stores you like best and where you will find the right doctor. Thus, hopefully, the act of forming a relationship creates a win-win situation. This is of course until one or both parties of the relationship begin to feel that the relationship is no longer fulfilling their needs and they could then probably be better served elsewhere.

On that note, would you have an interpersonal relationship with someone you do not trust? Why or why not? Usually the answer depends on what you have to gain and what you have to lose. What are the risks and what are the rewards? Of course, as with all relationships in life and in business, there are risks and rewards. Maybe you have a relationship with someone you do not like but he or she is family. Maintaining civil harmony within your family becomes a greater reward than the risk of whatever it is about the family member that annoys you. In business, the greatest risk is financial, but there are also many other types of risk, such as time and ego risks. But from the customer's perspective, with greater and greater saturation of markets, why would you ever do business with someone you did not trust? And more importantly, once trust is broken, would you ever continue to conduct business with that person or company? What if you just heard from a *trusted* friend or colleague that an establishment or salesperson is untrustworthy? The answers to these questions are fairly obvious to most of us. Unless that business has something that we really want or need, that we cannot get anywhere else, the lesson is very simple—no trust, no sale.

REPUTATION IS EVERYTHING: GUARD IT WITH YOUR LIFE

Reputation is all about consistency. Honest people should work for honest companies and vice versa (honest companies should hire honest people). Trust can be viewed from the perspective of the salesperson and how salespeople can be perceived to be more honest. However, in the 21st century it is just as important to trust the company as it is to trust the salesperson. Once again, would you do business with someone you do not trust? NO! Thus the basic elements of public relations, reputation management, and corporate identity are critical in the 21st century.

This means it is crucial for businesses to manage and guard their reputations and to be seen as trustworthy. In the 21st century, if you do not have a good, healthy corporate image, your firm is at a serious competitive disadvantage. At the end of the day, unless you have a trustworthy sales force and a solid corporate image, you have got nothing.

KNOWING AND UNDERSTANDING THE COMPETITOR

In light of the extreme importance of strategy, it would be utterly foolish to examine any strategy, even a sales strategy, without giving careful consideration to the competition. Nobody operates in a vacuum. We are constantly dealing with competition from every angle. And even with the most trustworthy sales force and the best corporate image, competition can come in and disrupt the equation and cause the best planned strategies to fail. This raises an important and often forgotten point. When you are a salesperson, who is your competition? Is it the competing businesses? Is it their products and/or services? As an individual out in the field, it is much more basic than that. Your primary competition at this level is the other salespeople. The business environment of the 21st century is one of hypercompetition (extreme competition), created from fragmented and saturated markets, more knowledgeable consumers, greater technology, and more globalization, just to name a few. So, when you are out in the trenches, what distinguishes you from the competition? What sets you apart? Well, the easiest answer is you!

It is up to each and every individual salesperson to build an ongoing, solid, lasting relationship with each customer. When that loyalty is built, then you have a differential advantage. It is also up to each salesperson to learn and understand how the other salespeople in the industry behave and build relationships. No matter how great the technology and innovation of the 21st century is, we are all still just people selling products and services to other people. And given the increased changes, this concept becomes even more important than ever. We are right back to the basic principle of relationship marketing, which is once again why it is so incredibly important to focus our "selling" and "sales management" activities on relationships.

KEYS TO SUCCESS FROM THE INSIDE OUT: BUILDING A SUCCESSFUL SALES FORCE IN THE 21st CENTURY

According to the president of a shoe company, two shoe salespeople were sent to a poverty-stricken country. The first wrote the president and said, "Returning home immediately. No one wears shoes here." The second, more optimistic salesperson approached the situation in a very different way. She described the situation to management as "unlimited possibilities. Millions of people here are still without shoes."

This story illustrates that one of the most important jobs sales managers perform is the personnel function. The work of sales managers in personnel activities starts with finding and hiring individuals for sales slots in the organization—people who are both interested in sales jobs and qualified to fill them. An organization cannot survive without a good, competent, energetic, and creative sales force.

As a business owner, the utmost important thing is to always have a clear strategy. This must come first. Thus just as in all other areas of managing a 21st-century sales force, your guiding principles and choices of action must be rooted in a carefully planned and deeply rooted strategic mission and vision statement. From this statement, more specific, tangible objectives can be established. These goals and procedures not only must have strategy as their guiding principles, but must also emerge from a set of ethical standards. Does this line of thought seem repetitive at this point? Good! A well-developed strategic direction that is founded on a solid ethical foundation is the single most important step.

Once these tasks are accomplished, then sales managers can begin the tasks of hiring, training, motivating, and keeping employees who take special care of the customer. Profitability stems from customer satisfaction, and customer satisfaction and loyalty are deeply rooted in employee satisfaction and loyalty. Just as many businesses have learned this lesson the hard way, so did T.G.I. Friday's. After years of very dismal store results, T.G.I. Friday's started focusing on internal operations such as the cleanliness of the store and the happiness and the attitude of the servers. When they did this, sales doubled in six months.[1]

Few businesses want to look inward to find fault for problems. It is always easier to blame something external. We have almost an instinctual response left over from the 20th century to try to dig out of sales slumps by increasing advertising spending. Pumping thousands of dollars into promotion is not going to solve problems that form the very backbone of relationship marketing. Who do customers actually have a relationship with? It is the business, but more specifically, they remember the waitress who actually waited on them or in the case of sales, the salesperson who took care of them. These issues are not human resources problems and they cannot be left to HR departments to solve. Instead, they must become central to any marketing and sales campaign and must be integrated into the total efforts. Finding and keeping the best sales talent is a key competitive weapon of the 21st century.

SALES EFFECTIVENESS, MONEY, AND THE BOTTOM LINE

What is the end result of all this fluffy relationship stuff? Hopefully, it is money, of course! A reoccurring theme of the 21st century is hypercompetition. Competition is more than just potential competition for your customers; it also includes competition for your employees. Relationship marketing is just as much about the relationships with your employees as it is about the relationships with your customers. Customer satisfaction and loyalty come from employee satisfaction and loyalty. So how do you get satisfied, loyal employees? Studies have shown that more than 80 percent of all behavior is determined by the reward system. As a consequence, 80 percent of behavior is within your control as a manager. You must pay employees correctly and you must use a proper balance of the other types of motivational tools.

Then, it is just as critical that you enact the proper mix of measurement tools, for both the sales force and the organization. You cannot know what to fix if you do not know what is broken. As this chapter describes, many performance indicators must be collected. Simply looking at financial indicators is not sufficient. After all, money is a lagging indicator, meaning that once you are looking at an income statement, the mistake (or accomplishment) has already happened in the past. Customers must be enticed to buy first, must be satisfied, must have time to tell their friends and/or coworkers, and must have time to possibly rebuy or look elsewhere before the outcomes of their behaviors will show up on an income statement. Thus it is critical to take a multifaceted approach to evaluating effectiveness.

LEARNING FROM YOUR CUSTOMERS TO INCREASE INNOVATION

Once we have taken care of some basic strategic decisions, built a great company from the inside out through the development of a great sales force, and paid very careful attention to the competition, we have to remember the most important component of the relationship. Who are we trying to build a relationship with? It is the customer of course! Customer relationship management (CRM) has become a very popular term of this century. The term CRM is frequently used to refer to software packages that have become commonplace in the 21st century for managing and handling consumer data. However, CRM goes beyond software applications. The term encompasses a total strategic approach to managing customer relationships. Specifically, CRM is the processes that identify customers, create knowledge about those customers, build customer relationships, and shape customers' perceptions of a firm and its products and/or services. One of the most important parts of the CRM process is the knowledge-building component. What do your customers want and how do you modify your product based on that? How do you get them to talk to you so that you can find out what they want? How do you interpret what they say? Understanding innovation and adaptability, and more importantly how to be innovative, is a necessity in an age of such turbulence.

KEY ACCOUNT MANAGEMENT IN THE 21st CENTURY

CRM of the 21st century also involves a very strategic handling and managing of accounts. Since partnerships are hopefully long term, you need and will have tons of data about customers. These data need to be stored and utilized to make key decisions. Then, salespeople need to use this information to determine which accounts to serve and what levels of service to provide each account. Some accounts just want a phone call every now and then. Others need personal visits every week. Key account management in the 21st century requires careful consideration of these questions. Key account management is simply about learning who the most profitable customers are. The 80/20 rule, that 80 percent of your sales come from 20 percent of your customers, holds true. Thus sales managers and salespeople need to make key decisions to determine who those 20 percent are. But it goes much further than that. What do you do with the other 80 percent? They need careful consideration and classification as well. What if you could take some of that 80 percent and "move them up" or get them to purchase more?

There is also the issue of the key account management equation. How do you organize your sales force around these accounts as well as all other accounts? Territory management of the 21st century has become harder than ever before. On one hand, as a sales manager you want to utilize whatever system is most efficient and effective and allows the customers to have the best possible service available. On the other hand, you want to be fair to your salespeople. Sometimes sales representatives perform poorly not because of their own skills and abilities, but instead because they are simply in a bad territory. It can and does happen frequently. If your compensation and motivation systems are based on this, you have problems. Therefore just as relationship marketing has caused us to take a more careful and strategic approach to account management, sales managers must also take a more careful and strategic approach to sales force and territory management.

Sales managers want to get the most bang for their buck no matter how they make decisions. They want value. Value refers to the perception that the rewards exceed the costs associated with continuing the business relationship—on all sides of the equation. For the seller, investments in building the business relationship may be considerable, but a highly committed buyer may be the seller's most important asset. The seller can leverage skills and resources, build strong competitive positions, and enjoy the benefits of a long-term relationship without continuing to experience customer search costs. Buyers also enjoy the benefit of long-term business relationships. They can avoid costs associated with extensive product search procedures, receive favored treatment from suppliers, and often achieve a reduction in total costs, even if the price is the same as (or even higher) than that charged by others.

The value and efficiency, which both the buyer and the seller want, make the tedious process of customer relationship management, key account management, and territory management worth it in the long run. However, these are processes that require a great deal of skill and effort. The sales manager and salespeople of the 21st century must understand these principles.

GETTING RID OF THOSE THAT ARE NOT PROFITABLE

In the 21st century, many companies are operating on even tighter margins and managers are forced to be more accountable. Thus, just as the tried-and-true approaches of the past are still necessary, 21st-century sales managers must learn when to get rid of customers just like they must know when to get rid of certain employees. Keep in mind the definition of relationship marketing, which was mentioned earlier in this chapter. Relationship marketing is a total strategy focused on creating and maintaining long-term, *mutually* beneficial relationships. As we just saw in the key account management discussion above, through our efforts we will find that some accounts are not as profitable as others.

A recent analysis of customers of a major bank in Australia revealed that 12 percent of its customers contributed to the majority of the profits, 60 percent were at a break-even level, and the remaining 28 percent cost the bank money. Other studies from the largest banks in the United States found that only 6 percent of the customers were the most profitable. On average, they produced $1,600 in revenue and cost $350 to serve. Compared to this, 14 percent of customers contributed to loss and produced only $230 in revenue while costing $700 to serve. The percentage of profitable customers varied from a mere 7 percent of the customers for a software company to 16 percent for a media company.

We all know it is true to some degree, but the actual statistics presented can be somewhat daunting. These numbers may make sales managers want to consider whether or not they have been segmenting their accounts correctly. Key account management also needs to incorporate other variables into the equation, which adds the costs associated with serving each customer. If you are making a lot from a customer but calling on them every day and refunding their purchasing constantly, they still may not be profitable. Now the tricky part: what do you do with unprofitable customers? Depending upon the situation there may be a number of strategies and alternatives to take care of these accounts. In the 21st century, managers must consider these crucial elements along with their customer relationship management and key account management decisions. Margins are simply too tight in this century.

UTILIZING INTEGRATED MARKETING COMMUNICATIONS IN SMALL BUSINESSES

Because the 21st century is all about customer relationship management, it is also necessary to discuss some of the special types of businesses and customers and their respective needs. Small businesses have always existed. In fact, the origins of all businesses were in small businesses. However, the 21st century has brought with it changes that have transformed and will continue to transform the role small businesses play in our economy. In some ways, it is easier than ever to thrive and succeed with a small business. In others, it is harder and harder to succeed when faced with competition from major corporations and their megabrands. So, what are the alternatives for selling in small businesses in the 21st century?

As with so many other things that we have seen, it all comes back to strategy. Many feel that the 21st century will see a continued dominance of "pull" strategies instead of "push" strategies—meaning, instead of companies pushing the product to the consumer with mass advertising and a heavy sales force presence, consumers will pull the product through the channel. They will do so because they are so educated these days. With blogs and all other forms of technology and word of mouth, customers can find out information about products and services as soon as, if not before, they hit the market. Thus strategies for the 21st century have and will continue to change.

Luckily, the 21st century has brought amazing advancements in technology, which can help the small-business owner succeed. These are all basically "tools" that sales managers can add to their "tool box" and utilize to communicate with the customer. The author of chapter 10 discusses direct marketing, database marketing, e-mail marketing, using websites, and utilizing search engine technology. For the small-business owner with a considerably smaller sales force, many members of which are performing multiple functions, these technological tools make the small-business owner an equal competitor in this century. It all comes back to strategy, because even with the use of these tools, they all must be integrated back into the company's strategy to send one consistent and unified message to the customer about the company's products and services. If the messages say the same thing, it really does not matter what the "channel" or "medium" is. As long as the customer receives correct, timely, and relevant information, the technological breakthroughs of this century help the small-business owner succeed right alongside large companies.

UNDERSTANDING DIVERSE ORGANIZATIONAL BUYERS

Once again, with customer relationship management and key account management being two crucial elements of a relationship marketing strategy, it is vitally important to understand a firm's largest accounts. Usually, just due to sheer purchasing power, the largest accounts are the industrial and other business-to-business accounts. These customers have many distinct differences from ultimate consumers in the marketplace. Many of these differences are the same as they have always been throughout the 20th century. However, some of these aspects are so important that they deserve repeating. On the other hand, just like everything else, the dramatic changes of the 21st century have brought dramatic changes in organizational selling characteristics and processes.

Some of the biggest changes that have occurred in the 21st century, with regard to business-to-business purchasing, deal with the purchasing and buying center functions of the organization. Many of these changes were brought about by the same forces that are requiring changes in all organizations—increased accountability and lower operating margins. There is not as much room for trial and error in this century. Salespeople calling on business-to-business and industrial accounts need to recognize these changes and deal with them effectively. Although the changes mentioned in this chapter are unique to business-to-business and industrial selling, the solutions are the same. To succeed in this century we need to have a greater emphasis on relationship marketing.

THE ETHICS OF MANAGING CUSTOMER INFORMATION

Finally, all of our customer relationship management efforts have brought with them one tremendous opportunity and challenge: What do we do with all this information? What are the ethical issues involved? What about consumer privacy—does it matter? First and foremost, salespeople have to reach the customer. All the information that exists has, quite frankly, produced "information overload." Therefore from a sales perspective, it has become harder and harder to reach customers. So, the first question managers must answer is how to reach customers through the clutter of information. Then, if you do reach the customers, you then have a whole new set of issues around managing their information.

Moreover, it can be a benefit to your company if you manage this information correctly. Just as companies that mishandle consumer data can end up in a public relations nightmare, companies that learn to properly use and respect consumer information gain an added advantage of enhancing their reputation.

CONCLUSION

The only way to survive in the 21st century is by building relationships. Relationship marketing seems like a term caught between a cliché and common sense. However, no matter how clichéd and like common sense it may seem, it is a complex set of processes that must be utilized to cope with the rapid changes of this century. By accepting the strategies and tactics of relationship marketing, companies can forge stronger bonds with their customers to build relationships and create better success and hopefully, ultimately, greater profitability.

NOTE

1. Michael LeBoeuf, *How to Win Customers and Keep Them for Life* (New York: Berkley, 2000).

CHAPTER 2

BUILDING A SUCCESSFUL SALES FORCE IN THE 21ST CENTURY

Daniel J. Leslie

INTRODUCTION

Greater attention to recruiting, hiring, training, developing, evaluating, and motivating great salespeople can increase a company's profitability. However, creating a successful sales force in the 21st century is becoming more difficult in light of the many challenges that are present today. More competition, more sophisticated customers armed with more information, issues regarding technology, communication issues, meetings, and many other distractions are but a few of the challenges. In this chapter, I will talk about what I believe to be the core building blocks of building a successful sales force and building a successful organization no matter what your endeavor, and I will help guide you to answer the following questions:

- What is your purpose for being in business?
- What are the values that guide your decision-making progress?
- How do you develop these values?
- What vision have you created to share with your people to get them excited?
- How are you using your vision to attract good people and what selection process do you have in place?
- What are you doing to develop your people and to help them achieve their personal goals as well as your company's goals?
- What program do you have in place to begin to develop leadership within your organization and to develop your second-line management?

This chapter is meant to provide awareness of the things that will help you to make a good sales force even better. Or if you are starting from scratch, this chapter can provide a road map and an outline for success from a 30,000-foot point of view. The details and the work involved will be up to you to explore further. Obviously, all of the aspects of building a successful sales force cannot be covered in one chapter. For example, many important human resource management issues are not included. Most notably, the legal aspects of human resources are not discussed. Just as everything else is rapidly changing in the 21st century, so are the laws and the legal ramifications for breaking those laws. As a sales manager or business owner, you must either have a legal department to advise you on such matters or pursue additional training in business law. As you read this chapter, one of the most important things you can do is to create an action plan. Think of the outline for this chapter as your action plan for the next 12 months. Get out your calendar and plug in when you and your leadership team will tackle these issues. At the end of 12 months, you will be amazed at how far you have come!

IDENTIFYING VALUES

In order for a sales organization to be successful, they must firmly believe in a core set of values. Values are those things that are constant, that never change. They provide us direction in times of uncertainty. They are the foundation of any great organization. These values guide us when things are difficult and decisions are not clear. The values of your organization will help you to manage and select good people. They will help you create successful policies and procedures.

In order to determine an organization's values, I recommend taking time away from the office and out of the field. Bring your leadership team together and have a discussion about values. Determine as a group the values that really dictate the direction of the organization. What are the things that are important to the individuals and ultimately to the organization? Agree on three to four values to introduce to your business and your personal lives. Here are the values of our sales organization at Northwestern Mutual Financial Network: professionalism, integrity, and excellence. They are the values that guide our organization and they will continue to guide me as a person. What are your values? How will you lead your organization into the future?

- Professionalism: doing the very best for your client and recommending to your client what you would want recommended if you were in your client's situation. Professionalism means attaining the highest level of competency in your field.

- Integrity: My simple definition of integrity is doing what you say you will do and following through.

- Excellence: Excellence simply means if it is worth doing, it is worth doing the very best that you possibly can and directing all of your energy and resources to accomplish the goal or the task.

Recently, in an effort to merge two of our existing offices, we began to have discussions about our shared values. Our leadership teams met to discuss what values we have in common and what they really mean to us. Out of the discussion came some definitions of values.

One person said values are "those things that guide you when others aren't looking." Someone else said values are "those things that help keep you accountable to what you know are right." Another person said values are "your beliefs put into action." Others said that values really equate to leadership.

I like to think of values as a compass that will guide any person or any organization through difficult times when a decision is not always clear. Would you go sailing out on the ocean without a compass or other forms of instrumentation? Of course not. Why? The potential consequence would be too great. What about your business? What are the consequences for not having clearly defined values and sticking to them?

Think about your current sales force in your business. What happens when a salesperson does not do what he or she says he or she will do? What are the consequences? What happens if all of your salespeople accomplish a goal except for one person? And what if that salesperson is someone whom you have a great relationship with and someone with whom you have forged a friendship outside of business? What do you do? Does that salesperson come along for the reward just because he or she is a nice person or because he or she has been with the company for a long time? Do your values permit that? If they do, what will that do to the rest of the group the next time you have a goal? Once you have established your core values, there must be consequences. You are doing no one any favors by allowing them to fail. A great manager of people has to make tough decisions like this because if you do not, you are actually holding your people back. I believe that holding people accountable will eventually do one of two things. Either it will help your salespeople to be the best at their profession. Or, it will help to coach them get out of the business so that they can find out what they are good at doing. Everyone has something that they will excel in naturally and some do not naturally excel in sales. I have heard it said that only 20 percent of the entire population has the capacity for sales. What kind of impact will it have on your culture to have people on your sales staff who will do anything to make a sale, even if it is unethical? What about borderline unethical? This is where values come in. What are your values? Below are some others that our leadership team came up with that day.

Integrity	Intensity
Growth	Honesty

Family	Consistency
Fun	Passion
Self-understanding	Desire
Loyalty	Courage
Tenacity	Abundance
Follow-through	Accepting change

Your values will directly impact your culture. Do you have a culture of mentoring? Do you have a culture in which your veteran salespeople help your newer salespeople, or is it a culture of hoarding ideas and not sharing? Do you have a culture of people showing up to training sessions, on time and eager to learn and to grow? Do you have a culture of being professional and doing what is right for the customer? If you do, defining your values will protect that culture. If not and you desire to improve your culture, defining your values will be the first start to turning your culture around.

Now that you have your values clearly defined, communicate and promote them to your organization as regularly as possible. Promote your firm's values by including them in your bulletins; display them in your training rooms. When appropriate, you should also have discussions about how recent actions or decisions were consistent or inconsistent with the organizations values. Having your values clearly defined will help you manage your salespeople to reach a higher standard. Being consistent with your message and actions will help you create a culture of success.

DEFINING YOUR MISSION

Once you determine your values, it is important to create a mission statement. Many times I hear people downplay the importance of the mission statement. A mission statement answers why we exist and what our purpose is. It defines what your organization or your business brings to the marketplace and your clients. It should communicate what value your business brings to your clients and how you accomplish your mission. These are the three main points to a good mission statement. It should be relatively short and simple and should provide a clear road map for making decisions in good times and bad. My personal mission statement as a financial advisor is as follows:

My mission as a financial advisor with the Northwestern Mutual Financial network is to help quality individuals, families, and businesses maximize their true financial potential and gain confidence through the realization of their goals, objectives, and dreams. To achieve this, I will assist them in overcoming procrastination by simplifying the ever-changing and complex world of business and personal finance. I am committed to recommending solutions to my clients that I would want recommended to me. My goal is to establish strong, long-lasting relationships of trust that are mutually beneficial. I ultimately believe the greatest gift you can provide to your family is to plan ahead and be prepared.

This is my professional mission statement. This is what guides me on a daily basis. It reminds me of why I am in business. What is your personal mission statement? Why do you exist as a professional? As a salesperson, what value do you bring? What sets you apart from other professionals in your industry? Why are you in business? I firmly believe that it is also important to touch upon this point: I believe that anyone in a for-profit business needs to be in business first and foremost to make money. As I talk to classes at our local universities, I find that a lot of young people are sometimes confused by this. If you are profitable, you will be able to achieve your mission. You cannot accomplish your mission as a sales organization if you are not profitable and if you are not able to be financially solvent. Some may disagree with that, but I feel those people put the cart before the horse. As a business, you must be profitable, and by being profitable you will accomplish the mission of your organization or business.

DEVELOPING A COMPELLING VISION

Once a company's values are determined and the mission statement has been laid out, the next step is the creation of a vision statement. If a mission statement expresses an idea of where your company is and what it stands for, a vision statement provides clarity for the future. Without a vision statement, how does a company know where it is headed, and in turn, how do your people know what they are striving to achieve? Good leaders are always providing a vision. A vision statement is a written, detailed account of where that business will be in 5 or 10 years. In our organization, we work on a 5-year time frame. We believe that you have real control only over what happens in the next five years. The important thing about a vision statement is that it provides inspiration and motivation to the people who are involved. Another important thing to remember is that your vision statement may or may not come true. Circumstances in the future might dictate that the vision that is clearly laid out today, 2, or 3 years from now might be different based on circumstances outside of your company's control. Your vision statement still provides a target.

Many companies consistently provide good service to their clients and have strong sales, but over time fail to grow and fail to keep up with the competition. This is sometimes true because they do not have a clear vision of the future. To be a great manager, you need to help your salespeople have a clear vision for their future.

As I suggested when you are deciding upon your organization's values, the best way to complete a vision statement for your sales organization and each individual salesperson is to have a retreat outside of the office. Take time out from working

If the applicant's resume indicates that he or she is a loner, a recruiter may consider that possibility worthy of further investigation.

There are also many computer-based analytical tools to help companies select the right people for the right positions. One example of these is the Harrison Assessment. The candidate is asked to answer numerous questions to help identify personality traits as well as the candidate's strengths and weakness pertaining to a specific employment opportunity. An important benefit of these tools is the ability to identify potential challenges that the candidate might have. By knowing these challenges ahead of time, you can decide if you will be able to train this person to overcome those challenges. On the other hand, by using these tools and identifying the challenges, you will again have a better idea if this candidate fits the job description. This will not only save the company a lot of time and money by not hiring the wrong person, but you also save the candidate from coming into a culture where he or she probably will not fit due to personality or lack of skills to do the job.

Related to this point is the matter of testing. Certainly, no personality test or other test proves that a person will or will not be a good salesperson, and this fact concerns job applicants who feel that they have been denied a position on the basis of a pencil-and-paper quiz. Sales managers are willing to admit that no test is right in every case. However, many sales organizations continue to use tests as one form of input in the selection process because the test results have shown some validity over a long period of time. Thus, although tests are not right all the time, they may serve to improve the odds of making a correct choice.

Finally, you must determine where your best candidates come from. Where are you maximizing your recruiting efforts? Career changers? Clubs or professional associations? Career fairs? The Internet? College campuses? How about within your own organization? The best selection tool you have could be the people in your office right now. Do you have a culture in which your people refer other good people to your company on a consistent basis? Communicate to your existing employees the type of people you are looking for to join the group. Have your director of recruitment meet with the salespeople on a regular basis to help people brainstorm. You may even want to put in place some incentives for referring a qualified person who ultimately gets hired. The other sources of recruitment are good, but nothing beats a referral.

Creating a successful internship program is also a great way to identify and select the right people. An internship gives you an early opportunity to identify good people with career potential. You can then mold them into successful salespeople. The second reason to have an internship is to make an impact on young people and encourage them to become a fan and an advocate of your organization for the rest of their life. I have heard some people say that they went to college to avoid being a salesperson. I find that ridiculous because almost every job involves some form of sales. I make it a point to speak to students at nearby universities to share with them the terrific opportunities in sales. What many young people want is exactly what a career in sales can give them. You can communicate that to them through giving back to the community and speaking to classes and helping young people see the positive impact they can have on their lives and the lives of others.

Another benefit to students participating in an internship is the opportunity to explore a career in sales while they are still in school and in a safe environment. Whether they stay with your company or not, this experience will give them a huge head start, and if they do pursue a career in sales, your organization will most likely be the choice they make.

An internship is also a great way to develop your people early on. It allows young people through trial and error to learn the business prior to them making a large financial or personal commitment. They are able to learn without much risk and we all know that we learn best from our failures. Done correctly, interns will never forget the experience they had while working with your company, and whether they make a career with you or not, they will always be an ally.

TRAINING AND DEVELOPMENT

Now that you have chosen the right people, it is important to have a system in place to develop your sales force, both from the beginning and in an ongoing way. This is important for different reasons. First, people with a lot of potential want to work in a predictable environment. They want to know that there are consistent ways for them to grow with a support system in place to help them accomplish their goals. People who strive to be successful want to work in an environment where they are challenged. This will help you with your retention. In addition to this, as a manager you want to be assured that there are proven, time-tested ways for your salespeople to advance. Remember, to the extent that you are able to meet the needs of your clients (your salespeople) your needs will be met.

I believe there are three main pillars of development. The first pillar is your formal training curriculum. This is the pertinent information for a new person joining your organization. What information is critical for a new person in your business to know immediately to help him or her have a profitable fast start? I recommend that you break this training up throughout a two- to three-week period. For example, during the first week you might decide to have your new recruits in a classroom setting for the first three days and then out in the field with a mentor for the next two. You may want to continue a schedule like this for the next two weeks. In addition to initial training, what kind of follow-up training is there? Provide at least one or two opportunities a week for your salespeople to learn and to grow in terms of their product development, their people skills, and personally. In our office, we do this on both a group and an individual basis. We will discuss this more in the Coaching section.

While companies vary in terms of length, location, and even method of the initial formal training, it is imperative that this is done correctly and thoroughly. You may find that formal classroom instruction that is onsite works better than watching videos and running through computer simulations at a national convention of all the trainees in Hawaii. What is important is that the formal initial training program covers six basic areas of training. In an effort to rush the sales force out "into the field," some companies forget to cover some of these important topic areas. These six areas are listed below:

- *Sales techniques*: While it is true that some people just cannot sell, I will put it another way. People must be born with certain personality characteristics that make them better salespeople; other things must be learned!

- *Product/service knowledge*: To sell a product you must understand the product. This includes everything about a product or service: its features, advantages, and benefits, how it is made, how it will be delivered, its accompanying warranties, its price, and everything else about it.

- *Customer knowledge*: Consumers of the 21st century are smarter, have better technical skills, and are more diverse. It is critical to understand everything about customers including why they buy what they buy and how they buy it. For new salespeople, it is useful to have cross-cultural training since the world of today is so global and cultures can be so different.

- *Supplier knowledge*: Since 21st-century relationships are so important, it is just as important to understand the complete value chain. If you are selling a service, and two or three other companies will be a part of this service at some point along the way, you must understand what role these intermediaries and third-party firms play in the total product package.

- *Competitor knowledge*: Understanding the competition is critical!

- *Individual time and territory management*: Many great salespeople fail because they are so poor at managing their time and territories. You want your salespeople to work smarter not harder.

Training goes beyond the initial training. Also, do not forget about your veteran salespeople. It is sometimes easy to assume that your veterans are okay, and they probably are most of the time. But your veterans need ways to grow and to continue learning as well. Invest in them by bringing in outside speakers or giving them incentives to join study groups or attend industry functions. Make sure they know they are not forgotten. A great way to continue to give your veterans an opportunity to grow is to put them in a teaching or training situation. This is consistent with the mantra of "see, do, teach." Sometimes the best way to improve and refine your skills is to teach. You might be surprised by how flattered some people will be by asking them to participate in teaching and training of others.

The second pillar of development is what that person will learn in the field. As I mentioned earlier, encourage people to go out into the field early on in the training process and to push the limits of what they are comfortable doing. Salespeople will learn the most in the field, interacting with clients and watching their mentors. You can put salespeople in training for six months and they will not learn as much as they will one week in the field. Encourage your salespeople to go out and implement the things they learn in training and to partner with a veteran to maximize their learning. If this is not already a part of your culture, find a veteran salesperson who is inspired by helping others and pair him or her up with a new salesperson. If done right, you will see the production of the new sales representative go up as well as the veteran's production. Once others see the results, they will want to pitch in and help out as well. Again, is giving back a value within your organization? Is it part of your culture?

The third pillar of professional development is what a salesperson does in his or her spare time. Are they using their spare time effectively? Encourage your salespeople to utilize their spare time. Direct them to the learning resources you might have on your intranet or direct them to sales tapes and CDs or product information so that they can learn and fill in the gaps on their own. Some companies pay the membership fees for their sales force to join local organizations. This creates not only a culture of continued learning but also opportunities for networking. In summary, your salespeople should always be striving for continuing education. If this is available to them in your industry, then that should be a priority. Is this a value? Is personal growth and excellence a value of your organization? If not, it should be or your development initiatives will not reach their full potential.

I find that these three pillars create a stable foundation for the development of a salesperson, creating almost a vortex of learning that builds up steam and momentum. Taking away one of the pillars will hold a salesperson back from achieving his or her potential. Managers should be able to expect that their salespeople will go the extra mile to learn, to develop themselves, to improve their product knowledge, and to further enhance their people skills. Do this and you will have salespeople who are growing as people as well as making sales for your organization.

ACCOUNTABILITY: CREATING A CULTURE OF SUCCESS

Once your values, mission statement, and vision statement are complete, and you have recruited and developed people consistent with those values, you now have the building blocks of creating your culture of success. We now need to take action. I believe the culture of success has three primary areas that need to be developed thoroughly to have a successful sales force. They need to be clearly defined and communicated expectations of professionalism, activity, and production. They must be consistent in every situation and there must be a strong system of accountability to those expectations. What is your culture? Is it based on your values? Over the past decade or so, it seems that many organizations' cultures have begun to be eroded or dictated by the casual dress that many companies now promote. What is your culture? Is it okay for salespeople to come in wearing polo shirts and wrinkled khakis? Or does it make sense to create a successful environment with people that are dressed and look the part? It has been said that you dress to pay respect to yourself and to the people you meet that day. Is that going on in your office? What impression are your salespeople giving your prospects and clients? Are they paying respect? This, of course, is just a small example of a culture. Again, I am not suggesting that everybody in every sales situation wear a suit and tie or that it would even be appropriate, but it might be more appropriate than you might think. It all comes down to this issue that you must consider: what culture have you created regarding sales activity in your office? Remember, everything else will filter down from the overarching strategy, culture, and values.

Habits are the key to success, and creating a culture of success means creating an environment that promotes good habits. What does a good environment look like and what are the specific activities that should be in place on a daily, weekly, and monthly basis to develop successful salespeople? First, remember that successful people make habits out of doing things that unsuccessful people do not like to do. Successful people also have a strong desire to succeed. Having a system of accountability in place will build on the strengths of your people and will help them succeed.

It is important to meet with new sales professionals every day. This should be done by a mentor, a coach, or someone designated to hold your salespeople accountable every day. If not, the new sales professional will quickly fall into bad habits and ultimately fail. Remember, it is all about setting goals and objectives (which we covered in the beginning), and salespeople must be held accountable to their individual goals just like corporations should be held accountable to their corporate goals.

In order to instill the habits of a successful salesperson, there must be daily accountability in the first 90 to 180 days. These meetings should be brief and ideally held first thing in the morning. Hold the meetings between 7:30 and 8:00 a.m. every day. During that time, record the activity of the salesperson from the previous day and then compare that to the expectations set by him or her and the organization. In addition to that, discuss the present day and make sure that the salesperson is properly prepared. Allow for no more than 15 to 20 minutes per person. Remember, these morning meetings should be moderated by someone who has a leadership role, but not someone in senior management. It is important that the moderator hold the salespeople accountable. This is not an easy job. It is important for the moderator to ask the tough questions and help keep the salespeople on track. Eventually, if the salespeople are successful and stay with the organization, they will realize that having the moderator do his or her job is one of the many reasons they are so successful. Pair these brief morning meetings with a weekly one-on-one meeting with the sales manager or mentor.

Between these two meetings you will create a high-touch atmosphere and head off any problems or bad habits. You must have accountability to help in developing the habits that will make the new salesperson successful.

Once new salespeople have succeeded in their first 90 to 180 days, do not think that they will fly all on their own. Move the accountability to a weekly basis or at a minimum, for your very senior salespeople, monthly. Remember, if you are selecting highly motivated, driven people, they want to be held accountable. Even the most motivated people can get distracted by all the noise and issues on a daily basis. Having the opportunity for the sales manager to look at the weekly activity from an objective point of view should often identify what is holding them back.

COACHING

This, then, leads us to having a good coaching process. You have the right people based on your values and mission statements. They have gone through initial training and they have had a successful 180 days in the business. Now what? This is when the one-on-one meetings become even more important. Depending on the success of the salesperson, we may end the daily morning meetings and begin one weekly individual meeting and one group meeting. Having group meetings provides an environment of accountability. Individual meetings allow the new or veteran salesperson to discuss more personal issues. If you eliminate the one-on-one session, you are putting yourself and your people at a disadvantage. During these individual meetings you may discover the real reason that the salesperson is struggling. It could be problems with a marriage or issues with his or her children. You just do not know prior to this, and group meetings will not bring these to attention.

One of the biggest challenges that companies of the 21st century face is having a span of control that is simply too large. This is partly due to the rampant downsizing and lay-offs of the 20th century. But whatever the cause, the result has been that some managers are now managing double-digit if not even triple-digit numbers of salespeople. Most scholars feel that the appropriate span of control is anywhere between 6 and 18 depending on the type of work and type of employee. It is a lot easier to manage veteran salespeople than it is to manage new salespeople. Whatever the case, the coaching step is critical to the success of each salesperson and then ultimately to the whole company. A first-level supervisor must be able to spend adequate one-on-one time with all subordinate employees.

The most difficult and most important part of coaching is holding people accountable. As we discussed earlier, we are not doing any favors when we help people fail. In your own business, do you currently have a process in place of consequences to implement when people do not do what is expected? Now is when we refer back to your organization's values. By having clearly defined values, your second-line management will be able to coach to those values. For example, let's pretend that a salesperson is not doing what he or she says he or she will do, and that is in direct conflict with your definition of integrity, which is one of your values. So, instead of your manager spending time on the actual activity that was not done, he or she could have a conversation about integrity and how the salesperson's actions do not reflect your expectations. The employees should also know that they are not living up to the values of your organization. Find out how they feel about that. Of course, the salesperson is not going to feel good about letting down his or her manager or mentor, let alone being in conflict with the values that helped bring that person to you in the first place. This kind of a discussion is much more productive if you go back to the values and to coaching versus using strong-arm tactics.

As I mentioned before, this is not an easy job for the second-line management. These managers will build great relationships with the sales force and will most likely be friends. It is a difficult job to hold your friends accountable. It is impossible to do without being able to fall back on the values. Your second-line management will be much less stressed, and your salespeople will understand that their performance is measured not just through the eyes of their manager or through potential forms of punishment, but that they actually are not living up to the values that they agreed on when they joined the organization.

Ultimately, if a salesperson does not come through and does not follow through on the clearly defined expectations, then it is the values that are not in alignment. It is not a personal situation; it is just a values discussion. That way, if that happens, the person will leave knowing that, for whatever reason, he or she did not live up to the values and it was not personal. This creates the culture of not letting people who should not be around hang around any longer and erode your culture. How many times have you seen a situation where people lingered in an organization and eroded the culture because nobody had the guts to let them go because they have a personal relationship? Define your values, communicate them, and then coach to them. That is how to treat your salespeople like clients.

Helping people work through what they really want and dispelling any fear of failure will help your salespeople push and strive to do bigger and better things. One of the things I think we do so well in our organization is to get our younger and newer salespeople exposed to what the possibilities are. We will have picnics and get-togethers at some of the veteran financial representatives' homes to see the level of success they have. Some of our salespeople have homes down on a lake for the summer, and they will have our young interns or our new salespeople down for a weekend just to see what it is like and what the possibilities are. I find that so many people who want to be successful sometimes actually have a fear of success, and if you fear success, how can you create a culture of success? Give them the ammunition they need to learn about themselves and to learn about the possibilities, and your salespeople will go above and beyond and accomplish not only your company's goals but their own as well.

Invite your salespeople to sit down and have dinner with you and your spouse, and get their spouse involved. The more the spouses are involved in the career of your people, the more in harmony their family will be and ultimately the more productive your salesperson will be. By treating your salespeople like a customer or a client, you will create a culture of success. It will help you deliver on the promise of your mission and achieve your vision for the future. Not only will this help the company, but it will help you attract and retain your good people, knowing that there is room for them to grow in the future.

DEVELOPING YOUR NEXT LINE OF MANAGEMENT

As I work to continue to build a successful sales force, I am reminded of these words: great managers surround themselves with great people. By doing this, whatever task is at hand will be done efficiently and done well. Bad managers surround themselves with less effective people. The reason they do this is to make sure that they always look good in comparison. They are threatened if someone is more intelligent or a better people person. It is critical when building a successful sales force to keep this in mind. We must surround ourselves with people who do not always think alike but have the same core organizational values.

One of the biggest challenges that many companies face is developing leadership for the future. Attracting good people to your organization and helping your people create a vision for themselves means giving them an opportunity to become leaders. What kind of leadership development program do you have in your company? Are you identifying people early on and teaching them about leadership? Are you giving them leadership responsibilities and having them learn from those responsibilities and thereby positioning them for future? Do not make the mistake of not developing your second-line management. If you make that mistake, the success you have today will soon come to a screeching halt, your people will be looking for direction, and they will go elsewhere to find it if they do not find it there.

Invest in leadership development. You can buy leadership books and schedule weekly or monthly meetings to discuss them. Hire outside consultants who you get references from that promote leadership. Spend time going to other successful sales organizations inside or outside your industry to get perspective and to share ideas. Build a special relationship with your leadership team by going on retreats away from the office. Invite your up-and-coming leaders to your main leadership team's meetings. Pair them up so your senior leaders can mentor your emerging leaders. Whatever you do, investing in leadership is a tax deductible investment in your company's future success.

CONCLUSION

Building a successful sales force in the 21st century is an incredibly challenging and rewarding endeavor. It is my hope that this chapter will better enable you to build a successful sales force for your organization. By following through on the outline of this chapter, and implementing this as part of your action plan for the year, it will force you to spend time working on your business and on your sales force. Take time out of working in your business and work on it. The basics of sales have not changed over the past 50 years, but the backdrop has changed dramatically. Salespeople are more sophisticated, as are our customers and clients. Dealing with the large amount of information can become distracting, and the amount of time spent in meetings and communicating and follow-through can be daunting.

Remember to run your business based on your values, use these values to select the right people, and then manage and coach them to their fullest potential. A plan for developing and coaching and a strategy for developing second-line management will allow your company and your sales organization to thrive, not only today but into the competitive and ever-challenging future. Your sales force is your best client, so treat them as such. Yes, it takes time and a lot of patience, but most of all, it takes great leadership.

All of these things will allow your salespeople, and your organization, to be highly rewarded beyond your wildest dreams. These rewards will not only be financial, but you also will have built incredible relationships. Best of all you will have made a lasting impact on the people you work with and on your community.

CHAPTER 3

LEARNING FROM YOUR CUSTOMERS: BUILDING MARKET FEEDBACK INTO STRATEGY AND INNOVATION

Jason DiLauro and Linda M. Orr

INTRODUCTION

If we make products or offer services that do not fulfill our customers' needs, sales will suffer. In most companies, research and development (R&D) and product development are separate departments. This separation was brought about by the creation of functional silos, which were created in many organizations in order to operate more efficiently. By the very definition of the name, R&D usually has their own research function, which possibly forms focus groups, or looks at last year's sales and products, or looks at what the competition has done. This set of processes, many of which were created in an attempt to be customer driven, or emerged out of "customer relationship management" (CRM) strategies, have unfortunately resulted in being anything but customer driven. However, we know that in the competitive landscape of the 21st century, businesses that do not employ CRM strategies will probably not be as successful as those that do.

Given CRM's great potential, some have been disappointed with the results to date. There are many reasons for the fact that the implementation of CRM strategies has not resulted in a greater focus on customers and their needs. The very people who understand the customers the most, who deal with them every day, who understand their needs, and who make daily attempts to find products and services to fulfill these needs, are frequently the last ones consulted in the product development processes. Salespeople, who are serving on the front lines, are excellent sources of knowledge for improving and upgrading product and service offerings. Involving the sales force in the product development process indirectly brings the customers directly into the process through the sales force's daily associations with their customers. Companies that truly can bring their customers into the product development process will benefit from greater customer satisfaction and loyalty. Thus, even though sales forces of the 21st century are finding greater responsibilities, across broader functions of the organization, one of those added responsibilities must be a strategic involvement in the CRM and product development processes. Figure 3.1 demonstrates the customer relationship and product development processes.[1]

CRM is a set of business processes, which are strategically embedded within a company, that create the value propositions and linkages between the firm and all of its external stakeholders. As shown in Figure 3.1, companies must first gain

Figure 3.1
CRM Processes

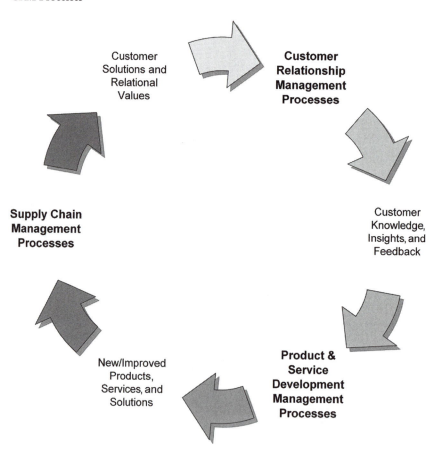

Customer Solutions and Relational Values

Customer Relationship Management Processes

Supply Chain Management Processes

Customer Knowledge, Insights, and Feedback

New/Improved Products, Services, and Solutions

Product & Service Development Management Processes

customer knowledge and insights. One of the easiest and most accurate ways to do this is through a company's sales force. After a firm gathers knowledge, they must then relate that information into ways to upgrade and adapt new products and services, if that is what the market wants. Additionally, it is important to note that new products and services may need consistent adapting to appeal to the needs of all stakeholders, including suppliers. Thus 21st-century salespeople must be gatherers and distributors of customer information and they must be entrepreneurial in order to understand how to best utilize this information in terms of providing solutions to customer needs. Saying that 21st-century sales forces need to be entrepreneurial, or creative, or innovative means more than just utilizing information to provide customer solutions. Salespeople must be innovative across many parts of their jobs, from more innovative prospecting methods to even finding out more creative ways to gather information from customers.

Customers today are busier and more distracted. Many times, customers do not even know exactly what they need, and good salespeople can help find the right products and services for customers to fit these needs. This chapter will first discuss the process of gathering feedback from the marketplace from the perspective of the "ideal client." Some of the topics covered are how to identify your ideal client, how to then understand why they are an ideal client, and then learn how to replicate your ideal client. We will do this by analyzing our existing clients by categorizing them, asking them questions based on the service we provide and how we can improve this service, making changes based on analysis to improve our relationships, and changing and becoming adaptive in terms of product and service offerings. Finally, we will examine working with our clients to help grow our business, more effectively and efficiently. But first, we need to understand why adaptability is so vitally important in the 21st century.

ADAPTABILITY AND INNOVATIVENESS

Salespeople do more great things for a company than merely listening to and understanding the growing and changing needs of the customers. Contrary to the typical way in which businesses are set up to have functional silos, salespeople can make the best innovators of a business. Not only do they listen to the customer, but studies show that salespeople share personality variables that enable them to be more innovative and creative than some other employees.[2] These common characteristics are that salespeople tend to be achievement oriented, persistent, persuasive, assertive, more likely to take initiative, versatile, perceptive, energetic, self-confident, independent, more likely to have an internal locus of control, more likely to have a tendency toward risk taking, creative, resourceful, likely to be an opportunity seeker, comfortable with ambiguity, hardworking, and well organized. These types of personality variables enable salespeople to think of the most innovative creative solutions to business problems. In the 21st century, innovativeness is imperative.

Several significant changes that have occurred recently in the business arena have caused a true realization of the statement "Change is the only thing that remains the same." Some have termed the 21st century as "the next industrial revolution." Some of the changes are: (1) the pace of economic change is accelerating, (2) there is explosion of innovation and new knowledge generation, (3) competitive pressures are intensifying, (4) manufacturing can now take place almost anywhere, (5) new organizational structures are emerging, (6) international trade is being liberalized through trade agreements, and (7) company actions are becoming increasingly visible.

In light of this environmental turbulence and competitive intensity, many feel that the only way to succeed today is through learning and adaptation. The simple process of listening to and learning from the customers can be a sustainable competitive advantage that cannot be easily imitated or eroded away by competitors. The ability to learn faster than competitors may be the *only* real source of sustainable competitive advantage in the 21st century. Organizations that are adept at learning are more adaptable to change and better equipped to undertake the processes of strategic renewal. Strategies can no longer be designed without allowing for and capturing what is emergent in contemporary situations as they unfold.

Innovations, whether they are small changes to products or services or radical innovations of new products or services, better enable businesses to fulfill customers' needs. Studies have shown that returns on innovation can account for as much as 50 percent or more of corporate revenue.[3] Continuous innovation is a necessary condition for a focus on total customer satisfaction. Innovation creates new processes, both administrative and technical, that can create and produce products and services in more efficient ways.

The need and impetus to be innovative has emerged from more than just a desire to create new products that will sell better, therefore increasing profitability. Even in the most low-tech situations, it would be essentially impossible to find an industry that is not engaged in continuous or periodic innovation and reorientation due to the dynamic nature of most markets. Further, intensifying competition and environmental uncertainty has made innovation increasingly important as a means of survival. Innovativeness shows a strong, positive link with performance because innovations serve to accommodate the uncertainties (i.e., market and technological turbulence) a firm faces in its environment. Innovations set companies apart from their competitors in turbulent environments. The differentiation that can arise from innovations provides firms with competitive advantages.

Unfortunately, in this era of hypercompetitive and mature markets, most marketing programs fall short in terms of innovation and creativity, which results in markets overflowing with very similar "me-too" products and even downright failures. For example, 80 to 94 percent of all new grocery products are outright failures.[4] No one seems to understand all the elements of innovative idea generation. One of the nation's largest health care and beauty aids manufacturer found that almost 95 percent of all its innovations were minor package changes, line extensions, and other incremental improvements. These simple improvements were mostly me-too products that had relatively little effect on the company's bottom line.[5]

Thus, in light of the importance of innovation in the competitive marketplace, it is vital that business owners gain an understanding of how to increase innovative thinking that can lead to a competitive advantage. A solid competitive advantage is one that cannot be easily eroded away by competitors. As companies like the ones used in the previous examples have found out, the innovation of each individual new product or product improvement by itself is not the most important component of the successful business model. Single new products or new product improvements, whether they are tangible products or improvements in services, may easily be copied by the competition.

The key to developing innovative programs does not lie in each single innovation, but instead lies in a company's ability to be innovative on a consistent and continual basis. Firms that have a customer-focused vision realize that their success lies in the processes or capabilities, not specific resources. Once a firm becomes adept at the capabilities or processes that are utilized to create each innovation, they can then use those processes to create other forms of innovative products or services. Thus the firm's competitive position is not dependent on each single innovation, which may succeed or fail. The firm instead builds and attempts to become proficient at the capabilities of the firm, which can then create and consistently renew the firm's strategies and products and therefore create constant innovation.

Thus the firm's competitive advantage becomes the processes or capabilities that create innovation, not the innovations themselves. So, what are these processes? What can we do as a company to find out our customers' needs? How can we fully utilize the full potential of our sales force? As mentioned, adaptability is crucial for a sustainable competitive advantage and success in this century. Salespeople by nature have personality characteristics that make them more likely to be the great innovators of the firm. The following sections will explain how salespeople can, very specifically, first identify the "ideal client" to provide feedback, and then the steps a salesperson must take to get this feedback and ultimately interpret it to help provide better products and services.

THE IDEAL CLIENT

In the early stages of your sales career, you are usually forced to grasp onto any piece of business you can get. No matter how small or large the client is, you open the account without a single thought about the long-term consequences. What tends to happen is that the first accounts you open receive all of your attention, all your best effort, time, and service. What happens over time is you develop a larger group of clientele with larger average client sizes. When the larger clients start to eat most of your time and the smaller ones no longer receive the service they once did, you start to lose them. This is not necessarily a bad thing, but it is not the ideal situation. You would ideally bring on a partner to continue to give good service to the lower tier of clients or create a team structure so they are provided the attention they deserve. The point is, your ideal client will grow and emerge and change as your business changes, so it is vital that we realize this and learn how to develop a business plan that accommodates this change. The ideal client for any business is a nice person who needs you, appreciates you, is willing to pay for your service, and can make decisions. This is the same for all businesses. Of course we want to deal with only nice people, but we want the customer to need us. If they need us and we provide the product or service they need with reasonable service, then they will appreciate us. If they appreciate us and feel that we provide a good value, then they are willing to pay for our service or product. To be able to provide excellent service, the person or business has to be able to make decisions in a timely manner. Add to these traits one more very important quality and you have the perfect client: a person who is willing to refer you to other potential clients. If we can replicate this person or business over and over again, this creates opportunities to grow at a more rapid pace than ever found before.

INTERVIEW YOUR CLIENTS

So how do you ask your clients to help you? What are the different ways of gathering this information? The conservative way is to send out a survey. The most efficient way is to conduct an interview over the phone. The most *effective* way is to sit down with them and conduct a face-to-face interview. This is not to be taken lightly. When an important client is taking time out of their busy schedule to help you, you owe them the courtesy of sitting down with them, giving them the respect of going to a place they are comfortable, and showing them the appreciation you have for giving you this opportunity. There are many reasons this is so very important; to name a few: First, the client needs to understand how important this feedback is to you. If you send a survey, it is very easy for a client to discard it, and quite honestly, they view it as a nuisance. If you conduct the interview over the phone, while it saves you time the same amount of sincerity will not come through over the phone as it would in a face-to-face meeting. Second, the face-to-face interview gives you the opportunity to express your gratitude for them being with you.

How do we set up this meeting? By using your segmentation look at all of your "A" clients. Which of them think you are wonderful? Which clients have sent you referrals in the past? Which clients have told you how much they appreciate you, and the service you provide? These are the ones we talk to first. Starting with the people who really like you will make this difficult process a little easier. We can work on tougher challenges later. Now that you have identified a few of your favorite clients, it is time to make phone calls. When you call your client, tell them you need a favor: "I would like to have your opinion on the service we are currently providing you. As a matter of fact, we are in the process of making our service model more efficient, and we would like to have input from our best clients." Let them know they are one of the best; after all, a little flattery never hurts. Then say, "Would you be willing to share some thoughts with me?"

By doing this, you will get many different responses, but the most typical will be "ABSOLUTELY!" When you make this call to your lesser clients, who do not get as much of your attention, you will receive a different response, which will typically be a pause, with a "why me?" type of comment. There are many ways to look at this. You can shut down, get nervous, and not push the issue, or you can look at this as an opportunity to find out what you have been doing wrong. Spend time with the client to learn what you can do better, and then reestablish the relationship and make it stronger. The reason your best clients will react favorably is because they have a bond with you on a higher level. They trust you, they understand you, and they appreciate what you offer them, and more importantly, they *know that you appreciate them*. Simply put, people stay where they are appreciated; they go where they are invited. The reason lower-tier clients will not act favorably to this type of questioning is because they do not have this comfort level with you. They do not necessarily feel appreciated; they definitely do not feel important. This is where we discover the opportunity. The client wants to feel important. Just like us as individuals, clients want attention. Give it to them and let them know we hear what they are saying, verbally and nonverbally.

WHAT DO WE ASK?

The answer to this question depends on which response you get to the initial call. The positive response leads to a very direct line of questioning. The negative response offers a challenge in that you need to initially find out what is making the client uncomfortable.

Let's first look at the positive response. When together remind the client why you asked them to meet you. They are here so you can ask questions about the service you have provided them in the past. Not only that, but what changes would they recommend to make it even better? Ask them what they feel differentiates you from your competitors. What you are really asking is why they are doing business with you, but doing so in a way that tells you your competitive advantages. When they offer their suggestions, and opinions, ask them what they mean. Why is it important to them? What we really want to find is: *where do they see value in the relationship*? You will hear answers that will surprise you. You will hear answers that upset you. Either way, we are learning what your clients like and what they dislike about your offering.

Of course answers will differ dramatically depending on your industry, but some of the most common positive responses in financial services are: you return phone calls in a timely fashion, your office staff is very supportive, you are consistent in delivery, you help my organization run more efficiently, your prices are better than others, and the consistency of your service allows us to focus on other things that are more important. While all of these are nice responses, which ones carry the most power and meaning? Returning all of the phone calls and a nice office staff should be a given in today's business, but surprisingly this is not the case. Answers like "You help us run more efficiently," or "Your consistency allows us to focus on more important things," are much more meaningful. The reason they are so important is that the client is telling you where they see value in your relationship; they are telling you where you help them the most. They are telling you loud and clear the strongest characteristics of your service model and what it is that makes them stay with you.

A small caveat about comment on price is warranted. Price is a double-edged sword. It is positive from the aspect that you have earned their business. But it is a negative from the aspect that they will be gone the next time someone offers them a better price. Be careful. Instead of stopping on these comments, push a little deeper. Just like in a sales situation, when a prospect starts making price objections there is usually a much deeper hidden objection that you must find. Also, keep in mind that from a competitive standpoint, 21st-century strategic business models that have a sustainable competitive advantage are much more likely to be successful if there is a differential advantage. Just having a lower price is not necessarily something that will enable a competitor to keep clients in the long run. If you are truly seeking to learn from your clients, going beyond price and money will almost always enable you to reap richer information.

When the client tells you that you have freed up time for them to concentrate on other things, ask them to give you an example. This is important. It is just like the metaphor that a picture is worth a thousand words. Stories and examples provide clients the ability to elaborate. When they start elaborating, you have a better chance of uncovering deeper needs and concerns. Also, by digging deeper into the details of each example, the client is reinforcing in their own mind how important you are to their business. When they answer a few questions like this, they are ready for you to press forward. This is when you ask if there are other businesses or people that share the same need for a service like the one you provide. Off the top of their head, they may not be able to think of anyone or any organization immediately. Give them a moment, and interject by asking, "Do you *feel* it would be a good idea for me to offer my services to others in your field?" They know the answer is yes, but are they willing to share you with anyone else? You have to ask. If clients are not completely satisfied with your offerings, they will not refer you to someone else. Most clients will say yes and will tell you that it is a good idea that you pursue more opportunities in that field, as long as it is not at their expense. After they have told you about their own field, ask them if there are any related areas that would benefit from your service as well. You will be surprised that many clients at this point put on their thinking cap and start to become your marketing department. They will come up with suggestions you have never thought of. They will come up with specific names for you to call and maybe even make the calls for you to make the introduction.

WHAT HAVE WE LEARNED FROM THIS EXAMPLE?

We have definitely discovered that our clients are willing to help us. They want us to learn. We have learned that our clients have a good understanding of what they need from us. We have found where they see value in our relationship with them. We have found that the client appreciates what we do for them. And finally, we have found that if given the opportunity, our client may send us referrals based on the service we have provided to them in the past. The key is you have to EARN the right to get the referrals. Remember that 21st-century selling is all about the relationship. Referrals are not to be expected; they are to be earned. Clients will give you the opportunity to meet their peers if they feel you will not embarrass them and if they feel you can truly help others. When you develop the relationship at this level you know you have a client for life. This is the ideal situation.

LET US NOW TAKE A LOOK AT A NEGATIVE RESPONSE TO OUR INITIAL QUESTION

Keep this in mind. It will be rare that a good client will turn down the opportunity to give you feedback. If a client tells you that they would rather not have this conversation with you, you must do a quick self-analysis to see if this is the type of client who has always been withdrawn, which is all right. Or is this a client who is unhappy, one who feels unappreciated or mishandled? If it is a client who just truly is not a person who will typically share their opinion, thank the client and move on. If you feel that there is a possibility the client is not happy, this is your opportunity to take a step back and ask the client, "If there is one thing about our relationship you could change, what would it be?" This gives them the opportunity to speak their mind and give you some feedback that will allow you to repair the relationship. There is a good chance the client will tell you there is nothing wrong. But you have to have the courage to push and find out if there is the slightest issue. If there is, and you do not uncover it, eventually another organization will come along with something better, whether it is price, service, reporting, etc., and you will lose the client. You must discover what the issue is.

Many times, by going through this process the client will appreciate your effort and will rediscover why they chose to work with you in the first place. This type of communication will repair the relationship, and maybe even give you the chance to do more business than what you did in the past with this client.

On the other hand, you may also learn that the client just does not fit your profile anymore, and that it may just be best to part ways. This is a tough pill to swallow, but what you will find, in time, is that the sales industry is difficult enough on normal days. If you add to your typical day angry clients, unappreciative clients, clients who are not willing to make decisions, clients who are unwilling to pay, or clients who do not see the value you provide, you will soon be miserable in your position. The point is, work with nice people. People you want to work with. People who are willing to pay for your service, appreciate your time, and are willing to make decisions. We all have had to open accounts and do business with people we do not necessarily like, but if you can minimize this type of person, your days will be better, with much less stress.

What have we learned from the negative response? We have learned that negative responses can sometimes create an opportunity. An opportunity to ask the questions about what has happened in the past, and what we can do to fix it, or make it better. We have learned that an unhappy client can be brought back to positive status with proper handling. In fact, sometimes the most loyal customers can be those that had a problem that you corrected. These opportunities can create very strong, long-lasting relationships. We have learned that some clients will just not give feedback. They may just want to keep their opinions to themselves. From them you must learn by their behavior and their reaction to the way you work with them. This may be a big challenge, but it is a skill you must develop to be successful in sales and marketing.

WHAT DO WE DO WITH THIS FEEDBACK?

The reasons for segmenting clients, asking difficult questions, and challenging them to give us detailed answers are to learn more about what will make our business successful and what makes our business vulnerable, and most importantly, to help us take better care of our clients. By interviewing each level of client, we gain a better knowledge of our service model on all levels. If we were to look only at our top-tier clients, we may get false sense of reality. Our top clients will typically love us because they are getting all of our attention. Our lower-level clients will typically share their displeasure with us, because their experience is not quite as positive. With the positive comments, what we want to do is obvious. Continue to do it! With the negative comments, correct them! This is not a quick fix. We cannot just flip the switch and be done with what we have done for entire time it has taken to build a business. We will have to take baby steps. Find the most common complaint and start from there. Once we have solved this issue, we move on to the next most common complaint, and so on. By doing this we will gradually improve the quality of service we are providing to each and every client.

THE FOLLOW-UP

The best way to find out if it is working is to go back to the interview section of the process. Go back to the same people we interviewed in the past. First, ask them if they have recognized any of the specific changes we implemented. Then ask if they like these changes. Since they were the ones who suggested the changes, typically the answer will be a resounding yes. If it is not, we have to go back to the interview part and ask what needs to be adjusted. For the most part you will hear many positives. The few negatives you do receive will be from people who just want something to complain about. Most of our clients will be so happy we listened to and executed their suggestions, they will feel closer to us and will appreciate the fact that we care enough to listen. This will prove to be invaluable as the relationship continues to grow—no matter the level of client. They will respect us for listening and making the effort to follow through.

HOW DO WE IMPROVE OUR BUSINESS BY IMPROVING OUR BEHAVIORS?

Remember that old motto of the 20th century? "It's all about location, location, location." There should be a new motto for the 21st century: "listen, listen, and listen!" Our clients will tell us what we need to do. Listen to their needs, listen to their suggestions, listen to complaints, listen to their compliments, and we will find what it is that they really want. The sales and marketing representative who understands the "gift of gab" is nice to have for social events, but the true art of sales starts with a better understanding of silence. The ability to ask open-ended questions that give the client the opportunity to *share* their thoughts is what will help us understand their true needs. If we ask the right questions, and our line of questioning is leading, we help the client discover that they need us. They realize that we are asking all of the appropriate questions, helping them understand that we have the product or service that solves their issues. This allows us to be an advisor, or a valued salesperson, instead of a vendor. Vendors may get business a few times, but they will never be able to hold a candle to a consultative advisor, who is appreciated by the client. Our ability to listen to clients, and interpret clearly what exactly is needed or wanted, gives us the ability to analyze the situation and respond in a more appropriate manner. This behavior creates a better atmosphere for our clients.

Our ultimate goal should be to make our customers feel important and to treat them like no one else will. If our clients feel appreciated, they will stay with us and continue to introduce us to more people who can benefit as well. By taking the measures discussed in this chapter, you will be able to create a business structure that will allow you to be efficient, effective, and successful. We can do this only by learning directly from our clients. And then, it is that learning that can help us provide better, more innovative solutions to the needs of our customers. The 21st century is one of rapid change, and we must learn to listen to the customer, find out their needs, and incorporate these changes into our business. The independent, creative, risk-taking salesperson is best suited for this job. Successful 21st-century companies will realize what a gem they have in their sales force and utilize this gem to learn from the customer in order to constantly improve their business, business model, and its products and services.

NOTES

1. The Sales Educators, *Strategic Sales Leadership: Breakthrough Thinking for Breakthrough Results* (Mason, OH: Thompson Higher Education, 2006).

2. Ibid.

3. Jin K. Han, Namwoon Kim, and Rajendra K. Srivastava, "Market Orientation and Organization Performance: Is Innovation the Missing Link?," *Journal of Marketing* 62, no. 4 (1998): 30–44.

4. Robert M. McMath, "Kellogg's Cereal Mates," *Failure Magazine* July (2000), http://failuremag.com/arch_mcmath_kelloggs.html (accessed September 21, 2006).

5. George S. Day, "Feeding the Growth Strategy," *Marketing Management* 12, no. 6 (November/December 2003): 15–21.

CHAPTER 4

NEGOTIATING COMPANY AND CUSTOMER RELATIONSHIPS

Jon M. Hawes

INTRODUCTION

As relationships become more and more complex during the 21st century, the use of negotiations within company and customer relationships has become even more prevalent. What is negotiation? "Negotiation is a decision-making process by which two or more parties agree how to allocate scarce resources."[1] Inherent in this definition are a number of important factors. First, two or more parties are involved. The company, of course, can be one party and the customer can be the second party. In some cases, there may be more parties involved. For example, governmental agencies impact the dealings between sellers and buyers of electricity. The media may also impact buyer-seller relationships in some settings. As a case in point, Walmart currently receives so much scrutiny from the media that any negotiation in which the firm is involved will certainly be influenced by the potential public relations impact of any deal that might be reached.

Another important factor in the definition of negotiation is the allocation of scarce resources. Within a buying-selling situation, the allocation of scarce resources can simply be the products to be sold and the money needed to secure them. Obviously, the seller would like to get more money for fewer goods while the buyer would like to get more goods for less money. Often, however, more is involved. The utility or satisfaction to be obtained by participants of the exchange represents a broader and perhaps more meaningful conceptualization of this notion of scarce resources. Often, emotional considerations represent a significant consideration when determining the total satisfaction obtained by each party to an exchange.

Central to the notion of negotiation is the expectation of give-and-take. Rather than accepting an initial offer from the other side, we negotiate whenever we ask for an adaptation of what the other party initially offers to us. Negotiation involves offers, counteroffers, adjustments, and revisions. We expect to make concessions, but we also expect the other side to do the same. As nice as it would be, give-and-take does not mean take and take and take and take. The norm of reciprocity creates an expectation of some degree of parity in terms of the pattern and number of concessions across the parties.

Consequently, anytime that buyer and seller do not accept the initial offer of the other side and instead propose a modification of the terms to that agreement, negotiation has occurred. The decision-making procedure that occurs among the affected parties to achieve this is negotiation. This process can be tough on relationships, or the parties can work together for the common good. Hopefully, the latter approach is used.

What are the alternatives to negotiation? What could we do when confronted with a situation rather than negotiate a solution with the opponent? The first alternative that can be easily identified is to simply capitulate or give in to the other side. While we would not get what we want, we would avoid the effort needed to negotiate with the opponent. Rather than capitulate, we could instead just break off contact with the other side and hope we never see them again. We might also take the dispute to a third party for potential resolution. Better Business Bureaus often get involved with commercial disputes. Some contracts also call for other forms of mediation or third-party resolution of disputes. Obviously, legal action in a court is a form of third-party resolution. Yet another option is just to hope that the other side will give in and change their practices in a way that suits our needs. Do not hold your breath for this to occur! Finally, physically fighting with the other side is an alternative to negotiation. This does not represent a reasonable alternative within commerce, but this what nations do when they go to war rather than negotiate a peaceful resolution to their differences.

With such a broad definition of negotiations, it is clear that many people engage in negotiations on a frequent and regular basis. In fact, we can argue that everyone does it, almost daily. Interestingly, while negotiating is so abundant within company and customer relationships, most of the participants have not received any training on the subject. Usually, people just "wing it" with their best seat-of-the-pants judgment on how to handle a negotiation. Unfortunately, the result is often poor tangible outcomes along with damaged relationships, even when both parties' intentions have been honorable.

The good news here is that there is clearly much room for improvement here. While many firms have made considerable improvements in efficiency for a variety of other organizational functions, there is great potential for increased effectiveness both in terms of the tangible outcomes as well as in terms of improved relationships with others relative to the negotiation processes. With the stakes so high and with the historical level of training so low, even modest investments in better understanding the process of negotiation are likely to pay very high dividends. Considerable movement along the learning curve is likely and welcome for all concerned.

FUNDAMENTAL APPROACHES TO NEGOTIATION

There are two fundamental approaches to negotiation between a company and its customers. The first type of negotiation is distributive negotiation, sometimes called "bargaining" in the negotiation literature. In the popular press, this may also be called the "win-lose" approach. In this highly competitive situation, one or both parties view the allocation of scarce resources as a zero-sum gain where my loss is your gain (or my gain is your loss). In other words, I can get more only if you get less. The entire focus is upon claiming for your side all of the value that is possible while still convincing the other side to agree to the deal. Historically, this has been how many people approached negotiations. While it is sometimes the appropriate frame of reference, this style can be hard on relationships.

The second and perhaps more enlightened approach is known as integrative negotiation, or as a "win-win" agreement. Here, both sides recognize that the scarce resources can be expanded through cooperation or perhaps by creative thinking. This can result in a larger pool of resources that then will need to be claimed by each side. The fundamental difference between a distributive and an integrative agreement is whether or not the pool of resources or the "pie" gets enlarged. If it does, the agreement is said to be integrative.

DISTRIBUTIVE BARGAINING

Even in the 21st century, there are some times when distributive bargaining is the appropriate approach. This can be the case when there is no potential for relationship development, when the other side is focused only on price, or when time pressures prevent the development of trust or the sharing of interests. But when a negotiation participant seeks only to claim value by gaining through the other's loss as is the case in distributive bargaining, all sorts of aggressive tactics can be expected. Under this competitive context, the focus is on getting all you can get out of this deal without much consideration of the impact on any future interactions because there may not be any more deals. This is a very Adam Smith type of view in which short-term profit maximization is the name of the game. Transaction-oriented rather than relationship-oriented selling would appear to be consistent with distributive bargaining.

Setting Distributive Goals

Preparation for a distributive negotiation should involve setting a target point, a reservation point, and an asking price (seller) or an initial offer (buyer). The target point is the best-case scenario on how the deal will end. For the seller, this would involve the most optimistic (high) price and quantity of goods that they could expect to sell. For the buyer, this would involve getting the best (lowest) price in the quantity needed.

Research has shown that ambitious targets are directly related to better outcomes. Negotiators who have high expectations often come closer to fulfilling them. Especially within the distributive context, target points should represent aggressive goals. They should be set high but not so high that they are viewed as unrealistic and therefore not worthy of discussion by the other side. Targets should be ambitious but discussable.

While the target point is the ideal outcome hoped for, the reservation point is the worst deal that you would still accept. The reservation point provides guidance on the most that you would be willing to "give" and still do business with the other side rather than select your best alternative to a negotiated agreement (BATNA) with this party. BATNA is a very important concept within distributive negotiation. It suggests that there is more than one opponent with whom you could work. It implies competition within that market and multiple attractive sources. The most attractive of those available sources provides your best alternative to the negotiated agreement under consideration. Obviously, it would make no sense to accept an offer from the current opponent that is worse than what one of its competitors has already offered to you. In many cases, however, under the heat of battle in a highly competitive distributive situation, this unfortunately is sometimes done. The development of a reservation point prior to the interaction is an attempt to avoid this type of a mistake during the bargaining session. Thinking ahead is better than thinking behind and in hindsight wishing that you had made a different choice.

The third important element to effectively planning for a distributive negotiation is to determine what your first offer should be. Since the process of give-and-take is a central element in the negotiation process, the first offer is very much influenced by subsequent concessions, and this will be covered in the next section.

Making Concessions

The seller's asking price and the buyer's first offer impact the settlement price. In many cases, these initial values become anchors that influence subsequent discussions about price. When the two parties ultimately agree to "split the difference," a very common method for finalizing the settlement, the first offers are directly related to the final outcome. In order to provide some room for give-

and-take, the seller's first offer should be higher than the target point. This enables the seller to make concessions (decreases in price) yet still achieve the target price. For the buyer, the converse is true. The initial offer should be low enough to enable concessions (increases in price) but still achieve the buyer's target price.

Beyond the first offer, it is also important to more broadly consider the role of concessions within a negotiation. Remember that once the parties consider the interaction to be a negotiation, there is an expectation of give-and-take. This implies a belief as well about the pattern of concessions that are likely to occur. Without concessions on the part of either side, the negotiation is likely deadlocked. There is no positive movement and an agreement is not likely.

An extreme case of this has become known as "boulewarism," named after Lemuel Bouleware who was the chief labor relations negotiator for General Electric many years ago. He became famous for his "take it or leave it" approach to union contracts. Mr. Bouleware's strategy was to offer the union leaders what he called GE's first, best, and only offer without an opportunity for give-and-take. Imagine the level of distress the union leaders would face if they informed their dues-paying membership that they had accepted the company's first offer. Union members would likely question the need for a union! Instead, the union leaders effectively argued that Bouleware's strategy was unacceptable and filed an unfair-labor charge against GE. This charge was upheld under the Wagner Act, forcing GE to bargain in good faith, meaning that it must engage in give-and-take.

Consequently, there is a very strong social norm for give-and-take during a negotiation. But beyond the avoidance of a take-it-or-leave-it offer, what else is involved in the process of give and take? Three very important elements of give-and-take are the magnitude, the pattern, and the timing of concessions. First of all, let's consider the magnitude of concession. This can be expressed as a dollar or a percentage amount and it should be viewed by the other side as reasonable. This usually means that the magnitude of each side's concessions relative to the opponent is reasonably similar. The second aspect of concessions involves the pattern. Generally the recommendation here is for each subsequent concession to be of lesser value, signaling to the other side that there is little to be gained by holding out for yet one more concession and that the negotiator has no more to give. Finally, the amount of time it takes to respond to the other side's most recent offer also sends a signal. The longer it takes to make the counteroffer, the less likely the opponent will try to hold out for yet one more concession.

As a practical example of this, I recently received a neighborhood newsletter from a realtor that included recent home sales along with various information relating to those transactions. One interesting statistic was the percentage of transaction value to asking price. Within this neighborhood, the recent statistic was 92 percent. In other words, homes sold on average for 92 percent of what the asking price had been. What a valuable statistic for a potential buyer trying to determine her first offer on a property within this neighborhood! Knowing that

8 percent was the average amount that recent sellers had been willing to discount home prices suggests that an aggressive but discussable first offer might be perhaps 15 percent under listing price. If this amount is not accepted (and in all likelihood it would not be), the seller would likely make a counteroffer since the first offer had been "discussable." The potential buyer can then react to that new discounted price. If the seller offers a reduction off list price of, for example, 3 percent, the potential buyer's next offer should be commensurate with the sacrifice that the seller offered from the listing price. In this case, the buyer should up her offer to about 3 percent more than her first offer. This would take the current bid to about 12 percent under the original list. If this is not accepted by the seller, another counteroffer is likely. If that comes in at about 2 percent under what they had proposed as the first counteroffer, the seller knows that he is getting close to what the "average" home has been netting and may accept the offer. There could be, however, another round of concessions. Assume that the buyer counters this most recent offer by increasing her last offer by 1 percent. What would you expect to happen? My guess is that if the house had been on the market for more than the average number of days to sell (another statistic reported in the newsletter), the seller would accept the most recent offer and a deal would be made.

What can be learned from this real estate example? First, the amount of each concession was reasonably similar in magnitude, demonstrating to the other side that there was reciprocation for their sacrifices. Furthermore, the pattern of concessions signaled that the negotiation was nearing an end. The amount of each concession narrowed over time, logically indicating to the other side that as these values approached zero, there simply was no more room for bargaining. Taking longer to make each concession can also signal that the making of concessions is almost over.

Dealing with Dirty Tricks

While the distributive negotiation approach is sometimes appropriate, when this win-lose approach to negotiation is used relationships can suffer and some too-agreeable parties can be taken advantage of by tough opponents. If the other side uses a dirty trick, the best defense is early recognition of the tactic to enable an appropriate response. In the next section, we will describe some of the most frequently used aggressive tactics in an attempt to help you identify these early. Before we cover that, let's discuss your options. The best way to deal with the use of these dirty tricks is to minimize the chance for usage by creating a personal relationship with the opponent early in the interaction. An opponent is less likely to attempt the use of an aggressive tactic of questionable ethics on a person with whom she has a positive, personal relationship. Consequently, co-opting the tactic by befriending the other side before it is used is a good place to start.

If that does not work and you suspect that your opponent is using a dirty trick, most experts recommend that your first response should be to ignore it. There is a chance that you are mistaken in your identification of the tactic. In addition, it is possible that the tactic will not be repeated. As long as you do not give up pie because of the tactic, a strategy of simply ignoring it and continuing to bargain in good faith as you attempt to reach your negotiation goals makes sense.

What if the opponent then uses another highly aggressive tactic or a dirty trick? At this point, it makes sense to call them on it or to discuss their use of the tactics and suggest a return to more professional ways of interacting. Maybe the opponent can be persuaded in this manner to stop using these unpleasant approaches to negotiation.

But what if the opponent persists? The next suggestion is one of the following depending upon your BATNA. If your BATNA is highly attractive, you should simply walk away from an opponent using the dirty tricks. You can do better and suffer less stress from dealing with one of the competitors. If the opponent is this unprofessional during the negotiation, imagine the difficulty that you may face in obtaining compliance to the terms of the agreement after the sale. Do not waste your time dealing with this unpleasantness.

On the other hand, what if your BATNA is lousy? In that case, you might (or might not depending upon the circumstances) want to respond in kind to the dirty trick. If the opponent is yelling at you, yell back at him. If this opponent plays chicken (see next section) with you, you have the option of playing chicken with him. Sometimes, an opponent may just be trying to see how far you can be pushed. Once you fight back, it is possible that he will stop the aggressive use of dirty tricks for fear of your reciprocation. Be careful, however, because this response can put you in the same category as the nasty opponent. Do you really need this deal with this particular opponent enough to risk this type of behavior? Furthermore, what are the odds of full compliance to the terms of the agreement by the opponent after the transaction has been made? This might just be a deal you are better off not making.

Frequently Used Dirty Tricks

So what kinds of dirty tricks do some of these opponents use? Remember, the objective of this list is not to encourage you to use the tactics. Instead, the goal is to enable the reader to recognize these techniques early in an interaction so you will not fall prey to the opponent. By no means is this list complete. There are hundreds of gambits for aggressively persuading others to accept your offers.[2] And there are a hundred variations on how each tactic can be used. Be careful!

When there are multiple people on an opposing negotiating team, the *good cop/ bad cop* is often used. This dirty trick is very simple and straightforward, yet highly effective. One person takes a highly aggressive, unyielding approach to the negotiations. This is the bad cop. He becomes unpleasant and highly annoying during the interaction. Another member on the team takes a much softer approach during the interaction. This good cop smiles occasionally and is reasonably pleasant during the negotiation. Due to the psychological impact of the so-called contrast effect, she seems REALLY nice in comparison to the bad cop.

At some point during the interaction the bad cop excuses himself, perhaps to retrieve something from his car or to use the restroom. When he is gone, the good cop sympathizes with you about the difficulty of dealing with the bad cop. She then offers to work out a deal while he is gone, saving you from the unpleasantness of dealing with him. While the deal she offers you would normally not be viewed all that favorably, it sounds great in comparison to the alternative of dealing with the bad cop upon his return. Their hope is that you will readily agree to the good cop's terms prior to the return of the bad cop.

Another frequently used dirty trick is *the highball/lowball tactic*.[3] This takes on two basic forms. The first application of the highball/lowball also has its power based on the contrast effect. With apologies to my friends in the used-car business, please consider the following example of a highball/lowball application.

You are shopping for a used car; let's say a 2001 Chevy Cavalier. You have a fairly good knowledge of the market after having visited several other dealerships. You arrive at the next dealership, notice a nice-looking green 2001 Chevy Cavalier (the color you prefer) on the lot, and begin inspecting it. Soon a salesperson approaches you and asks what you think of the car. In response, you ask what the price is. He promptly responds that the price is $,9600. You realize that this is way too much money for the car and exclaim, "You have got to be kidding me!" The salesperson says, "Well, let me go inside and check my numbers. Would you please wait here while I check?" When he returns in a few minutes, he offers you what appears to be a sincere apology and says that the price is only $6,900 and that he could not be sorrier for transposing the numbers.

What is your reaction to this? Most of us would feel vindicated for our good understanding of the market. Due to the contrast effect, we also feel that we have just received a discount of $2,700. For many shoppers, this car really begins to look attractive at this point. And, we feel a strong obligation to continue in the "negotiation" because we have already extracted such a major "concession" from the salesperson. In this situation, many buyers do not bargain hard for significant additional concessions and the negotiation very likely concludes with a purchase of the car at nearly $6,900. Had the salesperson started by saying that the car is $6,900, most buyers would work much harder at attaining major concessions from that value.

The other application of this basic tactic really could be better described as the lowball/highball trick. There are a thousand variations of this scam, but it works something like this. A customer buys a new car and get what she believes to be an exceptionally good price. She finances it at the dealership and drives it home that day. She pays $1,000 down and is told (in writing) that her payments will be $237 per month for 48 months. Of course, she parks it in the driveway and all of her neighbors, family, and friends come over to see it. What a beautiful car!

Early on the third day, she gets a call from the salesperson, who tells her that there was an error in the financing and that they have to come to her house to pick up the car. She fears the embarrassment of people finding out that she no longer has the new car and is afraid that they will think the car was repossessed or at least that her credit was not approved. Due to this social risk as well as the concept of cognitive commitment, many people in this situation will respond to the return request by saying something like "Isn't there any other way to resolve this? I really like the car." Often, the salesperson will reply "The number of payments was incorrectly listed—you would need to make 60 payments of $237, not 48" or "The numbers were transposed on the paperwork and your payments would need to be $273 per month." Often, the customer agrees to the new terms without bargaining or even making a counteroffer.

Chicken

"The game of chicken (also referred to as playing chicken) is a 'game' in which two players engage in an activity that will result in serious harm unless one of them backs down."[4] Remember the movie *Rebel without a Cause*? In that movie, two characters drive cars at top speed toward a cliff. To the idiots involved in the madness, the one who swerves first loses and is identified within that peer group as the "chicken."

The same type of game also happens during a negotiation. "If you don't drop your price by 10 percent, we will pull you from the approved vendor list!" "If you don't deliver to us in three days, we will bad-mouth you to the point where you will never sell another product in this city!" These and similar outrageous threats are made by customers all too frequently in commerce. Failure to comply with such a serious threat from the opponent carries considerable risk. The best defense to this type of extreme demand is to have really attractive alternatives to this deal with other clients.

The Nibble

Speaking of chicken, how about the nibble? This is a much less intense form of dirty trick. The nibble is done almost at the point of deal completion, usually by the buyer but the seller could also get involved. This tactic is executed just prior to signing on the dotted line by making one more request for a small concession. When done by the customer, the request could be for a cash discount, a "baker's dozen," a free gift with the purchase, or a free tank of gas when buying a car. If the seller is the initiator, the request could be for a small unexpected prepayment prior to delivery, for a special rush-order fee, for an "order-processing fee," or some other form of deal sweetener to improve the seller's margin on the deal.

The reason the nibble is so often used is because it so often works, even though it can be hard on relationships. At this point in the process, the opponent usually feels like the negotiation is over and may conceptually breathe a sigh of relief. In addition, many of us are reluctant to risk losing the deal by refusing to make such a small concession now given how far we have come in the process. The best defense against the nibble is a comment like "I am sorry, but we just can't do that." If that does not work, consider making a counter "nibble" of slightly higher magnitude. Fortunately, not all distributive negotiations involve dirty tricks. In fact, some interactions lead to an integrative outcome and a discussion of this follows.

INTEGRATIVE NEGOTIATIONS

The fundamental difference between a distributive and integrative negotiation is whether the pool of exchanged resources (the "pie") gets expanded. Pie expansion is a thing of beauty. When both sides get all that they want instead of only part (maybe only half in a classic compromise), there is just cause for celebration. Participants in such a negotiation are often quite satisfied with the deal, and the relationship between the parties often flourishes as a result.

The classic example of an integrative negotiation involves two sisters. There is only one orange in the house. Both girls simultaneously decide that they want the orange. Both run to the kitchen to claim the last remaining orange. Consider how this dilemma would be resolved in a distributive negotiation. Under the classic compromise situation, one girl would cut the orange in half and the other would get to select her half of the orange while the other gets the remaining half. To be sure, each girl would get about half of what she wanted. Now, consider an integrative resolution. Here, each sister would discuss the situation. Interests would be shared. Questions about why the orange was wanted would be asked. Time would be taken to consider a variety of potential resolutions to the issue.

In this classic example of sisters each wanting the last remaining orange in the house, it becomes apparent that an integrative solution is possible in which both girls can get all that is wanted. When asked *why* she wants the orange, the first sister says that she wants to eat the pulp. No big surprise here. But when the second sister is asked *why* she wants the orange, she responds that she needs the peel as an ingredient for a recipe she is preparing. So, the first sister takes all of the pulp as she wanted and the second takes all of the peel as she wanted. By asking questions, sharing information, taking some time to think, and creatively resolving the problem, each girl has all of her interests fulfilled.

With such an ideal outcome, why are not all negotiations resolved integratively? Unfortunately, it is not always possible. But it is possible far more often that most negotiators believe to be the case. As a matter of fact, most negotiations have the potential for at least some pie expansion even though participants believe that that most negotiations are a zero-sum game.

It should also be mentioned that integrative outcomes are harder to achieve. Integrative negotiation takes longer, involves creative thinking, and requires a higher level of trust among the participants so that they become willing to share interests rather than just positions. Interests are the fundamental, underlying, and often hidden needs that a party is trying to achieve from a deal. Positions are what a party says it wants and are exemplified by the terms of sale that are quoted to the other side.

Even with a solid recognition of the benefits of integrative negotiation, that outcome is often hard to achieve. An important factor here is the fact that conflict tends to prevail over cooperation in many negotiating settings. Furthermore, often parties come to a negotiation with a past history that makes trust building and information sharing difficult to achieve. Consider, for example, the next negotiation between the National Hockey League Players Association and owners of those teams. Given the history of lockouts and strikes in the past, there is not much love in the room when these parties get together.

So how can negotiators experience the benefits of an integrative outcome? How can each side get more pie than would be obtained under a distributive outcome? The next section describes five methods for expanding the pie.

Pie Expansion Tactics

There are at least five tactics that can be used to expand the pie and create an integrative solution within a negotiation.[5] These can best be explained by way of the following example. Consider the negotiation between a happily married husband and wife concerning their next vacation. Here are the facts. They want to go together. Each works outside the home and gets two weeks of vacation time. If requested soon enough, each can pick almost any two weeks in the year. The husband says that he would like to go to the mountains and the wife says that she would like to go to the ocean. The classic distributive solution would be to spend perhaps one week at the ocean, then travel to the mountains for the second week. While they would be together, each party gets only one week at the first-choice location. Another popular distributive choice would a form of turn taking. The wife could get her ocean vacation this year but plan on a trip to the mountains next year. Integratively negotiated outcomes are better.

The first type of an integratively negotiated outcome is very straightforward, but often overlooked: *expand the pie*. Each party could ask the respective boss for more vacation time. Occasionally, the supervisor will approve this request. If not asked for, there is no likelihood of the boss voluntarily offering the extra time. Why not ask?

Another way to create an integrative outcome in which there is more pie to share across the participants is through the use of *nonspecific compensation*. In this tactic, one side gets her way and the other side is "paid back" for compliance in an unrelated way. In the current example, the couple could go to the ocean for their vacation, but the husband could receive nonspecific compensation. For example, suppose that the husband had been asking for his wife's permission to allow him to start a part-time career in NASCAR but that she had so far refused to give it. She might get her preference on the ocean vacation, but then relent and grant permission for the husband's NASCAR ambitions. A key issue here is that the payback be unrelated to the vacation. The pie would be expanded because the wife gets all she wants (100%) relative to the ocean vacation and the husband gets something that until now was unattainable, creating additional satisfaction or utility for him as well.

Another related tactic is called *cost cutting*. In this situation, one side gets its way. The cost for the other side's compliance with this outcome is also considered, however, and reductions are sought, enabling a more positive outcome than would otherwise have been the case. In our vacation example, let's assume once more that the wife gets her way. The couple plans an ocean vacation. But the wife, in the spirit of true cooperation, asks the husband what it is about ocean vacations that he does not like. If what he does not like includes noise and crowds, the wife could select a relatively quiet and sparsely populated spot for their ocean vacation, which would cut the husband's cost for complying with the decision. She gets her first wish fulfilled, but his utility is improved by the removal of what he disliked about vacationing near the ocean.

A fourth method for securing an integrative negotiation is through the use of *logrolling*. This tactic requires that at least two issues be under consideration in the negotiation. Let's reframe the current vacation example as a two-issue problem. We already have the issue of location: mountains or ocean. A second issue might involve hotel quality: high or low.

We already know about each party's preferences about location. How about hotel quality? Perhaps the wife has a preference for high-quality hotels while the husband prefers a low-quality hotel due to the cheaper price. In addition, perhaps each party also has a different valuation relative to the importance for the two issues of location and hotel quality. Maybe the wife is more concerned about hotel quality than location and the husband is more concerned about location than hotel quality. This is an ideal setting for logrolling. If each party gets to its first choice on the most important issue, the vacation will take place at a high-quality hotel (wife) in the mountains (husband). Since the decision is based on what is most important to each party, each gets more than half of what was wanted, enabling pie expansion.

Finally, we come to the most difficult opportunity to achieve an integrative outcome. This method is called *bridging* and involves conceptualizing the problem in a radical new way. Suppose that instead of selecting one of the stated positions (mountains or ocean) that is already on the table, the husband and wife search for a solution that fulfills their more fundamental interests. The husband can ask the wife, "*Why* do you like vacations at the ocean?" or similar questions. The wife should also ask the husband, "*What* is it that attracts you to vacationing at a mountain location?" By exploring their reasons behind their originally stated positions, they may be able to find a solution to the problem that they both like.

For example, let's suppose that the wife likes the ocean for vacations because when she goes there she enjoys sunbathing and swimming in the pool. Perhaps the husband likes the mountains because when he is there he finds many opportunities for hunting and fishing due to the remoteness of the site. If they give this some further thought and freely share with each other what they fundamentally enjoy about the vacation experience, the couple may determine, for example, that a two-week vacation together in a hotel near a highly remote Canadian lake in July enables both to get all of what they want. This is an optimal solution that was possible only because both sides worked together to explore creative solutions that were not initially considered.

CONCLUSION

Negotiation is hard work, but the payback can be very attractive. Now more than ever, the opportunity to work with others to explore modification and improvement of offerings enables greater productivity, higher customer satisfaction, and often more profitable deals for both parties involved. When buyers and sellers negotiate issues of concern rather than simply seeking out alternative partners, working relationships often improve and long-term strategic alliances become more likely.

Here is some good advice on negotiations. Prepare well, set ambitious but discussable goals, seek and develop more attractive BATNAs (best alternatives to negotiated agreements), be honest, and treat opponents with respect. When the time is right share your interests, not just your positions, with the other side. Furthermore, learn from your previous negotiation encounters. Identify where you have done well and in what areas you should work for improvement. If you do these things, you will be well positioned for negotiation success.

NOTES

1. Leigh Thompson, *The Mind and Heart of the Negotiator* (Upper Saddle River, NJ: Prentice Hall, 1998), 2.

2. For many examples of gambits, see Roger Dawson, *Secrets of Power Negotiating* (New York: Career Press, 2000).

3. "The #1 Sales Scam," *Reader's Digest* 164, no. 982 (February 2004): 138–41.

4. "Game of Chicken," *Answers.com*, http:www.answers.com/topic/game-of-chicken (accessed August 22, 2006).

5. Roy J. Lewicki, David M. Saunders, and Bruce Barry, *Negotiation*, 5th ed. (Boston: McGraw-Hill Irwin, 2006), 84–86.

Part II

INTEGRATED MARKETING: THE PRODUCT-CUSTOMER CONNECTION

CHAPTER 5

PATH-FORWARD THINKING: CORE COMPETENCIES AND THE VALUE PROPOSITION

Ken Dickey

INTRODUCTION

With all that has been written about the subject of core competence, why is it that the present-day strategic planning process has proven so frustratingly difficult and yielded continued poor operating results for so many companies? One wonders if the process of strategic thought, which must take place before action, can provide serious benefits. If so, can companies learn to utilize this powerful tool?

It seems that the concept of core competence is too abstract and theoretical for real-world consideration and use. Apparently, this is a topic for the classroom that corporations never apply to their strategic thought process. If this concept of strategic thought anchored by the core competency process is to deliver on the promise of the future, why do so many companies continue to struggle to implement it?

As a practical matter, many business leaders view the core competence subject in isolation, as though conversational mastery of this topic will prove to be the "secret ingredient" missing from their recipe for success. Often discussed as the latest and greatest one-minute business solution, "core competence" is interwoven with those classic phrases "back to basics" or "returning to our roots"; it is never really understood and therefore is superficially applied.

In reality, most strategic plans contain little genuine forward thought and are no more than an exercise in spreadsheet arithmetic. Companies take the year's numbers, add x percent, build a series of action steps that are good enough to get through the presentation meeting, and next year blame poor results on the economy, competition, weather, etc. The strategic planning process in use by companies who take the time to generate a long-term plan is similar. An abundance of numbers, data, charts, graphs, comparisons, analysis, plans, and action steps are all built through a backward-looking perspective; not a single eye looks to the horizon or what might lie beyond.

A quest for understanding is embedded in the core competence process. The real power of this understanding is in the intellectual work and thought process, which involves dynamic discussions, tough introspective questions, and brutal intellectual honesty. The product of these efforts is a clear direction for the future of the enterprise, which will continue to produce increasingly superior results. "Superior results" means growth rates two to five times the industry norm, and financial results (measured by return on capital employed) of the same magnitude when compared to competition. The delight of customers who place serious value on their strategic relationship with the firm is the true testimony of the firm's success.

Addressing the real barriers requires intellectual honesty—something that not everyone finds easy. The intellectually honest discussion process that will soon be addressed is not for the timid, casual, or unwilling, as it will expose difficult, perhaps painful, and unpopular topics requiring attention. A commitment to producing superior results demands intellectual honest and open discussion on all subjects. Remember that if superior results were easy, everyone would do it.

Readers may find it amazing that so many companies continue to struggle year after year simply because they fail to address the most basic issues. Hopefully, the case examples given will be beneficial in making the connection from theory to practice.

CASE EXAMPLE 1: CONFLICTING FUNDAMENTALS

The owner of an enterprise makes all the politically correct statements about growth, long-term career opportunities, future plans, etc., but in fact is unwilling to fund growth projects. The owner's level of satisfaction for risk and complexity of the enterprise has been achieved, and additional capital investment or risk is not necessary for him to further benefit. The owner's desire to preserve the status quo remains unspoken, but the intellectual honesty required for the core competence process will quickly uncover this watershed issue. The enterprise cannot deliver on the promise of growth if its basic fundamentals are in conflict. The conflict between the personal life of the business owner and the needs, expectations, and aspirations of employees, customers, and vendors is ever present. There is no easy answer or quick fix, and the frustration of those team members trying to execute a long-term growth strategy will continue to grate against the true agenda of the owner until the problem is solved. Albert Einstein once said that the definition of insanity is doing the same thing over and over and expecting the same results; unfortunately, some companies do this.

For any plan to deliver on the promise of the future, the importance of every stakeholder must be acknowledged. The reality of expectations (business and personal) requires that a company consider the aspirations, desires, and needs of all stakeholders, not just the owners. The stakeholders' responses to future plans must also be considered; it is important to remember that all stakeholders have an opinion, positive or negative, about the future of the firm. Stakeholders are raised to the forefront of corporate attention depending on the issue, hence the need to recognize their importance.

Understanding and using core competence does not require investment, but the success and growth of customers will dictate future investment pace as the firm gains a greater share of an expanding market-based opportunity. Investment decisions should be centered on serving the needs of customers.

Building a great business, not just an average business, is a matter of conscious choices. The size of the company is no guarantee for success. In the example of the business owner who was satisfied with merely the status quo, the choice had been made, though probably never discussed, to accept the concept that "okay is good enough." Usually these owner-focused companies slowly settle and fade over time. Bright new employees are not attracted, vendors share their new ideas with companies on the move, customers look elsewhere for value innovation, and lending institutions view the lack of growth as a sign of management weakness and stagnation.

The greater the need for superior performance, the more critical the task of comprehensive strategic thought becomes. An understanding of core competence is at the heart of this process.

The strategic thought process utilizing core competence as a driver is difficult, painful, and awkward. It requires one to think on multiple levels (vertical, horizontal, and concentric), deal with an unknown number of variables (including business and personal), and recognize the simultaneous occurrence of those variables. In this example, the business owner has made a personal choice, factoring in comfort level, risk tolerance, family status, etc. This basic unspoken decision will drive the future of the enterprise, for better or worse. This example used a small business as a case model; however, larger firms are subject to their own series of barriers and blinders. Size or product diversity is no guarantee for success.

The process to harness the power of core competence is not a stand-alone, one-time event; the discussions usually span months and are conducted best by a neutral moderator. Furthermore, the process includes the key people running the business. These busy people are stressed already with the events of the day. Most managers are short-term tacticians; they look for immediate resolution of "today" issues. Unfortunately, many of their tactics prove toxic to the long-term success. Many times the flood of everyday activity and their training or instincts prevent them from seeing the world from a position of opportunity driven by understanding, a position that comes from the core competence process.

Some team members may have difficulty grasping or accepting the concept of core competency, while others may fear change and take on obstructionist roles. In many companies that I have had the opportunity to assist, we have found that time to understand and digest this new lens to the world is a great ally in gaining an opportunistic perspective.

An open discussion process often reveals strong differing opinions about what the company actually does and what it needs to do. As employees have an opportunity to speak openly about their feelings regarding what they believe is really happening in the company, these latent feelings and issues will surface. The example's small-business owner might be surprised at his employees' reactions to his speech about growth. Their reactions would show him the reality of the consequences that flow from his unspoken agenda. His agenda may have greater influence on the business than any other single issue.

Keeping all stakeholders in mind, a company must decide what it wants to do and does not want to do, how it wants to do it, what needs to happen and when, and how it will deal with the variables.

CASE EXAMPLE 2: BOEING AIRPLANE COMPANY

Not long ago, Boeing referred to their firm as being in the "transportation business." This comprehensive, all-inclusive corporate direction led to multiple paths. Transportation includes everything from planes, boats, cars, bikes, elevators, trains, and walking, and some of these ideas may have been good for Boeing. In reality, however, the heart of Boeing was airplanes. So after years of less than satisfactory operating results, Boeing was forced into serious reconsideration, and attention was again focused on the core competence of Boeing: airplane design and manufacturing. As an affirmation of their newfound focus, Boeing even began calling themselves The Boeing Airplane Company. Today, Boeing is the world leader in commercial aircraft and the envy of global competitors.

Imagine the vigorous discussion at Boeing during this period of self-examination, particularly between the corporate managers defending the transportation theme and the operating people opposing it. In the end, they achieved success by hearing the voice and needs of the customer, initiating the core competence process, and forging the value proposition.

In an article in *BusinessWeek*, Stanley Holmes writes, "Another success driver [is] Boeing's newfound discipline on the factory floor. It has come a long way from the troubles it faced in 1997, when production problems shut down two assembly lines and cost the company $2.5 billion."[1] Boeing's core competence and discipline to the design and manufacturing of commercial and military aircraft is at the heart of its success.

Core competence is a way of thinking about the total enterprise and how the people within it view the world served by their customers. Cultivating and developing a thought process centered on core competency does not require outspending competitors on research and development. The core competency process has nothing to do with vertical integration. Outsourcing is a tool, while a thorough understanding of the company is the true value.

Consider the issue of the stakeholders in a business and which of the stakeholders has the most significant stake. These stakeholders are united in their desire for a successful business, each for their own reasons.

The listing of stakeholders includes but is not limited to employees, customers, vendors, the financial community, shareholders, union leaders, joint development partners, distributors, representatives, dealers, integrators, users, original equipment manufacturers, etc. All of the stakeholders are important, but only one can reside at the top of this list: customers.

To emphasize this point, a company could ask each member of the strategic planning team to create his or her own list of the stakeholders in order of priority. This list will provide insight into how the employees see the company and whom the company should serve. Without customers, the remaining names on the list of stakeholders simply disappear. Serving customers better must be the first priority of all strategic thought process.

Sufficient time must be allowed for this early step since it will create the unity of purpose upon which the enterprise will rest. Team members will come to this strategic thought process with a narrow focus and must be given time to internalize the most fundamental reason why their enterprise is in business. Once customers favor them with orders, then all the stakeholders can share in the celebration. A simple review of how the enterprise responds to a business downturn validates this point; in a downturn, the company will launch a new marketing and sales theme focused on customers, which is quickly abandoned once the bookings crisis appears over. The company then moves on to the next hot topic, unaware that its path is circular.

Core competence discussion requires decisions concerning what the company is about and what it is not. Having had the opportunity to participate in this core competence process with many firms, I have found that many companies stall at this very first step. They simply cannot agree on what the business is about and what it is not. Management has allowed the direction of the business to be self-defined—that is, defined by the desires of individual self-serving units—to the point of paralysis. Nothing more can be accomplished until senior management clarifies this basic question, ironically a question that they have caused in the first place.

CASE EXAMPLE 3: SWISS WATCHES

One of the more widely discussed case studies used by universities is the example of the mechanical-watch business located in Switzerland. For years watches produced in Switzerland were the world hallmarks of fine watches. This precision mechanical manufacturing business, however, failed to notice the threat coming from the emerging market of electronic components in Japan. The Japanese competitors planned to compete through a complete change of technology. Electronic-component watches were cheaper, feature rich, more reliable, and easily mass-produced. In a period of a few years, more than 90 percent of the Swiss mechanical-watch business was gone, replaced by the new electronic watches from Japan. Thousands of employees who produced these fine parts were out of work, and the economy of Switzerland that depended on these craftsmen suffered.

In the aftermath of this market crash, the core competence process revealed to the Swiss leaders that their real competence was their ability to produce small precision mechanical parts. Watches just happened to be one of the uses for these precision parts, so any product that had a requirement for this level of precision could be considered to recover business losses.

While the list of potential consumer and industrial products was lengthy, one of the most promising possibilities was the upscale SLR camera product line. With the realization that Swiss precision parts competence could be applied to many products in multiple industries with customers worldwide, the Swiss turned their failure into success.

Although the Swiss were absolutely certain they were in the mechanical-watch business, when viewed through the lens of the core competence process they saw their business as a series of capabilities that extended far beyond watches.

The power of core competence is not visible unless a company looks for it in a deliberate manner, which is why it took such a long time for the Swiss to view themselves as having a series of competencies rather than just as producers of mechanical watches. The Swiss found that a useful core competence must be difficult for others to imitate, and it must make a significant contribution to the end product or service.

In consideration of the case of the Swiss watch industry, it is important to remember that the use of the core competency thought process is no guarantee or protection from competitors. Nothing the Swiss could have done would have prevented the Japanese from entering the watch business with new technology and creating a major market shift from mechanical to electronic watches. The metrics were in favor of the electronic components; it was the Swiss watchmakers' narrow perspective that caused the true damage.

It is important to realize that new and powerful competitors will enter the market from distant arenas using technology as their gateway. The Swiss business leaders did not realize this, and so they failed to see the threat from the Japanese electronics industry. A comprehensive understanding of their core competencies would have facilitated a far quicker response to the threat; it would have allowed them to expand into other products and markets that utilized their ability to produce fine mechanical components and parts.

CASE EXAMPLE 4: HONDA CORPORATION

If the Swiss watch industry is a negative example, Honda Corporation provides a positive example of core competency thought process. In my class studies, I ask the students to define Honda's core competency. Their responses are typically quality, value, choice, manufacturing, culture, engineering, or price. The correct answer surprises many.

At the heart of Honda's success resides a competence fired by passion to be the world's best designers and manufacturers of gasoline engines. Therefore any product or application that uses a gasoline engine as its prime fuel is fair game for the Honda product teams.

Just as the Swiss did not see the Japanese electronic threat coming from that distant arena, the U.S. lawn care industry did not see Honda coming into their industry. Until that point, Honda produced only cars and motorcycles, and these upscale transportation products were a long way from the business of consumer lawn care products. The Honda lawn care product, however, entered the market with a 30+ percent price premium and captured a significant share of market. When consumers are willing to pay a price premium for a product with demonstrated superior value and features, a competitive action based on lower price is not an effective response. The premium price serves as the point of validation for superior content.

The Honda business leaders clearly understand the power of core competency and have remained extremely loyal to the principles that differentiate competencies, technologies, and products.

Today, this portfolio of competencies allows Honda to participate in multiple products where the common link is a desire for a high-quality gasoline engine. The list continues to grow and currently includes standby power generators, lawnmowers, outboard marine engines, snowmobiles, automobiles, motorcycles, power sprayers, and their new venture aircraft engines. If a product utilizes a gasoline engine, consider it fair game for the Honda product teams. While competitors have tried to imitate the Honda business model, none have done it better.

Honda's success shows that core competence will provide access to a wide variety of markets. The Swiss watch industry was late to understand the value of their competency, while the leaders of Honda were early adapters and enjoyed a profitable growth curve for more than 50 years.

Honda's success also proves that it is important to differentiate competence, technologies, and products. Technology alone is not a core competence, but the organizational capacity to integrate human expertise across various levels of the organization is. Individual technology streams are not the issue, but the ability to harmonize the hard and soft issues across an enterprise is at the center of making competency an effective tool. In the case of Honda, they take the experience and knowledge gained from the racetrack and deliver that knowledge to various product design teams worldwide.

The knowledge gained from technology investments must have the capacity to move through the organization. It does little good to spend resources on technology development and then not have a competency to move that knowledge through the organization to people who can convert this knowledge into benefit for customers.

A company collectively learns and improves by developing a culture centered on learning, working together, and moving knowledge to those who need to know. Those responsible for stewardship of technology absolutely must have a shared understanding of customer needs and technical possibilities.

CASE EXAMPLE 5: LAWN TRACTORS

Recently, a local lawn implement dealer sent a very angry letter of resignation to the factory headquarters when his flagship supplier signed a national arrangement to source lawn and garden tractors to a national big box store organization. Until this time all lawn and garden tractor sales had gone through the exclusive dealer organizations, which enjoyed protected territories. The dealer could not understand how the loyal dealers could be expected to compete for new equipment sales against such a large-volume organization.

What the dealer did not realize was that his core competency was not new equipment sales, but it was supplying parts and service for the lawn care tractors. New product sales, as well as the employees, facility capability, revenue, and customer perception, were all based upon aftermarket parts and service. The competency to provide technical service and support to customers was a capability that few could imitate or duplicate. Thus his supplier's shift to a big box store that does not provide parts or service could only help his business.

CASE EXAMPLE 6: A FOOD PRODUCTS COMPANY

Lately, a large producer of processed foods decided to make a significant acquisition of a firm that used many of the same raw ingredients. The difference in the two firms was that one company used the national grocer's wholesale distributor's organization while the other company used the association of frozen food distributors. It seemed straightforward enough, as both frozen foods and dry goods foods used many of the same raw ingredients.

Unfortunately, because the original food products company had no competence in the frozen food industry and proved their ineptitude with their actions, the penalty administered by the frozen food distribution organization was a loss of revenue of more than 75 percent in the first 12 months. The frozen food acquisition was sold in less than 18 months and the food products company took a write-down on the acquisition of more than $80 million. It was an expensive lesson for such a basic principle.

Acquisitions made in the name of vertical integration, sourcing, raw materials, etc., are often the very worst performers because they are viewed from an incremental operations perspective and not from a core competency perspective. No one takes the time to examine the two companies in terms of a series of competencies. This example of the food products company is not extreme, but it is a real example in which the core competencies of the companies were not known or understood until well after the fact.

These six case studies illustrate the power of the core competency process to deliver on the promise of the future. Competency, or a portfolio of capabilities, is essential to a path-forward strategic thought process.

NOTE

1. Stanley Holmes. "Boeing Straightens Up and Flies Right," *BusinessWeek*, May 8, 2006, 69.

CHAPTER 6

FUTURING: ANTICIPATING THE EMERGING VOICE OF THE CUSTOMER

Stephen M. Millett

THE CHALLENGE

The cardinal rule of marketing has been, "Listen to the customer." The theory is that to be responsive to customer demand, marketers need to pay attention to what customers say they want. But what if they cannot express what they want? Sometimes, waiting for customers to state their needs results in being too slow and not sufficiently competitive to respond to customer demand. In still other cases customers may not be able to envision or articulate what they want. For example, Henry Ford allegedly asserted that "if I'd only listened to customers, I'd have developed faster horses."[1]

Traditional market research methods have proven to be very effective, even predictive, of identifying short-term and well-articulated customer wishes. Focus groups, interviews, and surveys have been invaluable when customers can see and react to the proposed new product or service. They can react to the tangible. The shorter the time frame, the more predictive the voice of the customer is. Yet these same market research tools typically fail when more abstract concepts and longer time periods are presented to customers. Customers generally find themselves unable to articulate what they will want in the extended future or whether or not they would buy at a specific price point until they can see and feel a product prototype.

What is an enterprise to do when the length of time it will take to bring a product or service to market is three years or more into the future? How can we know that a new product will sell when it reaches the market? How do we know what customers are willing to spend?

These questions pose a particularly troubling challenge to companies that pride themselves on innovation, original research and development (R&D), and being the first to market with new products and services. They must accurately anticipate customer demand in the future as well as respond to present customer demands without the information to make accurate assessments.

Futuring is emerging as a new tool for identifying likely consumer preferences and demands in the extended future when customers themselves cannot say what they will want. It employs a number of methods to explore likely states of customer behavior and needs yet unknown to customers themselves.

The purpose of this chapter is to explore the substance, methods, and applications of futuring as a potentially vital approach to marketing in the 21st century.

THE SUBSTANCE OF FUTURING

Futuring is the systematic study of long-term consumer trends and patterns of behavior in place of short-term consumer-articulated research. While straight trend extrapolations can be misleading, an understanding of how consumers have behaved in the past provides foresight into how they are likely to behave in the future.

One very important and often studied consumer trend is the composition of the consumer population, or demographics. An understanding of age, gender, ethnic origin, and other population characteristics has long been a part of market segmentation research. Futuring, however, extends the time horizon of market segmentation research to anticipate how people are likely to behave, under certain circumstances, in the future. A few examples illustrating the point follow.

In 1991, Strauss and Howe published a book in which they asserted that there had always been four basic types of generational cohorts in American history and that the generations followed predictable patterns of behavior.[2] By studying generational types, one could anticipate the predilections and preferences of generations. This principle could also be applied to consumer behavior. In an independent study, Yankelovich Partners built a database and provided an analysis of three generations in the 20th century: matures, boomers, and Gen X.[3] They claim to have established patterns of behavior that could be used to explain and anticipate how each generation would likely behave while passing through the stages of life. This analysis provided insights into new product and service development as well as marketing strategies. While generational trend analysis remained controversial into the 21st century, the concept of age as a demographic indicator of future consumer behavior is now widely accepted and practiced.

Generational analysis by itself, however, is not as robust as when it is combined with other demographic trends. One is life stage analysis, which was popularized by the best-selling book authored by Gail Sheehy in the 1970s.[4] Her adherents placed a heavy emphasis on life stage rather than generation cohort as the primary driver of consumer behavior. The emerging theory is that all generations have their own peculiar attitudes and preferences based on shared cultural and historical experiences, especially those of their youth. But all individuals and generations pass through stages of life, such as adolescence, marriage and early family raising, careers, midlife, retirement, and old age. Generational analysis tells us that all age groups do not act exactly the same way as they move through different life stages, but that life stages set up the aspirations, achievements, and frustrations that are common to everyone.

By way of illustrations, matures, or the World War II generation, typically accepted authority, worked very hard, and retired with occasional but rarely regular postcareer employment. They tended to have single marriages and careers. With fresh memories of the Great Depression, matures tended to spend within their financial means and saved money for their future. The baby boomers, who were born between 1946 and 1964, however, developed great skepticism about authority from their experiences of the Vietnam War, Watergate, and corporate layoffs. Their generation experienced higher divorce rates than in the past and many boomers have had multiple marriages, families, and careers. Boomers have consistently been heavy spenders and light savers. How they will behave in retirement is now a major question. The expectation is that they will continue working, at least part-time, well into their 80s, with many boomers starting their own businesses relative late in life.

While insightful, generation cohort behavior is not sufficient by itself to anticipate future behavior. One also has to understand life stage. At certain life stages, people face similar challenges, such as gaining an education, marrying and raising a family, pursuing a career, entering middle age, retirement, etc. Originally, it was believed that one only needed to understand life stage to predict consumer behavior. This is not true, because different generations have different styles based on their common life and historical experiences and respond differently to the challenges of various life stages. As mentioned above, the World War II generation, due to their military experiences, approached family life and their career-building challenges in the 1950s very differently than the baby boomer generation did in the 1980s. Accordingly, the boomers' style of retirement may prove to be very different.

By understanding generational and life stage behaviors, one can anticipate at least in general terms how certain consumers are likely to act and what they are likely to buy in the future even when the customers may not be able to articulate their wants and needs. Yet futuring must take into account additional demographic and economic trends.

While generation and age are important demographic indicators of the future, so is ethnic identity, especially in an era of heavy immigration into the United States. Of primary importance are Hispanics who are entering the United States from Mexico, Central America, South America, and the Caribbean, both legally and illegally. Counted as a distinct group, irrespective of country of origin, Hispanics are now the single largest minority group in the United States. While their presence is well known in the border states of Texas, New Mexico, Arizona, and California, they also represent a significant social group in such other states as Nevada, Florida, and New York.[5]

Is Hispanic consumer behavior in the United States the same as that of other Americans? Are the types of homes and neighborhoods in which they live reflective of their ethnic tastes, their economic strata, or some other factors? What evidence exists that indicates that given sufficient income, Hispanic consumers have a hunger for many of the same lifestyles and consumer products favored by American consumers? Oddly, we still do not fully know the answers to these and similar questions. It is assumed that Hispanic baby boomers, whether born in the United States or not, but living and working in the United States, behave generally the same as American-born baby boomers. However, we do not have the studies to confirm this.

Observations also tell us that while Hispanics may patronize Hispanic businesses, they will also shop extensively in the mainstream American marketplace. Therefore most consumer products and large retail chains will offer information in both English and Spanish.

Asians, who are a rapidly growing minority with approximately more than 4 percent of the total U.S. population, are another significant minority in the United States. Their lifestyles and spending patterns are noticeably different from both those who are American-born and Hispanics. They tend to have a very strong sense of Asian and family identity and will adhere to Asian ways to the greatest possible extent. They will shop largely within their own community for products ranging from groceries to financial services. This may be due to language problems, but it may also be due to cultural preferences and an associated trust of similar Asians with a corresponding distrust of native-born Americans. The historical pattern, however, is that second- and third-generation Asians born in the United States acculturate as quickly as any other ethnic group in American history.

Gender is another important demographic factor. The United States has slightly more females than males, and in many consumer niches, women are more likely to be the consumers as well as the primary decision makers. For example, it has been well known for years that women buy more men's clothes than men do. Yet so many men's clothing stores appeal to masculine rather than feminine tastes. Women are also the primary buyers of health care services. Yet, again, so many doctors, clinics, and hospitals are male rather than female in language, behavior, and culture. In still other cases, women have an increasingly major influence on the purchases of large-ticket purchases, such as homes (primary and resort), cars, and travel.

Futuring considers all of these demographic trends and sorts them out as to what outcomes are most likely to occur by what designated date in the future.

Demographics, as contextual as they are, do not tell the whole story of consumer behavior. One has to consider economics and technology as well. Economic forecasting, however, is notoriously difficult to do and mostly inaccurate. That is not for a lack of data or sophisticated modeling and simulation; it is due primarily to the dynamics of so many variables interacting with each other that make prediction difficult. For example, the events of September 11, which greatly impacted the American economy, were not predictable.

At the macroscopic level, with only a few years as exceptions, the U.S. economy has shown consistent positive annual growth since World War II. The average annual growth of the largest economy in the world is not likely to sustain more than 5 percent growth in the GDP. The United States is not likely to have the kind of hyper growth rates of China and India. More importantly, however, is the real GDP or the growth rate normalized into constant dollars. More important still are average household income and disposable income. These economics touch the lives of everyday consumers. While the data are readily available for household income, household wealth is very difficult to estimate.

The trend has been that average American household incomes have remained remarkably stable for nearly 10 years and that household wealth, which is difficult to measure, may actually be declining. Many of the apparent gains in income must be discounted by inflation (especially in the staples of housing, energy, and food). At the beginning of the 21st century, household wealth was increasing due to the rapid inflation of real estate prices. Unfortunately, the collapse of the real estate market resulted in a decline in household wealth. Equally troubling is the decline in pension wealth as a long-term household resource. Many corporations have eliminated or reduced their pension plans. On the other hand, while household finances have changed in the last 20 years, technologies have continuously improved the general quality of life with many products and services declining in prices due to technological advancements.

Health care insurance is also critically important. While many Americans are employed, they may be underemployed (meaning that their levels of responsibilities and their incomes may not be parallel with their education and past work experience) and have little or no health care insurance. It is estimated that nearly 50 million Americans have no health insurance at all at a time in history when a visit to the emergency room could cost $5,000 or more.

When thinking about the future of consumer behavior, one has to consider beyond income the matter of net household wealth. This takes into account debt versus wealth. With rising consumer debt, declining real estate prices, rising energy costs, and rising interest rates, net assets may begin falling rather than rising several years into the future. Such a trend would have potentially devastating impacts on the baby boomer generation as it enters its retirement years.

Futuring must also consider emerging technologies. Everyone has seen the enormous impacts on lifestyles, employment, productivity, and consuming caused by the personal computer and the Internet within just the last 20 years. What will be the next Internet? Computers will likely range in size and bandwidth, like TVs and telephones. Beyond the information technologies, there are the potentially important new energy technologies and biotechnologies. Breakthroughs in both could be as revolutionary in the marketplace as the personal computer was in the early 1980s and the Internet was in the late 1990s.

THE METHODS

All futuring methods generally fall into three categories: trend analysis, expert judgment, and alternative futures, or multioptions analysis.[6] A brief overview of each follows.

Trends

Some of the leading indicators of future consumer behavior have already been identified above. These are trends or patterns of behavior over time (as opposed to discrete events, which are very difficult, if not impossible, to predict).

Trend extrapolation continues to be the most frequently used method to make forecasts. All forecasters use trend data, because data exist only for the past and the present. No one has data from the future. Trend analysis can be very reliable in some cases, but it can only anticipate continuity. It cannot predict discontinuities.

I was asked once how many data points were required to draw a trend line. I thought the questioner was kidding me, so I said that I like at least two, but prefer three. He looked at me with a straight face and said that was odd because at his company they typically used only one. Obviously, predicting a trend for the future based on only one data point is risky business.

A common assumption is that additional data lead to better predictions. This may not be true. Indeed it may be the opposite, as past data may emphasize certain events or recent past events more than they should. Trends within an industry may be used to develop projections for shifts in purchase behaviors, due to changes in culture, tastes, fashion, or technology. Trend data are often collected and disseminated by associations or trade groups. For example, recent trend data published by the International Association of Culinary Professionals are shown in Figure 6.1, which shows several key trends, such as a trend toward lifestyle simplicity, that will likely impact consumer eating habits and purchases in the future.[7]

The theoretical problem with trend data, however, is not merely the amount of them or even their accuracy. The problem is the variability of the phenomena for

Figure 6.1
Key Consumer Food Trends

The focus is on healthy living
• People continue to cook, but want to take advantage of quick preparation time and convenience while taking advantage of healthy, fresh ingredients
• Focus on holistic health, including the mind, body, and waistline
Lifestyles are more casual
• Focus on simplicity and sharing
• More interest in local and regionally grown foods
• Slow cookers, aka crock pots, are experiencing a comeback
Ethnic Foods
• Italian and Mexican foods are no longer considered ethnic, but mainstream
• New ethnic trends are Thai, South American, and Mediterranean
Kids want food to be fun
• Enjoy a surprise element

Source: McLain, Cathy, *Forum Offers Food Marketers Trends Snapshot*, "The Hungry Mind," Quarterly Joint Publication of the Marketing Communicators Section of the International Association of Culinary Professionals and the Food and Beverage Section of the Public Relations Society of America (IACP and PRSA), Second Quarter 2004, p. 4.

which we gather data. In cases where the data are extensive and accurate and the phenomena are very stable, then trend analysis can be very accurate. Trend projections do work on many occasions, especially in the short term and for things known to vary little over time.

One very interesting trend is the shift in work in the United States over the past century. In 1900, over 40 percent of American working men were engaged in farming, fishing, and mining. By 2000, the proportion had dropped to about 4 percent. In the same 100 years, the proportion of professionals and retail male employees rose from 21 percent to 58 percent. Workers in production facilities, like mills and factories, and transportation rose from 38 percent in 1900 to a peak of about 50 percent by 1950, and then declined back to 38 percent by the end of the century.[8]

These trends reflect the economic shift from agriculture to manufacturing to retail and the "knowledge economy." However, even over long periods of time, will these trend lines be linear projections in the future? It is hard to image that agriculture will drop further, although a decline to 1 to 2 percent of the working population is certainly possible. Will manufacturing jobs in the future drop like agricultural jobs have? Considering trends in technology, especially information and communications technologies (ICTs), it seems likely that the proportion of manufacturing jobs may fall to 20 percent.

Trend analysis, however, breaks down when the data are not sufficient, data are inconsistent in accuracy, or the phenomena display a potential for great variability (or instability). The more complexity that exists in the phenomena (such as a large number of variables that are highly interactive with each other) and the longer the time horizon, the more there will be variability, risk, and uncertainty. For example, trend analysis is not very helpful in predicting fashion trends such as skirt length, tie widths, or baby names.

Trend analysis is another form of pattern recognition. In the many worlds of pattern recognition, there are fundamentally three categories of pattern recognition problems:

Type I: *Background Pattern Recognition.* The first type occurs when the background pattern is the principal focus of interest. It establishes what is the norm and the baseline of continuity. When the background is well understood, one looks for deviations ("signal") from the background to detect changes. One theory is that patterns of human living exist for long periods of time; the routines of everyday life endure despite periodic (and thankfully rare) great events of history.[9] In this context, the patterns have great stability, even though there may be relatively small deviations from time to time—and occasionally (but rarely) major disruptive events. One is impressed more with the continuities than the momentary exceptions. In this situation, trend analysis would generally be predictive.

Type II: *Signal Pattern Recognition.* The second type occurs when an event or a thing, called the signal, is the focus of interest rather than the background. One watches for the presence of the signal with little or no regard to the background (which may be only clutter confounding the detection of the signal). This perspective is the opposite of Type I; one is interested in the great events or discontinuities rather than the background, long-term patterns. Discontinuities do happen for all sorts of reasons, some of which are beyond the powers of humankind to control. Type II pattern recognition cannot be predicted from Type I analysis, although Type I trends are necessary to provide the context for understand the significance of Type II pattern recognition.

Type III: *Emerging Pattern Recognition.* In the third type, neither the background nor the pattern is known, so one collects data and searches for the pattern in them. Here is where both historians and futurists imagine all kinds of possibilities. The most favored Type III trend analysis is linear projections, even when complicated repression analysis has to be used to even find a line. It is possible that lines do exist, so a Type III analysis may lead to something that would fall into Type I. Another very popular pattern is cycles, whereby the analyst sees a consistent pattern of up and down curves.[10] A variation of cycles, called S-curves, have been developed to forecast the development of new technologies.[11] Cycles are very popular in all kinds of forecasting, but the periodicity of them and the exact replication of the curves over and over again is rarely achieved. The theory has great attraction, but the applications can be very messy.

In a true inductive style, one would need a great deal of data to be sure that the pattern would be repeatable over long periods of time. The pattern might be very irregular and have no similarity to either a line or a cycle. If the pattern did emerge, then Type III analysis would be a very effective way of discovering new Type I patterns.

Expert judgment is a form of intuitive forecasting. It is the only way, in most cases, to anticipate the discontinuities that cannot be predicted by trend analysis. In the ancient world, the experts with extraordinary predictive powers were called prophets, oracles, and soothsayers. Ultimately, in this historical context most of the predictions of such people came from their gods. Today, the experts are called analysts, professors, and consultants. Their inspirations come largely from their study of history, existing data, stringent logic, and the mental "black box" called intuition.

All expert judgments suffer from two major liabilities. One is the fact that no expert, contrary to what he or she may proclaim, can possibly know everything. The other is that all experts have their own biases. Therefore the best expert judgment methods involve many experts to fill in the gaps and smooth out the biases.

Expert judgment methods include interviews, questionnaires, surveys (both actual and virtual over the Internet), and group dynamics (such as brainstorming, variations on idea generation, and the Nominal Group Technique).[12]

Expert focus groups and expert judgment methods in general are used in ways very similar to the methods of short-term market research where the "experts" are the consumers themselves. The techniques for extracting judgments are about the same. The difference is largely in the pool of experts and the time frame of the questions. Whereas customers cannot articulate what they will likely do in the future, the experts who know about customers can make predictions based on their studies and their intuition. They may know more about the behavior patterns of customers than the customers know about themselves.

It should be noted in passing that all forms of modeling, even the most complex and quantitative, begin with expert judgment. Someone has to ask the focus question and select the variables that will be included and excluded from the model. Too often when futuring, there is no direct acknowledgment of this. In many cases the expert judgment, typically called assumption, is invisible in the construction of econometric and financial models. For example, assume we are interested in developing a model for predicting the number of students who would be available to attend state universities sometime in the future. We may include data on the number of high school students within the state, the present rate of college attendance, and the expected increase in tuition. Should this model also include students from outside the state; and what about students from other nations? What if we assume that the in-state tuition rate is extended to out-of-state students? Will this impact our results? What if the bias of the authors is that only legal residents should be able to attend the state university? Would this impact the result?

Alternative futures provide multiple possible futures. In trend analysis, there is an underlying assumption that there will be a single, most likely if not predetermined, future because of the momentum of the phenomena behind the trend data. There is a future and it is knowable. In expert judgment, there may be either singular or multiple predictions for the future. In alternative futures, the assumption is that there are multiple possible, even likely, futures and each requires examination. The most popular form of alternative futures today is scenario writing, although this category of methods also includes paths, trees, matrix analysis, and real options analysis.

The contemporary use of scenarios may be traced back to the RAND Corporation and the planning scenarios done for the U.S. Air Force in the 1950s. These scenarios were hypothetical, not predictive, sequences of cause-and-effect actions leading to a logically consistent end state. The RAND scenario method was adapted, with the help of Herman Kahn, by both GE and Shell in the early 1970s with a significantly different twist. In the applications of GE and Shell, scenarios became alternative end states with logically consistent components (trends, issues, factors, etc.) but without a presumed sequence of events. The Shell variation became highly publicized and the model for most scenario projects today.[13]

Depending upon their purposes and techniques, scenarios can be generated both intuitively, as a variation on expert judgment in a group setting with a potential for multiple (typically two to four) outcomes, and analytically using both expert judgment and trends analysis combined with probabilities, cross-impact analysis, and computer-based modeling and simulation.

Scenarios can be used a variety of ways just as they can be created in different ways. One use is contingency planning just as used by Kahn for the Air Force. The point of thinking about multiple endings (alternative futures) was to encourage the consideration of plans beyond the main one. For every Plan A there must be Plan B, C, D, etc., to cover possible alternative outcomes once a sequence of actions is put into motion. The military has been rigorous about contingency planning (at least at the tactical level), but businesses have not proven to be as flexible in their thinking and their actions as the military.

Another use of scenarios is the learning process itself. The scenarios are neither plans nor predictions, but rather a method for simulations of various complexity. Scenarios in the business context are similar to war games in the military sense.

They are hypothetical rehearsals of alternative, hypothetical futures. The benefits of the scenarios are derived from the insights gained in the process rather than the scenarios themselves. A secondary value is the team building that also comes from the process involving the social dynamics of the same people who will be responsible for the implementation of strategies that emerge from the scenario exercise.

A third application of scenarios is forecasting, but in a different way than in statistical, financial, and economic forecasting. Scenarios, at least analytical rather than intuitive scenarios, can be generated by modeling and simulation with or without a computer software program. As practiced by Battelle for over 20 years using the Interactive Futures Simulation (IFS) software program, scenarios begin with a topical question of importance to a client. The answers to the topical question will be used to make a decision in the near future about investments or strategies that will likely lead to desired outcomes in the long-term future. Expert judgment is used to identify the most important descriptors (trends, issues, factors, or variables) relative to the topical question. Trend analysis is performed for each descriptor. Then each descriptor is assigned alternative outcomes with a priori probabilities of occurrence by a target date.

While the software program provides the structure for cross-impact analysis of all the descriptors and their alternative outcomes with each other, the software program, using the judgments entered, also calculates adjusted probabilities of descriptor outcomes and arranges them in alternative sets (scenarios). The scenarios with the highest adjusted probabilities of occurrence are the scenarios that are most likely to occur given current information about trends. Desired scenarios may be included in the sets, although they may have low probabilities of occurrence. The desired scenarios provide foresights into what would need to occur, or what investments and strategies would have to be put in place in order to achieved desired outcomes (which provides more rigor and direction than just wishful thinking).[14]

CASE HISTORIES OF FUTURING

Two case histories will be offered to illustrate how futuring can be used to anticipate future consumer demand and to identify the emerging but yet unarticulated voices of customers. These come from the experience of Battelle, a large independent technology development, management, and commercialization firm headquartered in Columbus, Ohio.

The Case of the Intuitive Champion

The quotation by Henry Ford in the beginning of this chapter reflects the futuring of a new product champion, or one who sees the future with opportunities that few others do. It is the futuring of successful inventors and entrepreneurs. The first case history presented here tells the story of the origins of the Xerox machine when the intuitive futuring of the champion proved to be successful despite the flawed predictions of traditional market research.

In 1944 a patent lawyer from Battelle in Columbus, Ohio, met another patent lawyer in New York who was also an amateur inventor, named Chester Carlson. Carlson had a patent of his own invention for a dry, electrostatic copying machine. It was a revolutionary concept, but Carlson did not have the resources or the scope of complex technical knowledge to make it work beyond a benchtop model. So he joined forces with Battelle, which undertook at its own expense the development of an operational and commercially viable dry copying machine. Battelle's effort took 14 years! Along the way, a classics professor across the street at The Ohio State University suggested the brand name Xerox. The Xerox company was founded in Rochester, New York, to manufacture and distribute the machine. After many disappointments, the first commercially successful Xerox machine was offered on the market in 1960. It proved to be a huge success and emerged as one of the great technological innovations of its era.[15]

During the development of the Xerox process, Battelle and its partners commissioned a market research study. The study interviewed many potential customers and concluded that there was no market pull for a dry process copier. But Carlson, acting like a true new product champion, thought otherwise. He had his own view of the future. As a patent attorney, he knew from experience that there was no good process for him to make multiple copies of legal documents already in his possession. He personally knew trends in the law, government, and business. He knew that there would be a potential demand for offices to have their own copying capabilities. The people at Battelle and the Xerox Corporation agreed with him.

Why was the market study wrong in light of the later huge success of Xerox during the 1960s? The apparent reason was that the market study asked the wrong set of customers, who in turn could not verbalize their reactions to a totally unfamiliar product concept.

The market researchers went to secretaries, printers, and other people who generated copies. These people said they already had the tools that they needed and they did not see a role for a dry copier (which they apparently had a very difficult time visualizing in the framework of their normal work routines). When the Xerox machine was introduced and when people saw it and worked it, they came to see benefits not visualized or articulated before. It turned out that the customer base they had used was people who received, not generated, material. The original market research study had asked the wrong questions of the wrong potential customers and failed to anticipate several trends toward the explosion in business, legal, and academic paperwork.

Another point is that the Xerox Corporation was very clever to introduce a new business model for commercializing a new product. It was not only that the Xerox machine was a "better mousetrap" or that the Xerox Corporation was a better "mousetrap company," but that the business model for the new product was also a "better mousetrap value proposition." A major lesson here is that typically a new technology, especially a very novel one, requires a new business model.

The lesson of this case history is that, as asserted earlier, traditional market research methods fail when they ask prospective customers what they would buy in the future, especially when the product concept is not clearly developed understood or presented. Perhaps the market research went to the wrong target market (which frequently occurs); or it went to the right target market but asked the wrong questions (which also commonly happens). The point remains that the traditional market research came up with the wrong answer, which was ignored by the new product champion, who proved to be correct.

An important lesson is to understand that the customer of tomorrow may not be the customer of today. Who would have predicted 20 years ago that teenagers would be making the primary purchase decision for household telephones, for example? In this case, the expert judgment of Chester Carlson and his Battelle allies carried the day over the market research. Admittedly, they took huge technical and financial risks, but they were successful in implementing their vision of the future.

The Case of the Predictive Scenarios

The second case history also comes from Battelle and it is one in which this author was involved intimately. A consumer product company with a well-known corporate and brand name and with a common household product came to Battelle for futuring. The concept was to use futuring as a frame of reference for developing new products leveraged from existing capabilities. We used the IFS scenario method and supporting software program. The topic question concerned the future of American households and expectations for household cleaning. We conducted two expert focus groups (expert judgment), one with Battelle experts and one with corporate experts, from which we derived a number of demographic, social, economic, and technological descriptors. The core team, consisting of both Battelle and client project principals, performed trend analysis on the descriptors and projected the most likely alternative outcomes for each descriptor. The alternative outcomes (comprehensive, mutually exclusive, and numbering two to four for each descriptor) were assigned a priori probabilities of occurrence in the future based on trend analysis and expert judgment with peer review. Cross-impact analysis was performed with the IFS software program.

A large number of scenarios were generated by the software program. Most of them could easily be combined into five principal scenarios. With the scenarios giving us views to the future, we held yet another expert focus group at Battelle to derive product concepts from the scenarios. A materials engineer concluded that if people wanted cleaner homes, meaning more hygienic and free from illness-causing bacteria and viruses, but wanted to spend less time cleaning, then there was a potential market for a disposal wipe that would be impregnated with an antimicrobial substance. The product would be highly effective, easy to use, easy to throw away, and affordable.

The scenarios had stimulated a process of creating new product concepts. The client took the scenarios and their implications back to their R&D center, where they supplemented the scenarios with their own research and idea generation processes. The result was that within two years the corporation introduced a home-cleaning disposable wipe that became very popular as soon as consumers saw and tried the wipes.

When the scenarios were generated, we used a 10-year planning horizon. We asked the question in a way that gave a long-range perspective, but we never said that we had to wait 10 years to launch a new product. The client company introduced its wipe about three years after we began the scenario project. It made a likely future happen faster by being proactive rather than reactive to already existing and known consumer needs. Therefore the company seized all the competitive advantages of being first to market with an innovative product that captured people's imagination and store shelf space.

Futuring, particularly scenario analysis, proved to be the engine of innovation in new product development. It identified a potential consumer need in the future that had not been previously articulated in any meaningful way by traditional market research.

THE APPLICATIONS OF FUTURING

Looking into the future, four obvious applications of futuring come to mind, as follows:

R&D Investments and Portfolio Management. R&D organizations have the dilemma of developing technologies for future products with little or no direction on what consumers of the future will want. Some R&D organizations will conduct their own consumer but rarely market research. In too many companies, they get too little practical guidance from marketing. (In most companies there is a tension between marketing, which says to R&D, "Why can't you make what I can sell?," and R&D, which says to marketing, "Why can't you sell what I can make?") While the typical horizon of marketing organizations and traditional market research may be up to 1 year, the time horizon of R&D can be as far as 10 years into the future. Therefore R&D is turning to futuring as their long-term perspective on what technologies they should invest in and pursue.

Product Development. Both case histories above concerned futuring as the engine of innovation in new product development. In the past, new product development occurred primarily within R&D, but more recently new product development may be a separate function. Sometimes it falls under marketing rather than R&D. Some organizations will even have an innovation group and process separate from R&D and marketing. Whatever the structure, the question remains—what is the inspiration of innovation? Thinking about the future of customers, markets, and competitors provides an excellent avenue to stimulate innovation toward practical and successful new products and services.

Strategic Marketing. Marketing organizations need to do long-term thinking just as R&D groups must. Strategic marketing for the future addresses the issues of changing customers, shifting value propositions, and evolving market positioning of products and services. Skillful long-term marketing facilitates and reduces the costs of short-term selling.

Thought Leadership. Thought leadership occurs when a company takes ideas to its customers and shapes their very thinking. The object of thought leadership is mind share, which in the future of virtual networks will be like the shelf space of the future. It is the telling of a compelling story about the future to customers who are looking for answers they themselves do not have. Particularly in business-to-business relationships, buyers often look to their suppliers and partners to come up with new ideas for the future.

CONCLUSION

The purpose of this chapter was to explore the substance, methods, and applications of futuring as an emerging method for both companies and organizations to estimate the emerging, unarticulated voices of customers when customers themselves cannot say what they will want or buy in the future. "Customers" may be literally consumers or they may be stakeholders and constituents. It is important to remember that customers cannot always articulate what they will want in the future. Futuring is a way to anticipate the unarticulated voice of the customer based on various trends, including patterns of customer behavior. These patterns turn out to be better predictors of the future than what customers may say. In addition, futuring not only identifies potential new opportunities with existing customers; it may likely foresee new customers and growth opportunities.

NOTES

1. Thomas Goldbrunner, Richard Hauser, Georg List, and Steven Veldhoen, *The Four Dimensions of Intelligent Innovation: Winning the Race for Profitable Growth*, Booz Allen Hamilton, 2005, http://www.boozallen.com, 4.

2. William Strauss and Neil Howe, *Generations: The History of America's Future, 1584 to 2069* (New York: Morrow, 1991).

3. J. Walker Smith and Ann Clurman, *Rocking the Ages: The Yankelovich Report on Generational Marketing* (New York: Harper Business, 1997).

4. Gail Sheehy, *Passages: Predictable Crises of Adult Life* (New York: Dutton, 1976).

5. U.S. Census Bureau, *Statistical Abstract of the United States: 2004–2005*, 124th ed. (Washington, DC: U.S. Government Printing Office, 2004), 24.

6. Stephen M. Millett and Edward J. Honton, *A Manager's Guide to Technology Forecasting and Strategy Analysis Methods* (Columbus, OH: Battelle Press, 1991).

7. Cathy McLain, *Forum Offers Food Marketers Trends Snapshot*, "The Hungry Mind," Quarterly Joint Publication of the Marketing Communicators Section of the International Association of Culinary Professionals and the Food and Beverage Section of the Public Relations Society of America (IACP and PRSA), 2nd quarter 2004, 4.

8. Theodore Caplow, Louis Hicks, and Ben J. Wattenberg, *The First Measured Century: An Illustrated Guide to Trends in America, 1900–2000* (Washington, DC: AEI Press, 2001), 24–49.

9. Fernand Braudel, *Civilization and Capitalism, 15th–18th Century*, vol. 1, *The Structures of Everyday Life: The Limits of the Possible*, trans. and rev. Sian Reynolds (Berkeley: University of California Press, 1979/1992).

10. Strauss and Howe, *Generations*; Arthur M. Schlesinger Jr., *The Cycles of American History* (Boston: Mariner Books, 1999).

11. J. C. Fisher and R. H. Pry, "A Simple Substitution Model of Technology Change," *Technology Forecasting and Social Change* 3 (1971): 75–88.

12. Millett and Honton, *A Manager's Guide*, 43–61, 90.

13. Stephen M. Millett, "The Future of Scenarios: Challenges and Opportunities," *Strategy & Leadership* 31, no. 2 (2003): 16–24. Also see Liam Fahey and Robert M. Randall, eds., *Learning from the Future: Competitive Foresight Scenarios* (New York: Wiley, 1998).

14. See http://www.dr-futuring.com for more information about the Battelle approach to scenario generation. Also see William R. Huss and Edward J. Honton, "Scenario Planning—What Style Should You Use?," *Long Range Planning* 20, no. 4 (1987): 21–29; Stephen M. Millett, "Futuring and Visioning: Complementary Approaches to Strategic Decision Making," *Strategy & Leadership* 34, no. 3 (2006): 43–50.

15. Much of this case history is based on Battelle lore passed down by word of mouth. For Battelle's version of the Xerox story, see Clyde E. Williams, *Bridging the Gap: My Contributions to the Growth of Industrial Research* (Cincinnati, OH: Best Impression Corp., 1976), 95–104; George A. Boehm and Alex Groner, *Science in the Service of Mankind: The Battelle Story* (Columbus, OH: Battelle Press, 1981), 35–48.

CHAPTER 7

HOW TO CLEAN UP WITH A START-UP: TRICKS AND TIPS FROM ENTREPRENEURS

Robert Black

INTRODUCTION

You have come up with a smashing new labor-saving product for the home. You want homemakers everywhere to run out and buy it; what do you do? Clean Shower was introduced one bottle at a time. Samples were given to northern Florida employees of Winn Dixie supermarkets and their family members to try in their own homes. Company officials were lobbied until finally the store's buyer relented and agreed to allow the product on the shelves of the Jacksonville division. The inventor-entrepreneur-manufacturer-salesman then visited most of the 120 stores personally to ensure the product was available as agreed.

Then the creativity began. Beauty parlors near the Winn Dixie locations were targeted. Those beauty parlors were likely to contain local women who were careful about their appearance and their home's appearance. In the beauty parlor, they also had time to talk while waiting or even while sitting in the chair. The product was explained, some features were demonstrated, and then they received a free sample to try at home. "If you like it, buy it at Winn Dixie. If they're out, be sure to ask for more."

The captive audiences were captivated. Clean Shower took off. The rest, as they say, is history.

DEVELOPING PRODUCTS

Delivering new benefits or substantially improved benefits to the consumer is a must with a start-up company. To break through the noise and clutter, the offering must be outstanding in its own right. Me-too products will not work to kick-start a company. It is important to have a proprietary position. This can be as complex as securing patents or copyrights, registering trade names, or developing secret formulas or processes. It can be as simple as staking out a location on a busy street corner.

The most important proprietary position is the one in the mind of your customer. You and you alone occupy that place, nurture it, and defend it. Volvo established itself with a classic positioning on safety. Similarly, Rolls Royce laid claim to ultimate luxury. Clorox defended itself as "bleach" at the risk of becoming generic and being forced to share its position. As entrepreneurs, the first vital task is to set a goal for the positioning you want to establish for your new product. The rest of the introduction revolves around winning this spot and finding ways to defend it against intrusions from others.

How do you know you can achieve this unique positioning? There are many sources of statistics describing product launches, successes, and failures. It is claimed that only one out of five new products succeeds and that half of new products in the planning cycle are expected to generate less than $10 million in annual sales.[1] ACNielsen's consumer goods research operation, BASES, reported that in the year 2000, 30,000 new consumer brands were met with a 93 percent failure rate in the United States. The cost of these failures was put at a conservative $20 billion estimate.[2] Other sources cite somewhat different numbers, but the conclusion is inescapable: launching a successful product is very difficult.

One necessary but not sufficient requirement for success is that the innovation fulfills a need in the market. Ambi-Pure is a toilet-cleaning product sold by Sarah Lee. In its first year, sales grew astronomically. This said less about the product than about the market. Many new toilet-cleaning products enjoy excellent initial sales, then drop off. Customers continue to have a need for a better product in this market and are willing to try newcomers. None has been established as the dominant toilet cleaner.

In a classic product introduction, Crisco, the leading—almost sole—shortening available to homemakers was challenged by Spry. The introduction came with the marketing muscle of Lever Brothers. Although the challenge seemed insurmountable, the introduction succeeded. This was due in part to the fact that the market for shortening expanded as the fierce competition between Lever and Procter and Gamble reminded consumers of their needs in this category.[3]

The needs do not have to be significant or radical. Addressing small but lingering needs can lead to success as well. Take, for example, the fragrance of products that are not designed to provide or enhance fragrance. This characteristic is easily overlooked but can greatly influence purchase, use, reuse, and other desirable responses. Observing behavior at the retail shelf, shoppers will select those products that stand out, read some of the label, and then smell the product. Even some products in sealed metal cans are subjected to the smell test. Why? Consumers may be searching for indication of good products or merely trying to avoid bad (spoiled) ones. Once the product is in the consumer's hands, she is looking for confirmation that she has made the right decision or to discover a reason to put the product down and select another.

This rejection may not be the fault of the product at all, but due to some aspect of the package, merchandising, and the like. Staying with our olfactory example, a sealed and precooked canned ham may be rejected by a customer if the label's smell is reminiscent of a dead animal. (Some glues used to seal labels to containers still are made from rendered animal flesh.) Inside the can the product is perfect, but the marketing has been stymied by a label defect. This creates a secondary need for label printing that does not harm the ability to sell the labeled product, and might perhaps enhance the experience. A fragrance of cloves or other spice associated with ham will reinforce the decision to buy. One might ask, "Who cares what the label smells like?" The answer is: the consumer cares. The fragrance should be consistent with or even enhance expectations of product performance. A hammer's handle should smell like wood rather than like the fish oil preservative that has been used to treat the wood.

Delivering the right fragrance at the right time to communicate the right message may well be serving unmet needs. More attention is being paid now to the concept of headspace in products. Headspace is the volume of gas in the container or in the product that allows gasses to accumulate. The so-called new-car smell is the most recognizable and most often noted headspace example. Similarly, purses, makeup, chocolates, and other products have very familiar headspace aromas. Often the headspace is not representative of the product but rather is a by-product of production, packaging, or shipping. It takes time for the fragrance to develop, and it may be marred by outside events. Even "good" fragrance experiences may mask harmful chemicals (automobile headspace includes chemicals from colorings and adhesives).

A start-up would do well by attending to the fragrances of the business. Seeing that the aromas present an appealing mix with the product may move the customer to purchase. A purse that smells richly of leather is more apt to be purchased than one lacking this cue. Some leather preservatives, for example, contain formaldehyde, which would not offer customers as pleasant an experience. Research in psychology is only now beginning to document the strong relative influence of smell on memory and attitude. Entrepreneurs should keep this in mind in designing products and packaging or even in selecting conducive retail outlets.

RESEARCHING THE NEEDS

How do we discover the needs? Traditional marketing research methods such as focus groups, surveys, and in-depth interviews are obvious answers. The fragrance example above shows the power of programmed observation. Watching the consumption process from the first signs of need recognition through and past disposition may give insight into the choices, use patterns, and satisfaction with products.

One useful observation tactic takes disposition directly into account. Garbology, as the name suggests, is the study of garbage. There are many applications of this approach, including the archaeological examination of ancient or modern trash dumps. In a consumer setting, examining the garbage can tell us what has been consumed or not consumed and in what condition. USAIR's president had the airline's trash analyzed to better understand the customer preferences and satisfaction with meal selection and preparation. He knew intuitively that too much waste suggested poor choices by the dietary staff and used that to change menus and preparation methods. This was before garbology had taken hold as a respected scientific endeavor.[4]

Items do not have to end up in the trash to tell a story. Products left on the shelf or, worse, purchased and never opened or used also indicate problems detected by consumers. Apple's iPod may have run its product life cycle already or at least the growth stages. The market has slowed and people are using the technology less or not at all. As the mainstream entered the market, the innovators and early adopters (the earliest groups to adopt an innovation) appear to be turned off now that the product has become mainstream and boring. The effort required to locate, save, and program music is no longer rewarded with uniqueness and coolness. An effort to revitalize the market with video downloads of movies may not be sufficient to rejuvenate the brand. It depends on how many holiday-gifted iPods are returned or unopened because the market has moved on to the next technology.[5]

Frank Perdue, of Perdue chicken fame, saw that consumers could not find cues to quality in uncooked poultry so he created a market by creating new cues. Rejecting convenience for taste, Perdue emphasized that his birds were fresh, not frozen. Still requiring a cue by which consumers could judge the quality of uncooked poultry, he settled on the use of marigold leaves in the feed. Among the useful side effects of this nutrition decision was the fact that marigold leaves contained a substance that would change the skin color of the chickens to various shades of gold. This, then, becomes the immediate discriminatory variable in chicken selection. Watching customers in the store now, they can be seen to select chicken based on richness of color—as a surrogate for richness of taste or even nutritional quality.[6]

Others observe customers as well. The Perdue chickens do enjoy a better diet and better conditions, so the color marketing is not considered deceptive or dangerous. Marketers who create false attributes or overstate the usefulness of features may be in for trouble. Government interpretation of what is fair and appropriate can vary. In its early days, Coca-Cola suffered from intervention by the courts and the U.S. government. The product never contained cocaine, but adding caffeine prompted oversight and examination of consumers to see if they were being harmed by this substance. Eventually, the product was given the green light and no further attempts were made in the United States to intervene.[7]

A more recent beverage creation and introduction, Snapple, did not receive this kind of government scrutiny. The producers introduced natural bottled drinks using at the time unorthodox communication methods. The product was targeted to specific niches of customers identified by observing who was dissatisfied with what was available in the market.

Clean Shower was also designed for niche markets. The product and the approach were modified as feedback was gained by interviews and observation of the early trial markets. This research was tricky though. Many early triers were friends and family who may not have given the most realistic feedback versus offering "support from the family."

The Clean Shower customers being targeted were women more than 25 years old with a household income above $40,000 and below $200,000. Working women were a high priority. With many consumer goods, younger women are the more logical target. Observation of usage and discussion with customers convinced Clean Shower that they needed a different group. Women under 25 were not focused on cleaning techniques. Older women usually select their brand loyalties and are often not targeted, but this category was new and loyalties had not yet formed. So the age range was skewed upward. The narrow band of income may look odd, but there are reasons for this too. Below $40,000 the cost of the product seemed high and perhaps prohibitive. Those in the $200,000+ income groups often had maids to handle the cleaning duties and were unaware of the benefits offered by the product. Although men requested clean showers, they were seldom the ones doing the work so they were seldom targets for the company. Finally, it was found through observation that potential customers spent considerable time in the car commuting. This opened the door to some of the novel advertising techniques discussed below.

START-UPS AND NEW PRODUCT INTRODUCTIONS

A start-up has different characteristics than a more mature company. By definition, a start-up enters the world as naked as a baby—no products, no money, and no customers. The trick is to find a way to generate positive cash flow with initial successes. Once that has been accomplished, it is necessary to analyze what went right to develop a model that can then be replicated.

McDonald's started from just one location. Ray Kroc was selling milkshake mixers when he stumbled on a customer who wanted enough to make 48 milkshakes simultaneously. The smell of success was unmistakable, so Kroc went personally to investigate the techniques and processes being used. After a relatively short time, Kroc bought out the McDonald brothers and created a franchise system that ensured adequate cash flows and controls over quality and service.

McDonald's continues today in part by continuing to innovate. A successful product line and operating plan from the 1960s cannot survive in the 21st century, but a successful philosophy and value system can. McDonald's has maintained close contact with their customers and made changes along the way. Not everything works. Doing things that look dumb in retrospect are inevitable. The important thing is to do inexpensive dumb things (and learn from them). When something does work, understand how it works and replicate it.

NEW PRODUCT MANAGEMENT

One of the great success stories of product development happened almost by accident but has been replicated many times over. Coca-Cola began as a syrup for headaches and indigestion and was only incidentally mixed with carbonated water to become a beverage. The plans for bottling and distribution certainly were no accident, however.

Also not an accident was the selection of the name of the product. Coca-Cola was selected to be descriptive of the product and to be attractive in advertisements. The look of the name and the type style have been duplicated worldwide. Competitors and copycats still abound, much as other products with similar names were offered in the early 1900s: Candy Cola, Hoca-Nola, Kel Kola, and Kaw-Kala.[8]

Product naming itself is part science, part art, mixed with a bit of luck and a dash of magic. The name of the product and the name of the company should say what you do and why consumers should buy. The following are examples of product names that give a mental image and will attract the target customer:

- Tony's Deep-Dish Pizza
- Biker Pub and Grub
- Family Friendly Video
- Dermal Science Anti Aging Face Cream
- Nickermans Menswear
- Best Way Trucking

These names do part of the selling. Everyone has their own preconceived mental images associated with words and phrases. The start-up needs to take advantage of these images and use their name to send a message. Even if the founder's name is Edward Smith, a pizza shop needs an Italian name. People who ride motorcycles are shunned in some places and may think of themselves as part of a clique. A name like Biker Pub and Grub would attract bikers and probably repel many in search of a family-friendly or quiet dining establishment. The name itself helps to define the focus of the business and identify the niche market targeted.

Nickermans Menswear is the actual name of a tailor shop in Bangkok, Thailand. The owner is an East Indian. When asked where the name originated, the owner said that he thought a Jewish name would be more likely to attract European and American customers who had had good experiences with Jewish tailors in Europe and the United States. A nearby tailor shop that is also owned by an East Indian is called Raja's. We leave it to the reader to decide which shop is more likely to attract walk-in business from European and American men.

The concept works in the business-to-business sector as well. When placing purchase orders, purchasers sometimes specify the shipping company desired. Usually, the purchase order form has a place in which to indicate the transportation company. It was usual practice to select "best way" on the form when it was left to the supplier's discretion to pick the shipping company. By naming a trucking company Best Way, the founders took advantage of this custom. Stories abound that similar strategies were used in the days when telephone directory assistance was the primary method for long-distance shopping. Operators asked for the number for a local florist would find themselves giving the number for A Local Florist. Clever and innovative naming can reduce some of the need for media advertising.

A name is also a promise. It gives the consumer expectations. What is delivered must be congruent with what is expected. Miss Evelyn's Tea Shoppe needs china, crystal, and white lace tablecloths. Biker Pub and Grub needs Formica tabletops and Harley-Davidson décor. Potential customers would do an about-face at the front door of Miss Evelyn's if they saw Harley-Davidson décor in the seating area.

A name can also be limiting. Wile E. Coyote (the Roadrunner's foe in so many cartoons) had found that the Acme Company could supply him with many different products. Conversely, he is unlikely to try Beautyrest for explosives. Once a company name becomes associated with a product or line of products, it can create a negative attribution for incongruous products. Beautyrest has become linked with mattresses. Beautyrest ice cream will not work. Similarly, Sealtest mattresses might be a bad choice.

Some companies are, however, able to use brand names for their products that unlink the corporate name from the brand or product line. Sara Lee is a company that markets shoe polish along with their apple pies. The shoe polish is sold under the Kiwi brand, and the pies are sold proudly sporting the corporate name.

Names that are hard to pronounce or are spelled incorrectly to be clever can cause dissonance and may create consumer avoidance. Consumers do not want to be made to feel inadequate at not being able to pronounce or spell a name, and it makes it more difficult to establish a place in customers' memories. Some examples of difficult names might include Kwick Schop, Abdjinger, and La Pountinifique. As firms go global they increasingly seek to identify names that will be memorable, pronounceable, nonoffensive, and perhaps not restrictive in whatever language they are doing business. The lists of candidate names tend to run short as more firms seek names they can use.

McDonald's may be viewed as a nondescriptive name. The brothers who ran the original hamburger stand that grabbed Ray Kroc's attention were named McDonald and the name seemed adequate for their needs. Perhaps some of the expansion came about because the franchises opened with signs that read McDonalds 10-cent Hamburgers in a time when 25-cent hamburgers might have been considered the norm. Apparently the neutral name did not hurt the franchise system. Some businesses with good names have failed; others with names that do not convey value succeed. A good name choice does not guarantee success, but it may be considered to be of particular advantage for a start-up.

Start-up companies require innovative approaches to marketing. Large, mature companies like Procter and Gamble will spend years and millions of dollars developing a new product and researching the market. They will then launch a product with a media budget of $20 million plus while simultaneously sending out representatives to retail stores to ensure shelf space. The stores feel the market's pull pressure from consumers coming in to ask for the product in response to the advertisement. As a contrast, Clean Shower was launched with a $70,000 budget that included manufacturing, marketing, and overhead. Marketing was personal, the inventor selling one-on-one to prospects in informal surroundings. Store employees pulled the product into the stores, and consumers drew reorders.

Naturally, the different types of organizations have different expectations of the results they will achieve with these programs. In either case, results should be measured against objectives. One formula for setting objectives is the SMART model, which sets the dimensions of effective goals. Objectives need to be Specific, Measurable, Attainable, Relevant, and Time bound. This enables even the least organized entrepreneurs to establish a test of success or failure versus the standard that was set prior to launch.[9]

Traditional advertising is becoming less and less effective. The public is saturated with advertisements and turns them off mentally. New technology enables television viewers to skip the commercials or fast-forward through them. In an effort to grab attention, producers of advertising add comedy, sex, and special effects. Often these are the only parts of the commercial that are remembered. In the case of some of the most talked about and memorable Super Bowl or World Cup commercials, viewers often fail to accurately recall the brand advertised. One of the reasons is that the attention is on the comedy, sex, and special effects rather than on the product.

Another reason for the limited effectiveness of Super Bowl advertising is that one exposure has little impact on purchase. The objective is to create sufficient motivation within the consumer to drive purchase. Big companies use this in scheduling media. The classic metric used to choose and measure media campaigns is the reach (number of prospects seeing the ad) versus frequency (average number of times the ad is seen during a purchase cycle) trade-off. One exposure of an ad to 100,000 people will not drive as many purchases as will 10 exposures of that same ad to 10,000 audience members. In an introductory ad campaign, you have to reach beyond a minimal level of exposures and ensure that the target audience views the ad at least enough times to increase the probability of purchase. It is also possible to have too many advertisements. The trick is to select a frequency high enough to have the desired effect but not so high that the final exposures are wasted.

There are many ways to determine how much frequency is enough. Some large companies use the "rule of nine" as a guideline for new product introductions. If you are in their target audience, you can expect to hear the message more than nine times. The audience is selected based on the media they see and hear and how often the media overlap (the same people hear the same message in multiple places). The rule of nine is based on an average product, an average media presentation, and an average susceptible consumer. Therefore this is a rule that a start-up must break. For a start-up, the product must be better at delivering benefits, the media must be better at motivating the consumer to purchase, and the message must reach the most susceptible audience.

One way to excel at reach is through creative use of media. Radio is an oldie but a goodie. Consumers turn off advertisements on radio. They do this by pushing the next button on the car radio or simply by mentally turning them off. Ratings produced by independent companies measure the number of radios tuned to a particular station. Listening is another story. To be effective, the potential consumer must be tuned to the station and listening actively. This author changes the station at the first shout of a car advertisement.

To overcome this radio problem, only personality-driven programs are effective. Talk radio is good because the audience is tuning in to listen actively. Personality music can be good if the patter between songs keeps the audience listening actively. As soon as the consumer realizes the program has shifted to an advertisement, it is turned off physically or mentally. Early Clean Shower radio commercials were simply the radio personalities relating their true experiences with the product. The personality was given the product, allowed to use it, and asked to tell his or her story about the experience. These had sufficient impact such that in many cases one exposure was sufficient to obtain purchase by susceptible consumers.

These outside-the-box campaigns are hard to manage. An advertising agency on a 15 percent commission could not do this and remain profitable. One of the most economical radio purchases at Clean Shower was a Scandinavian music program in the Pacific Northwest. The audience actively listened to the host and when he said, "Buy Clean Shower," the Scandinavians purchased Clean Shower.

Another good example of successful radio is Snapple. Traveling salespeople use convenience stores to get snacks, use the comfort facilities, and get something to drink. Snapple was introduced with a wide mouth so that it was possible to drink out of the bottle while driving and reclose it between stops. Canned carbonated beverages were not reclosable and had small openings. Recognizing that music listening loses its appeal after hours in the car, Snapple ran commercials on Rush Limbaugh's program. Salespeople in his audience listened, asked for Snapple, and looked for a variety of Snapple products. This Limbaugh audience, salespeople in cars, sought out the wide-mouth container with the reclosable top in the noncarbonated product niche and made Snapple a success.

When a radio campaign is done properly, the results can be spectacular. On the other hand, giving radio personalities the freedom to tell their own story can lead them to make promises that the start-up company cannot fulfill. Undoing the problems can consume large amounts of time and money that are not readily available to start-ups.

WORD OF MOUTH

Radio personalities speaking on behalf of a product are spokespersons. Your neighbor telling you about a great new product is engaging in word-of-mouth communication. Word of mouth can be particularly helpful to the start-up. The product must be revolutionary and not an incremental improvement. Word of mouth is best with a product in a niche market. For example, an improvement in racing sail development would spread quickly through the sailboat racing community. If it is shiny, functional, and fits on a Harley Davidson, word of mouth will work in that community.

In the youth market, Homestar Runner is an entrepreneur with a series of comic figures. The company sells T-shirts, hats, posters, CDs, and other branded items through their website. The consumers are 9-, 10-, and 11-year-old children. The only marketing is the website itself and word of mouth among children. The target audience returns frequently to the website, and events on the site become a topic of conversation within that age group. The markup on the products is substantial, and the media budget is zero.

Giving Clean Shower away in beauty parlors in Winn-Dixie shopping centers was completely outside of any conventional marketing approach, yet generated considerable discussion about the labor-saving product. The idea started by thinking about people who would care about appearances, shower regularly, have sufficient disposable income, and a wish for more free time. The company found this group in beauty parlors, and they told their friends and family. It was successful, but beauty parlors no longer allow access to their customers, so this word-of-mouth experiment cannot be repeated.

Steve Marks and Harvey Nelsen founded Main Street Gourmet, a producer of muffins and muffin and cookie batter. Harvey wanted a broader distribution and to get the muffins into McDonald's restaurants. He arranged to play in a charity golf outing with the owner of a major franchise group and then got him to agree to a one-month trial of his muffins. To get business started, Harvey encouraged all of his friends to purchase the muffins—even handing out money for them to do so. This got people to try the muffins, share them with their friends, and talk about the experience. People liked the muffins, and as a result, he was able to generate sales that impressed the franchise owners enough that they expanded the product line.

Barry Easterling is another creator/entrepreneur. He designed a better surgical table that was attractive to surgeons. Prototypes were produced, and physician friends were recruited to try the product and get it placed in hospitals. Once placed and tried, the surgeons discussed the improvement among themselves and pulled more tables through distribution channels through their word of mouth.

Jerry Wilson wrote the book on *Word-of-Mouth Marketing*, literally.[10] He describes a word-of-mouth marketing blitz as a way to orchestrate discussions in launching a product or start-up company. The essential element is *to keep it simple and systematic*, streamline everything, and orient everything to action. Wilson describes the steps to creating communication through word-of-mouth networks by creating teams to work through planned tactics to achieve specific quantified objectives. The book itself was marketed successfully through these channels.

Word of mouth works both ways. One bad customer experience can be spread to large groups that will not patronize a product. Clean Shower found that negative word of mouth could be reversed. Customers who did not use the product correctly reported problems to friends and neighbors. When these customers called to accuse the company of fraud and threaten to complain to the Better Business Bureau, opportunities arose. The person who initially answered the phone was able to identify the problems and reinstruct in the use of the product. This turned the complainers into loyal customers, and they began to spread the word on how well it worked. The telephone specialist began training the customer service staff that was added to the company, and she later became the vice president of operations.

OTHER PROMOTION

The word-of-mouth and sampling strategy of Clean Shower as a start-up somewhat mirrors that used by Lever Brothers to introduce Spry shortening. To introduce the product, one-pound sample cans, recipe books, and coupons were sent to one-third of U.S. households. This was supplemented with a mobile cooking school, model kitchen, and eventually a cooking program on the radio. With over

4 million mid-1930s dollars spent on the campaign, the product became very popular and put a significant dent in Crisco's market. Of course, Spry is gone now and Crisco remains.[11]

True start-ups have it a little more difficult. A rule of thumb in the grocery business is that 60 percent of buying decisions are made at the shelf. An easy-to-read label that describes the benefits will go a long way. A recent example is Cleanest Dishwasher. The package has the product name in bold type and adds, "Cleans the machine that cleans the dishes." The need fulfillment is clear—who could resist the special value two-pack?

Color is important as well. If it is a consumer product, it should stand out on the shelf. If all of the competitors are dark blue, your label should be red and white. It is hard to go wrong with light and bright. Different and appealing are an absolute must. In the case of Cleanest Dishwasher, the aisle where it is likely to be located (dish and laundry detergents) has product labels that are dark with greens and blues. As a contrast, the product's package is white with a bright yellow label.

Labels and signs tend to collect text. The name, the logo, multiple messages, consumer suggestions, company name, admonitions, address, telephone number, and the like are all included. Remember—less is more. The rule of thumb is that a highway billboard should contain no more than seven words, two of which should be "This Exit." The front label on a start-up product is a billboard. It has to work as quickly as the highway sign. Cleanest Dishwasher has 14 items including the logo. Even this is pushing the envelope. The back label can contain the details. This too should be concise enough to be read quickly. Details like the company name and address can be in smaller print. The best billboard this author has seen is a McDonald's M followed by "Playland Next Exit." One letter and three words delivered a complete message. Consumers who do not like McDonald's are not going to patronize in any case. Consumers who like McDonald's and have children are very likely to stop. Children in the car may even lobby their parents to stop (to put it mildly!).

Beyond the label, the rest of the package has to appeal to the customer as well. A start-up needs to have a good "feel" to it to make the long trek from the shelf to the cart. Fine wines are now being introduced with screw caps in place of the traditional, but awkward and messy, corks—much to the delight of this author. Purchasing the product in its package should be pleasant. In the late 1960s and early 1970s, Hanes created a hosiery product that was meant to break into a new distribution channel. The product itself, pantyhose, was improved so that there was better fit with fewer individual sizes. The channel selected was supermarket distribution. The unique packaging, a large plastic egg, contributed to the visibility and memorability of the brand. It was easy for retailers to manage (and Hanes did much of the work). The package also felt good.[12]

Making products easy for the retailer is one way to break in. Start-up companies are tempted to try to push their product through the supply chain. Pushing is marketing to agents and distributors who are given an incentive to push the products through to retail outlets. These in turn are given an incentive to push the product to the customer. In each case, the next layer has other interests and usually has more pressing present business. This has been described as pushing a chain, and is about as effective as pushing an anchor chain. The alternative is the pull strategy described earlier in which, for example, Clean Shower prospects were encouraged to ask Winn-Dixie retailers to stock the product. The best alternative is to design a product and package that are good for the retailer then get the consumers to pull it into the store.

Hanes not only made the package attractive, they took the handling duties away from the retailer. The rack and product were delivered directly to each store, so the retailers' storage and delivery costs were zero. Afterward, restocking and other maintenance were performed by Hanes's "route girls." These women, in distinctive uniforms, oversaw the displays and gathered intelligence daily in the field. A start-up may offer to do this sort of consignment placement on much smaller scales to get a product established.

Establishing a product sometimes comes down to timing. If the three most important things in real estate are location, location, location, the three most important in business start-ups are timing, timing, timing. The Spry shortening product mentioned previously was developed and ready five years before it was introduced. The launch of the product was held up while the economy recovered enough that a new item might have been better received. Start-ups seldom have the luxury of waiting that long, but some entrepreneurs may choose not to make the shift until the timing is right.

CASE HISTORY

How did Clean Shower come to market anyway?

Fair is fair, so in return for help in the manufacturing company the author was helping around the house. One chore was cleaning the shower. After one cleaning, it was time for a trip to the store in search of a better product. Finding nothing, the author returned to the workbench and developed Clean Shower.

After trying it and discovering how well the product worked, friends, neighbors, and employees were encouraged to test it as well. One use cycle later the people who were trying it came back and demanded more: "I can't go back to cleaning the shower—you have to make me some more." So we applied for a patent, and developed a label, bottle, sprayer, boxes, and a manufacturer to put it all together. The first 4,000 units were produced and stored before getting placement in a local convenience store.

A local marketing company had a public relations person who was able to get the story on the local news. The news show drove customers into the convenience stores. Samples were then given to employees at the local stores in the Winn-Dixie supermarket chain. This created more local buzz. As mentioned above, it was at this point that sampling occurred in the beauty parlors that were often in the same plazas as the Winn-Dixie stores.

Within four weeks, Clean Shower became the number one seller on the household cleaner aisle. Additional television appearances and newspaper articles caused additional growth. With the initial success, investors were interested and funding became available. Then a Boston media buyer suggested talk radio as an advertising vehicle. The initial radio was a morning talk show featuring a liberal and a conservative. The commercials were simply the two personalities discussing their experiences with the product.

In less than four weeks, Clean Shower became the number one selling shower cleaner in the Boston area. The system of having a radio personality use the product and describing their life-changing experience was then replicated throughout the country. As the product rolled out and became available in new areas, new media vehicles were phased in. Clean Shower grew 20.6 percent per month for 34 months with a peak of over $10 million per month. (Author's note: This brief history does not include the stumbles, hiccoughs, and just plain dumb things that also happened along the way. Those come with the territory too!)

CONCLUSION

A start-up is a difficult, frustrating, time-intensive, labor-intensive, and fun enterprise. It also requires marketing techniques different from those used by established firms. Some of the ones that have been mentioned include the following:

- Me-too products do not launch start-up companies.
- Create a name that is easy to understand, pronounce, and spell, and that describes the company.
- Color should add to the message and not reduce legibility.
- Fragrance, sound, and feel of the package count.
- Word of mouth and public relations are low cost and high impact.
- You have to know your consumer and what makes your target market susceptible to your offering.

NOTES

1. Judann Pollack, "New Products, Same Old Mistakes," *Advertising Age* 67, no. 41 (October 7, 1996).

2. Mark Dominiak, "Avoid New Product Release Pitfalls," *Television Week* 24, no. 6 (February 7, 2005).

3. Robert F. Hartley, *Marketing Successes*, 2nd ed. (New York: Wiley, 1990).

4. Jerry R. Wilson, *Word-of-Mouth Marketing* (New York: Wiley 1994).

5. David Smith, "Why the iPod Is Losing Its Cool," *The Observer*, September 10, 2006.

6. Hartley, *Marketing Successes*.

7. Ibid.

8. Ibid.

9. Wilson, *Word-of-Mouth Marketing*.

10. Ibid.

11. Hartley, *Marketing Successes*.

12. Ibid.

CHAPTER 8

HOW TO USE SOCIAL MEDIA: FOSTERING CONNECTIONS IN A VIRTUAL MARKETPLACE

Gretchen M. Keillor

WHAT IS SOCIAL MEDIA, AND WHY SHOULD I USE IT?

People want to be connected. We are social beings. We want others to know us, and we want to know others. You can see it everywhere: in the way a man introduces his wife at a party, in the handshake and hug when two friends greet, in the delight of a customer greeted by name.

For most of humanity's history, these connections have occurred in physical, tangible spaces. They have occurred in villages and towns: women chatting in the marketplace, men gathering in the pub for a football game, children playing together in neighborhood parks. Traditionally, our community interactions exist in a physical space.

But in the last few years this has all changed. Now we have a virtual arena in which to commune. We have developed technology that enables us to connect from miles apart, in more intimate ways than ever before. Grandparents in Ohio can video chat with their grandchildren in Colorado, someone can snap a photo and instantly show it to a friend across the ocean, and we no longer have to wait for the postal service to deliver important news.

Put very simply, that is what social media is about: connecting people. Whether it is a shared laugh over a silly video or asking for a recipe just because someone took a photo of the meal they made, it is about interacting together. Not only does social media enable people to connect to each other (grandparents to grandchildren), but it also enables people to connect to the places they go and, most importantly for us, the businesses they buy from.

Social media for business, executed well, capitalizes on this essential facet: the connection between you and your customers. There are virtual venues in existence that enable you to reach your customers on a very personal level, and if you are smart, you will use them in the way they were designed to be used—namely, to foster relationships.

This is where many businesses go wrong. They see Facebook as merely a place to display their new ad campaign, YouTube as a place for their latest commercial, or Twitter as an opportunity to blast their special offers. Some of these more traditional activities are great to include in your social media strategy, but if that is all you do, you will come off as impersonal and far from genuine, and that is not what your customers want.

For your business, think of social media like a virtual marketplace. People mill around, inspecting the wares on each stand. They scold their children, chat with friends, and carefully pack their bags with purchases. You sell things, of course, and your customers buy, but it is much more than that. That woman with the red hat wants you to know her name and her favorite drink. You want to have a conversation with the man who plays piano, even if your business has nothing to do with pianos, just because you play piano and you know he does too. Or maybe the little girl over there wants to show you her new shoes. Of course these exact conversations will not necessarily happen via social media with your business, but that is not the point. It is the mentality of making connections, not simply selling, that is important.

There are two main advantages to using social media. First, if you execute properly with this connective mind-set, you will end up with a base of very loyal, connected, returning customers for your business. Ideally, these loyal customers will also recommend your business and advocate for you in their own community circles. Second, social media is incredibly cost-effective; many of the channels that we will discuss are completely free to at least get started with, and even when you reach the point of paying for promotions, it is still much less expensive than traditional advertising and promotion.

More strongly connected and loyal customers for just a fraction of your marketing budget? Let's go!

KNOW YOUR BUSINESS LANDSCAPE: YOUR CUSTOMERS, YOUR COMMUNITY, AND YOURSELF

Before we can even talk about the types of social media or how to use them, you need to be very familiar with the three players involved: your customers, your community, and yourself. Because social media is all about making connections, knowing who you are and who you will be making connections with (or who you *want* to be making connections with) is paramount. You should already be intimate with these players from your business plan or overall marketing strategy, so it is just a matter of applying that knowledge to the venue of social media.

Social media is not an end in itself. It is just a venue that enables you to interact with your customers and your community, and it is up to you to choose *how* you will do so. Knowing your business landscape will help you to do this; it will shape a defining structure for your use of social media. It will empower you to choose which social media channels to use (i.e., YouTube or Twitter?), how often to use them (three times a day or three times a week?), and what kinds of content, tone, and imagery to use too.

First, know your customers, both your current customers and the kinds of customers that you *want* to have. Basic demographics are useful here. How old are they? Are they male or female? How much money do they make? What is their education level? Where do they live? What do they care about? Think about your ideal customer.

For example, I worked with a fine-dining restaurant to tackle this question. The restaurant was known for its locally sourced, elaborate culinary creations, as well as for its award-winning wine and beer selection. They also featured local artists, with new paintings on the walls each month and a new band in the bar area. As a result, their customers were mostly upper-middle-class, well-educated creatives who wanted to enjoy a hand-crafted cocktail or five-course meal while at the same time supporting their local community.

The next step is to think about your customers and social media. How do they use social media? How often? Which channels? If you do not have the time or resources to extensively research this (i.e., focus groups and data tables), then simply ask around. Find that one customer of yours who fulfills most of the items on your "ideal customer" checklist, and ask them if they have a Twitter account or if they know what Instagram is. And do not forget to consider, too: what do your customers want to hear from you? Information about exclusive deals, upcoming events, general information on a topic, or something else altogether?

Returning to our example of the restaurant, we discovered that a surprising number of their customers used Twitter on a daily basis, and so part of our social media strategy was to go where they already were—on Twitter, daily. In terms of content, many of them were interested in experiencing and educating themselves about craft microbrews, so we kept them updated whenever a new beer of note went on tap, and we also linked to interesting articles that related to craft beer. Their customers were also interested in supporting local artists, as I mentioned above, and so we posted about upcoming bands and artist openings as well. By knowing its customers, this restaurant was able to speak directly to what they cared about on a personal level, and as a result received much more interaction, both online and in-store.

The second aspect of knowing your social media players is to know your community. Because social media is about making personal connections, it is especially important to remember that your business does not exist in a vacuum.

There are two main advantages to knowing your community and interacting with it. First, if your customers see you supporting other businesses that they also like, they will feel even better about supporting you because you "get it," because you understand what they are about. Second, your customers want to know that you are not entirely self-centered. We will talk more about this later, but in this age, a company that is only self-interested will not get far. If your customers see you supporting something besides yourself, they will feel even better about supporting you.

So you have neighbors, friends with mutual interests, an overall community that you are a part of, and your customers want to see that you know that. What does your community look like? And what kind of culture do you want to contribute to, connect with, or be associated with?

Think about, say, a deli in a college town. Their community is the stand at the farmers market where they buy produce each week, the tattoo shop next door whose employees order to-go every night, the students who work for them, and the music shop around the corner who shares a parking lot with them. These are all opportunities for the deli to branch out and make connections. Perhaps the farmers market stand would like to feature a few of the deli sandwiches made with their produce next weekend, or the music shop would want to host an outdoor concert that the deli caters.

These are huge opportunities to share customers and participate in mutual promotion. Look for potential mutual partners—not competition, but businesses that you can come alongside of and work together with for mutual benefit. It helps to think about where else your ideal customers go. Are they college students who visit delis and music shops and tattoo parlors? Or, in the case of the restaurant I mentioned before, are they educated middle-aged creatives who enjoy art galleries and high-fashion retail stores as well as craft beer?

Once you have an idea of your community and opportunities for mutual partners, remember that social media enables these connections to deepen. Social media is more personal and connective than any other form of marketing, so when you interact with a mutual partner through social media, you engage their customers as well as your own in a very personal way, and that is great. Go ahead and "like" the music shop on Facebook, follow that tattoo shop on Twitter, tag the farmers market stand in a photo of a sandwich. And then go further: retweet a photo of a beautiful tattoo from the tattoo shop, share the music shop's event to your own Facebook fans, publicly thank the farmers market stand for growing such great produce. These businesses will notice, and they will return the favor by promoting you as well, which means that you will be exposed to all of their fans and followers too. It is not a bad trade-off. It creates goodwill among your neighbors, it gives you major brownie points with customers for "getting it" and not being selfish about your business, and of course it broadens your exposure.

The final brick in the foundation is knowing yourself. You are speaking to your customers' wants and interacting with your community, but knowledge of your company's identity will guide how you express yourself in these interactions, in terms of tone, imagery, and content.

If you have not already defined this in your business plan or marketing strategy, one of my favorite ways to nail this down is to choose a celebrity that best fits how you want to be perceived. In the case of the fine-dining restaurant I mentioned, they wanted to be perceived as classy, confident, and sharp, but with a playful side to keep their customers feeling at ease. So we chose George Clooney. This helped to inform the tone of the copy we used on their new website, the sleek design for their menus, and even how servers interacted with tables. In the same way, define a personality (or celebrity) that you want to emulate and make sure to adhere to that personality each time you use social media.

Now that you have the foundation of knowledge of your customers, your community, and yourself, we can look more directly at social media itself.

DEFINE YOUR GOALS FOR SOCIAL MEDIA, AND MAKE THEM MEASURABLE

Social media is a big field. It is anomalous and ever-changing. There is an app for just about everything, and there are constantly new services and websites taking off that enable people to connect to each other in new ways. It can feel a bit like going down the rabbit hole when you begin; there is always something more that you could be doing to increase your online presence. That is why it is important to have clearly defined goals for what you want to accomplish with social media—goals laid out both in abstract idea-based format and in tangible, measurable numbers.

There are two basic ways to grow your business: breadth and depth. If you are most interested in simply gaining more customers, your goal is breadth. If you are most interested in deepening the relationships you have with current customers to ensure that they keep coming back, your goal is depth. Ideally, of course, your business will pursue both of these goals simultaneously. Because of the sheer vastness of social media options, though, choosing just one direction in which to work will help focus your efforts.

In terms of social media, increasing your business's breadth will basically be gaining more fans (more followers on Twitter, more "likes" on Facebook, more subscribers to your Tumblr, etc.). Luckily, this is a fairly easy goal to measure, because generally the numbers are right there in front of you, and all you have to do is choose a goal (i.e., we're going to increase the number of our Facebook likes from 500 to 750 by August 1st). The challenging part about increasing your business breadth, obviously, is to actually reach more people. There are a couple of ways to accomplish this.

First, make sure to advertise the fact that you are involved in social media. This might seem obvious, but it is often overlooked. Add a Facebook icon to your business cards, stick a "Follow us on Twitter!" sign in your front window, and encourage customers to check in at your store with Foursquare.

Second, ingratiate yourself into the existing online community. Like we discussed in the previous section, it is important to acknowledge and interact with your neighbors online. After you set up your Twitter account, for example, spend a good couple of hours finding people or businesses to follow based on your existing community, as well as the type of culture that you *want* to be affiliated with. Do this with all of your social media accounts, too, not just Twitter.

When a nonprofit I worked with delved into social media, we did exactly that. Since the nonprofit was focused on providing education and work opportunities to women around the globe, on our Twitter account we followed international nonprofits like UNICEF and Kiva, as well as women-focused organizations like Women for Women International and Vital Voices. But we also followed Equal Exchange Fair Trade company, because we believed in fair work opportunities for everyone. And we followed ArtPrize, because we believed in supporting local creativity. And so on. Not only did we follow these organizations on Twitter, but we interacted with them, too. We retweeted interesting posts of theirs, asked them questions, and encouraged them when they announced good news. They responded by following us back or retweeting interesting posts of ours, and as a result, we gained more followers.

My final suggestion to increase your social media breadth is to create exclusive content—that is, content that is accessible only to your fans and followers. While this is not exactly possible to do with every social media channel, do it where you can. Some businesses offer special discounts to customers who check in at their business on Foursquare, for example. Or some music bands, upon releasing a new song on Facebook, will make it accessible only to fans who have "liked" their page. Exclusive content gives customers a tangible reason to follow you, aside from just being supportive of your business.

Increasing the depth of your customer base, when it comes to social media, means coaxing your current followers and fans to interact with you. By stepping up the level of your interaction, your goal here is to create long-lasting relationships and loyal, repeating customers, aka "regulars."

This is more difficult to measure effectively, though most social media channels have built-in analytics that can help you to grasp how much interaction you are receiving. If not, you can make use of third-party programs to help track this. (Hootsuite is a particularly effective social media management system, for more reasons than just their tracking capabilities.) If you do not use an integrated third-party system, since each built-in analytics system is slightly different, you may have to define different goals for each social media platform. For example, you might measure Twitter interaction by the number of retweets you have, Facebook interaction by the number of people "talking about" you, and YouTube interaction by the number of comments on your videos in any given time period. It just depends how you most want your customers to interact with you.

While measuring can be tricky, executing for depth luckily comes a bit easier (i.e., feels less like pulling teeth) than trying to broaden your customer base. It basically comes down to engaging your audience by posting relevant content that they get excited about (remember "know your customers"?), by asking questions, by coming off as engaged and approachable yourself (remember "know your community"?), and more. We will discuss more specific ideas for content in the last section of this chapter.

Now that you have an idea of your goals for social media, let's look at the various channels you can use to accomplish those.

CHOOSE YOUR CHANNELS AND INTEGRATE THEM

The early days of simple social media profiles have evolved into a very complex and diversified field. There is now a separate platform for almost every feature of the original "profile"—Flickr for photos, YouTube for videos, Twitter for status updates, Spotify for music, for example—and there are several platforms that combine all of these things together for a holistic approach.

In this section, we will discuss the various types of social media and the front-runners in each category, with the aim of helping you to choose which channels will be most effective for you to use. Do not be overwhelmed; you do not have to be everywhere and everything in this field. You just have to be relevant to your customer base.

Social Networking

The most well-known category of social media is the communicative one: social networking. These are the holistic platforms, who incorporate a lot of different features to enable people to connect on as many levels as possible. This is Facebook, Google+, MySpace, and LinkedIn. All of these platforms offer businesses the option of creating a corporate page, solely for your business, which you should do on at least one of these sites.

Facebook is the dominant social networking platform out there, and that is where you should start. It rivals search engines when it comes to discovering information about a business; more and more often, it is the first place people look, even before a corporate website. Facebook also offers a ton of features for your business to make the most of its presence there, from analytics tracking to targeted advertisements, and they also have an exceptionally good help center that guides you through the process of creating a page and how to use it. Major props, highly recommended, you need to be on Facebook.

The other three—Google+, LinkedIn, and MySpace—are up to you.

Google+ was heralded as Facebook's new rival, but that was almost a year ago and it is still not rivaling. What is left, though, is a lot of people who were into that kind of thing in the first place (namely, techies). If your company has a particular customer base of techies, it might be worth pursuing.

LinkedIn is Facebook's more professional and corporate older brother. It is put together quite well, but distinctly lacking personality. It is generally used for resume building and career networking, not so much personal interaction, and because of this, LinkedIn users are generally older and career oriented, and use the platform less often.

And MySpace is the opposite, perhaps Facebook's younger wild sister who sleeps around. To be honest, it is disconcertingly poorly designed in terms of user experience. Once you think you have got the hang of it, there is a broken link or a bug and you have to start all over again. That being said, MySpace has carved out a niche in the music department; it is a hotspot for bands and artists, which caters directly to their younger, creative users. Again, if this is your customer base, it might be worth pulling your hair out over broken links.

Blogs and Microblogs

Blogs essentially started out as a place for you to post your angst-filled journal online for people to comment on (which was unexpectedly appealing to a lot of people). While some blogs are still used that way, the field has developed into much more. Good blogs today will center on a specific topic, like how to raise your kids vegetarian or design your home cheaply. Think of them like the online version of a weekly newspaper column. If you are seeking to be a real source of information for your customers, for them to look to you for answers about a particular field, then perhaps a blog is for you.

WordPress.com is my favorite blogging option. It is highly customizable, easy to use, and even offers a website creation platform (at WordPress.org), if you are seeking to set up a basic website cheaply. Blogger and LiveJournal are also well-established blog platforms.

Microblogs are similar, but instead of full-length articles, they snip information into bite-sized pieces. On a microblog, you will post much more often (two to three times a day, or sometimes hourly) in much smaller pieces (140 characters or less) about a wider range of topics. Microblogs are tricky to get right, as they are probably the most honest, genuine, and unstructured representation of your business. They are literally up-to-the-minute updates, as opposed to highly strategic campaigns (though that is not to say that you cannot be strategic with microblogs).

Twitter is the most widely used microblog. It is a platform entirely devoted to the idea of status updates. While it is incredibly simplified, there is often confusion at first as to how it "works." Here are a couple of tips:

- Twitter is truly a two-way street. If you are interested in receiving someone else's status updates, you can follow them. And if they are interested in receiving your status updates, they will follow you back. But if they have never heard of you and do not care, they will not follow you back and you will only receive their updates; they will not receive yours.

- You can speak to someone directly, but only by creating a new status yourself and tagging that person in it. For example, Joe says, "Wish the Browns had won last night—great game!" To reply to that, you'd say "@Joe the Browns suck, it was a terrible game, lying is wrong." Key point: everyone will see your reply to Joe, not just Joe, because first and foremost it is a public status update.

- You can contribute to a discussion on a particular topic, but only by creating a new status yourself and tagging it with a hashtag. For example, you see all these status updates about #worldpeace, and you want to be a part of that conversation, so you say something like "We totally support #worldpeace!" Since you tagged it with a hashtag, your status will be added to the #worldpeace discussion. To see the whole discussion, you can search Twitter for #worldpeace, and it will show you all the updates that have been tagged with that hashtag. Pretty neat! This feature enables global communication about a single subject, and also helps you to see which topics are trending worldwide.

Twitter is a highly involved form of social media that requires constant monitoring and interaction. It is also very limiting, as you can literally use only 140 characters per post. If you are smart, though, you will use Twitter as a way to drive traffic to your other social media outlets that are built for a deeper level of interaction (i.e., post a link on Twitter every time you add a new blog post at your full-length blog, or post a link to your freshly created Facebook event). And better yet, you will track the click-throughs on those links to see exactly how much traffic you are directing. But more on that later.

Tumblr is another form of microblog that is slightly less "micro" than Twitter. It falls somewhere between the 140 characters of Twitter and the full-length articles of traditional blogs. Most importantly, it allows for photographs and video implants. In this way, many artists use Tumblr as a feed for their most recent artwork or sources of inspiration. Tumblr's tagline is even "follow the world's creators." If your business is creative, but you do not want to invest the time into crafting a full-length blog and you have more to say than Twitter allows, Tumblr might be a good place for you to showcase your most recent works and inspiration.

Multimedia

There are also social media channels entirely devoted to multimedia. These channels capitalize on the fact that people have interests, hobbies, and preferences that they want to share with other people. Sometimes they are a little more difficult to access from a business point of view (as in, they do not always have preset profiles, like a Facebook page, that you can just plug your business's information into), but it is possible to do.

If your business relates directly to photography, the photo community of Flickr might be worth tapping into. You can create a photostream of your most recent photos, follow other photographers, and mark photos as favorites. Or if your business has a clientele of stay-at-home moms really into DIY projects, Pinterest could be just the ticket to reach them; you can create a business profile to promote your products. Spotify is the newest trend in music sharing—it is even integrated with Facebook—if your business is interested in tapping into a music-based community.

YouTube is one multimedia channel that is highly adaptable for businesses. People love rich media; they love to see photos and videos. Even if your business is not a film company, there are still many opportunities for creating simple videos. For example, an artist could show the before-and-after process involved in the artwork, a nonprofit could interview people it helps, and more. The downside is that this could potentially be a lot of investment, so make sure that your goals feed directly into creating videos. (For example, if you are a coffee shop that wants to be known for its espresso expertise, you post how-to videos on creating latte art.)

Location Based

An interesting trend that has taken off with the advent of mobile technology is location-based social media. These apps allow the user to "check in" wherever they are, using GPS technology, and then share that information with their friends.

Foursquare has pretty much cornered the market on this one. Foursquare has made "checking in" to places into a game. They provide perks for checking in, essentially making your trip to the gas station seem much more exciting than it actually is. The perks they provide are mostly within the app itself (for example, you receive points and badges for checking into places, you can leave "tips" for other visitors, and if you check into a place more than anyone else, you become the mayor of that particular place). But businesses have capitalized on this, and you can too, by offering tangible perks to your customers via Foursquare. For example, some restaurants offer discounts to diners who check in, or provide a monthly gift package to the "mayor" of their location. If your business has an actual location that customers visit, Foursquare might be worth checking into (pun!).

Facebook "Places" offers the same basic features of Foursquare, but it is less about being a fun little game and more about social interaction. It is designed to keep users updated on their friends' activity: when they are nearby, where they have been recently, etc. This might be a good way to introduce yourself (and your customers) to location-based services, as it is already linked to your Facebook page instead of being a completely separate app.

Other Categories

And there is so much more. There are games and entertainment platforms that are social that your business could tap into, depending on your customer base. There are administrative and collaborative platforms for your business to increase efficiency and productivity through online sharing (Google Docs, Dropbox, Creately). There are sites based on reviews and opinions alone, such as Yelp, eHow, and WikiAnswers, that might hold customer insights for you. There are crowdfunding sites (Kickstarter and IndieGoGo) if you are looking for a solution to jump-starting a project. And more, and more, and more—all of it social, all of it personal, people reaching people.

Integration

You are probably thinking now that this sounds like a lot of work. There are so many channels to take advantage of, and they all require separate profiles with separate interactions; just to establish a presence on all these channels would be overwhelming, much less maintaining that presence, etc.

Luckily, someone thought of that before you did. There are several services out there that focus entirely on integrating and managing your social media, precisely so that you do not waste time posting and reposting the same things.

Two of my personal favorites are Hootsuite and Tweetdeck. They both enable you to manage multiple accounts across several different platforms (Facebook pages, Twitter, Foursquare, LinkedIn, WordPress, to name a few), and also provide great perks like scheduling posts and customizing your feeds and mentions. Hootsuite offers a premium option that provides great analytics and tracking for your links, too, including insights into your followers. I started with Tweetdeck and now prefer Hootsuite, but depending on your needs and work style, you can choose whichever works best for you. They are both free to get started.

Now that you have chosen channels, let's talk about how to use them.

MAP OUT YOUR TIMING STRUCTURE

Timing your posts properly can be a difficult aspect of social media. Because no one is on social media 24/7, you will want to time your posts at the appropriate time of day to receive the most possible views. You will also want to make sure that you find a balance of how often to post. Everyone knows that avid Facebook user who posts every five minutes, and you do not want to be that, but you also do not want to be inactive either.

The time of day that you post really depends on your customer base (i.e., young people will probably interact with Facebook later into the evening than an older crowd), so you might have to do some investigating into when your customers are most active with social media. Your timing strategy will also vary a bit depending on which social media channel you are using, too (i.e., Twitter users behave slightly differently than Facebook users). Nevertheless, here are two basic guidelines that will serve as a general strategy:

1. Peak usage days of the week are midweek and Saturdays.
2. The "magic" times of day that will receive the most views and interaction are generally around lunchtime (11 a.m. or noon EST) and after work (5 or 6 p.m. EST).

Discovering how often to post depends almost entirely on which social media channel you are using instead of your customer base.

There are three categories:

1. Weekly
2. Multiple times a week
3. Daily (or more)

Generally, the longer the content, the less often you will want to use it. So a full-length blog or YouTube channel with videos would be best suited to the weekly category. The articles and videos you post involve a lot of time for you to develop, and also a significant amount of time for your users to consume them, so do not stress yourself out—or expect too much from your customers—by posting lengthy items too often.

A step up from weekly is the three to five times a week category. Facebook is the key channel here; it is well suited for medium-sized chunks of information, without the user commitment of an entire blog or video.

And finally, Twitter is the most involved channel of all; that requires daily (or even hourly) updates to keep your users interested. As we discussed in the previous section, these posts are bite-size—retweets of a post that you liked, or a quick photo of your new piece of furniture for the office—which makes them more manageable for you to produce and for your users to consume.

One tactic that I have found particularly helpful is to actually create a social media calendar based on the strategies outlined above. Color-code the calendar based on which channels you will be using, and then create a certain number of events for that channel per day, week, or month. Keep a list of notes for potential content, and then use it to fill in the events. The calendar planning will help you to stick to your strategy, and keeping a content database will also help you to stay consistent with posting in the slow times when there just is not much going on.

I have done this for a band that I manage (everyone needs to have some fun!). I knew we wanted to post on Facebook three times a week (at least), on Twitter daily, and on YouTube once a week. So I created a Google calendar with these color-coded categories, and then actually created events for the posts for six months out. As the band developed, I have kept track of content ideas—a photo we took at practice, a video from our latest show, a funny comment our drummer made, an album that was inspirational to the band, etc.—and filled them into the calendar: band practice photo on Monday to Facebook, funny comment to Twitter on Wednesday, video launch to YouTube (and subsequently Facebook and Twitter) on Friday, inspirational album share to Facebook the next Monday, and so on. The integration platforms (Hootsuite and Tweetdeck) that I mentioned earlier make this even easier for you through their postscheduling feature. You can sit down for two hours and plan your entire social media week, and they will execute it for you. It is great.

COME UP WITH CONTENT

You are all prepped and ready to go. You know your business's landscape; you have defined goals, chosen channels to use, and mapped them onto a calendar. We are into the meat and potatoes now: what do you actually say?

Developing content will be different for everyone reading this, as every business landscape is different. There are a few ground rules, though, that might help guide your thinking in that area.

First, vary the type of posts that you use. You should post about new product launches, upcoming events, and interesting developments in your business's industry, not simply your daily special discount. Based on your goals for social media and what your customers are interested in, define three to five categories that you want to post about, and then work them into your social media calendar.

Going back to the example of the band, the three categories I chose were community, inspiration, and band news. Not only did we want to promote our music, we wanted to be a source of inspiration for our users, as well as be well connected to the community we lived in. So Mondays were our "community" day, Fridays our "inspire" day, and Wednesday our "news" day, for Facebook at least. Some businesses even advertise these categories (i.e., "Today is self-improvement Sunday! Check out this article on eating healthier."), which is not a bad thing. It creates consistency and a certain amount of expectation from your customers.

The second rule dovetails into this: do not talk about yourself all the time. It is annoying. It is annoying to come across that trait in a person, as we all know, and because social media is such a personal medium, it is annoying to come across that trait on a business's Facebook page. You can get away with that in advertising (sort of), but remember that social media is not advertising, and it needs to be treated differently. Social media is a very personal and direct interaction with your customers, about cultivating relationships. And that is a give-and-take. So do not be self-involved.

This rule can be executed in a number of ways. You can promote community events, promote a neighboring business that you love, link to an informational article that is related to your industry—or even not related, maybe you just thought it was interesting and it promotes the type of culture that you want to be affiliated with. And do not forget that you can simply thank your customers every once in a while, too. Here again it might help to think of your business as a person, or as that celebrity that you chose earlier. What kinds of topics, aside from yourself, is your business interested in?

The third rule is similar: engage your audience. (Remember your goal of creating customer depth?) Sometimes people need a little encouragement to interact, especially in a realm as public as social media. Do not wait for them to offer their opinion; ask it of them. Instead of simply saying, "We're booking shows for the summer; get excited!," you can say "We're booking shows for the summer; what's YOUR favorite venue in the area?" You can also publicly ask for customer photos ("post your favorite photo you took in our coffee shop!"), share customer posts ("thanks to Sandy for sharing this, such a great article"), and encourage check-ins at your events. And always, always, always have the last word. Respond and reply to every interaction a customer offers. They want to know they are talking to *someone*, and that they are being heard.

The fourth rule is simple: use rich media as often as possible. Rich media is visual and interactive; it is photographs, videos, and click-through links. In my own experience, these types of posts receive about three times the interaction as simple text posts. We are visual beings by nature. Think how much more fun it is to look through a picture book than to read a textbook, or how much more moving it is to see a photograph than read a description. You should take advantage of that inclination in your social media, particularly because so many channels make it so easy to do. I cannot stress this enough: post as many photos, videos, and links as possible.

OKAY GO!

You should be well on your way to establishing (or improving) your social media presence. Knowing your business landscape is just the foundation. Developing measurable goals for social media is key, and then carefully choosing your channels will make your time spent most effective. And finally, actually using social media well, in terms of timing and content, is not difficult given the basic guidelines we have laid out.

Just remember that virtual marketplace we talked about, where you develop relationships with your customers instead of just selling to them. You want them to know your name, of course, but they want you to know their names, too.

Part III

MARKETING CHANNELS: THE NEW REALITIES

CHAPTER 9

ANYWHERE, ANYTIME, ANYWAY: THE MULTICHANNEL MARKETING JUGGERNAUT

Dale M. Lewison

INTRODUCTION

Future success in the highly competitive and diverse marketplace will require a carefully conceived process that is capable of formulating a unique business concept that is adept at gaining access to newly defined markets through uniquely designed pathways. This chapter will focus on a model of a multichannel marketing process that will assist in the conceptualization and implementation of a contemporary business model that is well suited to the multidimensional behavior of the 21st-century consumer.

In the new knowledge/experience/service economy of the 21st century, the most relevant unit of business competition is not your company or your product line; rather it is your concept of how to conduct business in a fashion that is uniquely advantageous to your firm and its stakeholders. Now and in the future, intangible assets (e.g., consumer perceptions of your distinctive way of doing business) will be as or more important to your success than tangible assets. The plasticity of multichannel direct-marketing practices allows you to create a concept of business that can be dramatically differentiated from the ordinary and overused "go-to-market" strategies of the past. The destruction of the mass market and its reconstruction into market segments, niches, micromarkets, and markets of one individual demands that future business models tell an interesting and compelling story of how your multichannel networks are capable of delivering a more customized shopping experience that is best suited to the individual needs and preferences of your targeted consumer segments.

Our multichannel marketing model is based on a five-phase marketing process that will guide you from unearthing potentially new and promising customer needs (analytical marketing), to mining and converting raw data into useful information (database marketing), to formulating new and successful ways of filling customer needs (strategic marketing), to building and operating a collection of pipelines capable of extracting sales (multichannel marketing), and finally, to managing and adapting the relationships required to directly serve chosen market prospects (relationship marketing). We begin where one should always begin, with an exploration of the marketplace and its happenings.

PHASE 1: ANALYTICAL MARKETING

The first phase of the multichannel marketing process deals with gathering, analyzing, and interpreting the marketplace intelligence needed to make informed decisions concerning the internal and external aspects of your marketing effort. Successful marketing operations necessitate a complete understanding of: (1) existing and potential customers, (2) external and internal environments, and (3) levels, types, and degrees of competition. We will introduce these issues here and explore them in more depth in latter chapters.

Customer Analysis

You need to know what customers think and how they act. Customer analysis is a hodgepodge of tools and techniques used in diagnosing past buying behavior and forecasting future buyer activities. Multichannel marketers must continuously gather relevant information about what, where, when, why, and how customers buy and behave. You will need to know how prospects and customers act and react to various situations involving the procurement of products and the adoption of ideas. The buying behavior of individual consumers and organizational buyers tends to be significantly different. How so? Let's find out.

Consumer Buyer Behavior

Consumers have become strategic shoppers with the knowledge and experience to go beyond simple searches for the cheapest or best-known products. Today, consumer buying activities have become mutlidimensional behaviors involving numerous marketing channels and a complex set of integrated and interacting forces. Consumer buying decisions, and the resulting patronage behavior, involve a problem-solving process in which consumers are swayed by a wide variety of internal and external influences.

The consumer buyer behavior process is a sequential series of actions that progresses from problem recognition, information search, alternative evaluation, response selection, to some form of a behavioral reaction and a purchase decision. This process is directed and influenced by a set of psychological, personal, social, and situational forces that have both a direct and indirect impact on the buying behavior of consumer groups and individual buyers.

Organizational Buying Behavior

Organizational buying behavior is the focus of business-to-business marketing. The types of products organizations buy and the methods used in procuring those products are significantly different from the consumer buying process. The organizational market is composed of several different markets. For example, there are industrial markets (buyers who make purchases in order to produce other goods and services), reseller markets (retailers and wholesalers who secure products in order to resell them), government markets (local, state, and federal agencies that need products in order to provide those services they are mandated to perform), and institutional markets (public and private, profit and nonprofit entities that use goods and services to achieve their mission).

Organizational buying tends to be more rational, systematic, complex, professional, and direct. Organizations tend to use some form of multirole buying centers wherein need initiators, decision influencers, gatekeepers, decision makers, purchasing agents, and product users interact in a variety of ways to arrive at a purchase decision.

While the complexity of the organizational buying process is difficult to generalize, it tends to be a five-stage series of activities that is similar to the individual buyer buying process. The five steps of organizational buying typically consist of: (1) need recognition and specification, (2) vendor identification and consideration, (3) proposal solicitation and evaluation, (4) vender selection and order placement, and (5) product inspection and performance evaluation.

Environmental Analysis

The second component of analytical marketing is assessing the external and internal environments that create the key possibilities of the competitive playing field and determining the core competencies of each market player. External environment analytics requires a decision based on the opportunities and threats discovered in this assessment of the marketplace. In other words, what are the key possibilities or prospects offered by the market? The flip side of an external environmental analysis is an internal exploration of the firm's core competencies. What is the firm capable of doing? How do the firm's strengths and weaknesses impact its capabilities? Can the firm develop sustainable competitive advantages that will support the organization well into the future?

External Environmental Possibilities

Awareness, understanding, and appreciation of external marketplace environments are crucial steps in your successful detection of the key market possibilities facing your organization now and in the future. In this role, you become the eyes and ears of the organization's effort to monitor and interpret the patterns and trends that characterize the competitive external marketplace. Given the largely uncontrollable nature of this complex environment, you need to identify and react to these dynamics on a timely basis. As a marketer you have the best chance to detect pattern occurrences and emerging trends that define future market directions (possibilities) for a product or industry. Patterns and trends are systematic, repetitive, and detectable arrangements of marketplace phenomena that express a meaningful mosaic of occurrences that form consequential correlations, associations, or linkages between those occurrences and successful marketing outcomes.

The external marketplace environment encompasses all of the realities of the surroundings, conditions, circumstances, and forces that influence and modify the behavior of your organization. Typically, an external marketplace scan includes monitoring and assessing all relevant political and legal issues, social and cultural influences, technological and informational advances, economic and competitive forces, population and demographic trends, as well as physical and geographical surroundings. Your analysis of the marketplace begins with the information-gathering process we term "possibilities scan." Using the information from the scan, analysis should continue with: (1) the identification of the major influential forces that drive a particular pattern or trend, (2) the delineation of the opportunities and threats emerging out of an identified pattern, and (3) a discovery of the competitive advantages resulting from the opportunities and threats assessment.

Internal Environment Capabilities

Does your organization have what it takes to do what it wants to do, to go where it wants to go, and to be what it wants to be? You need to have a clear idea of you organization's potential—what it is and what it is not. In this internal analysis you need to understand your organization's capabilities in terms of its people, processes, systems, structure, and culture. "Know thyself" are the watchwords for conducting a scan of the multichannel marketer's special abilities. The purpose of this inward-looking assessment is to gain an expansive view of the firm's core competencies and capacities for adapting to and taking advantage of selected key possibilities that make up the market.

What are your capabilities? A capability is any ability that you or your company possesses to perform a task or activity in an integrative fashion by deploying tangible and intangible resources in an efficient and effective fashion. In the knowledge/service/experience economy of today and tomorrow, intangible capital created by humans can often be the most important capabilities your firm possesses. In the economies of the future, your firm's intellectual capital in terms of knowledge and know-how will create the core competencies needed to progress in the murky environs of tomorrow's marketplace. When conducting a capabilities scan, you need to identify and assess strengths and weaknesses of your organization that impact your firm's ability to survive and thrive in future markets. All organizations need the capability to resist negative forces in the environment and endure hardships. These embedded capabilities will allow you to overcome environmental threats and take advantage of environmental opportunities. Weaknesses prevent the firm from withstanding attack and reaping benefits of new marketplace opportunities.

How do you develop the core competencies package needed to deal with the uncertainties of the marketplace of the future? What can your firm do to establish recourse in responding to environmental situations? What courses of action will your firm have to rise to the occasion? The answers to these questions lie with the strategic value of the firm's resources to create capabilities, core competencies, and ultimately, the sustainable competitive advantages needed to outmaneuver marketplace rivals. In the misty realm of tangible and intangible assets, it may behoove you to understand and appreciate this "resource-based view" of business and marketing strategy. A full assessment of the wide spectrum of resources is beyond the scope of this chapter. In general, strategic assets include all potential sources of future economic benefit that have a capacity to contribute to a company's overall value. Assets have a distinct life cycle—a beginning and an end to economic value. Asset categories include physical assets (land, buildings, equipment, and inventory), financial assets (cash, receivables, debt, investments, and equity), customer assets (customers, marketing channels and affiliates), stakeholder assets (employees, suppliers, and partners), and organizational assets (leadership, strategy, structure, culture, brands, knowledge, systems, and processes).

Competitor Analysis

The preceding customer and environmental assessments can provide you with enough intelligence to determine the overall potential of a marketplace; however, they cannot provide you with one critical bit of information—what share of that

total market you can reasonably expect to capture. Competitor analysis is concerned with profiling the competitive rivalry taking place in any market.
Changing competitive actions and responses between rivals for a competitive market position is an everyday occurrence in the dynamic global marketplace. You
will have to build and defend your competitive advantages and market positions
on a continuous basis. What do you need to consider when conducting a competitor analysis? Competition can be characterized in terms of different levels,
forms, and degrees. Let's examine these competitive nuances.

Level of Competition

One way to look at competition is to examine the directness and specificity of
the competition you face. As Figure 9.1 portrays, competition can be head-to-
head direct competition between two competitors for a specific product item. At
the other end of the continuum, the competition is fairly general and indirect;
nonetheless, it can be quite significant and disruptive. Competition can fall along
a continuum from item to category to substitute to generic competition. The nar-
rowest perspective on competition is item competition—the rivalry among firms
selling the equal or similar products to the same target market at comparable price
points. Item competition is specific because it involves direct competition among
product items in terms of brands, styles, sizes, models, and features. Category
competition consists of rivalry among marketers of closely related lines of products with similar features. For example, toys, books, apparel, home electronics,
office supplies, home and garden, and arts and crafts are all product categories
where heated competition is common. Substitute competition is less specific
and more general—where two different products (e.g., a movie or a football
game) try to satisfy the same basic need (entertainment). Finally, generic competition can best be described as the general competition that exists among

Figure 9.1
Continuum of Competition

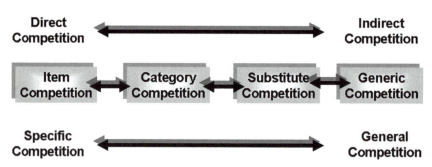

marketers of different goods and services for the limited income and patronage of the consuming public. If the consumer buys a new mobile phone, she or he may not have the money to go out to dinner and a movie,

Forms of Competition

The nature and structure of the relationship among various members of the marketing channel of distribution can greatly impact the form of competition that any particular firm might encounter. Within-channel and between-channel competition, as well as competition between two or more vertical marketing systems is common. Intratype competition is the rivalry between two marketers from different channels who occupy the same level with their respective channels of distribution. Walmart and Kmart engage in intratype competition. When competing parties from different channels use unlike business formats to serve the same target markets with comparable product offerings, the competitive form is referred to as intertype competition. The competition between Sear's and Baby Gap in infant apparel lines illustrates this intertype rivalry. There are times when you will have to compete with a member of your own channel of distribution. Vertical competition is the rivalry among members of the same channel—an apparel retailer who stocks and sells Levi jeans competes with factory outlet stores and direct-marketing channels operated by Levi Strauss. Systems competition is the rivalry among entire marketing channel systems; it is the competition that exists between two vertical marketing systems (an integrated production, wholesale, and retail operation). Home Depot and Lowe's are highly vertically integrated operations that compete as controlled and coordinated distribution and fulfillment systems.

Degrees of Competition

Competitive relationships range from hostile conflict to illegal collusion. The intensity of competition can be described along a continuum of competitor relations that reflect no competition to destructive competition. Figure 9.2 illustrates this continuum. Collusion is an illegal direct (person-to-person) or indirect (signaling) conspiracy to engage in cooperative behavior with the intent to injure a third party. Cooperation involves the consideration of a mutually beneficial relationship in which competing parties work together for a common goal. Indifference characterizes the coexistence strategy of competition—organizations seek to serve different core market niches and compete indirectly in peripheral market segments. By avoiding direct competition, coexisting competitors can pursue a live-and-let-live existence. Competition is an aggressive and confrontational degree of competition that will require that you meet or exceed customer

Figure 9.2
Competitive Intensity

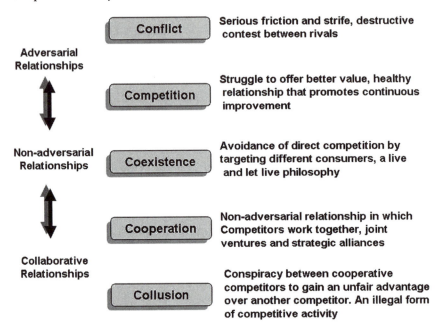

expectations by developing a better marketing program that offers the customer greater value. The hottest degree of competition is conflict—a serious confrontation between competitors that leads to harsh reactions and retaliatory measures.

It should be your goal to develop a competitor audit using the above factors to understand the current actions of competitors and predict probable future actions. A successful competitor audit form is able to serve as a diagnostic tool in identifying the strengths and weaknesses of competitive enterprises.

PHASE 2: DATABASE MARKETING

Database Analysis

Now that you have gathered and categorized information regarding your customers, competitors, and the environments and conditions under which you must operate, you need to change your static information into actionable intelligence. Extracting information from a database is more than just creating a new pile of facts and figures. Creating actionable intelligence requires that you first analyze and interpret the information, then use this newly minted intelligence to develop the marketing strategies and craft the creative appeals needed to take advantage of those intelligence opportunities that have been identified in the analysis process. Database analysis is all about transforming data into useful intelligence that allows you to develop successful operational marketing programs.

A database is a compilation of data that you can access and organize using computers to make queries, sort data, and extract information through the identification of patterns and trends. Database marketing focuses on discovering relevant trends and patterns in customer and competitive behavior as well as identifying the opportunities and threats that are inherent in the marketplace environment. The most common form of databases are those related to the following customer traits and activities: (1) purchase history in terms of what, how, and when of the customer's buying behavior, (2) the type and level of response to previous offers, (3) customer satisfaction levels with previous experiences, (4) demographic characteristics, (5) contact information, and (6) psychographic (interests, lifestyles, and activities) profiles.

Database marketing is a highly regarded marketing tool that will allow you to closely monitor your customers and permit you to categorize them in terms of their lifetime value to your organization. It allows you to identify the most profitable customers as well as those who are not worth the expense and effort of retaining them. Good database analysis is an essential tool to identifying market segments, selecting target markets, executing tailored marketing efforts, and developing cross-selling opportunities. Databases are very useful in providing a strong analytical foundation for your marketing plans and establishing the quantitative measures and successful implementation of those plans.

J.Jill, the Quincy, Massachusetts-based cataloger, started its push in 1999 to become a multichannel marketer by moving beyond its mail-order roots and launching a website and opening brick-and-mortar outlets. Over the years each channel developed its own database with little or no effort at integrating these sources of information. By keeping its information in separate silos, it was impossible to coordinate the marketing efforts of each channel. When J.Jill fully combined its databases in 2004, thereby going from a multiple-channel enterprise to a multichannel network, the firm saw a substantial 20 percent increase in sales.[1]

Market Analysis

The important tasks of identifying and analyzing markets are essential prerequisites for developing a viable marketing program and a successful multichannel approach to the marketplace. Poorly defined and profiled markets leads to poorly designed and executed marketing programs. Let's look at how we might define a market and effectively analyze it.

Figure 9.3
Defining Your Market

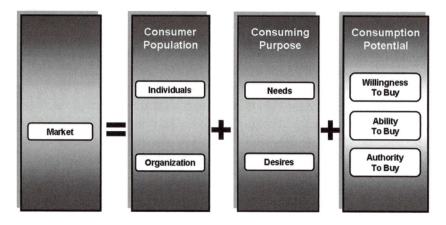

Defining Your Market

What is a market? We need to start with a common concept of what a market is. Our usage of the term "market" is very specific. As illustrated in Figure 9.3, a market has traditionally been a group of individuals or organizations (consumer population) who have needs and desires they want satisfied (consuming purpose) and who have willingness, ability, and authority to support a particular marketing effort by a given marketer. With advancing technologies and the availability of sophisticated direct-marketing capabilities, markets no longer have to be plural; a market can now be an individual or an organization.

Analyzing Your Market

The goals of market analysis are rather simple—to simplify and organize the rather complex marketplace by first identifying individual consumers or clusters of customers who have similar needs and exhibit similar buying behavior patterns. By grouping customers into more meaningful submarkets, you can select and target those individual customers or groups of customers that best match your marketing programs and operating competencies. As we shall find out later in this chapter, having a greater understanding of the marketplace will allow you to gain a competitive advantage by uniquely differentiating and positioning your marketing effort with regard to the specific needs and desires of a more homogeneous market. The rationale behind this market delineation and assessment process is to assist you in focusing your efforts on some of the most promising target markets.

The essential steps in analyzing a market include market segmentation (dividing the heterogeneous mass market into more homogeneous submarkets), market targeting (selecting one or more market segments to be targeted and developed), and market positioning (creating in the minds of target buyers a distinctive position or image for your firm and its products and marketing programs). Market segmentation can be accomplished using one or more of the following approaches:

- Geographic segmentation—delineating and describing market segments in terms of their physical location and aerial expanse

- Demographic segmentation—identifying and characterizing market segments based on the personal traits (e.g., age, gender, race, education, income, etc.) of the customers that make up the market

- Geodemographic segmentation—linking demographic characteristics with geographic locations in an attempt to isolate more defined market segments

- Psychographic segmentation—defining and profiling market segments using social class, lifestyle, and personality traits

- Behavioral segmentation—outlining and describing market segments that reflect usage characteristics (user status, usage rate, usage occasion, and usage regularity).

- Benefit segmentation—identifying and profiling market segments on the basis of the primary benefit or benefits sought when buying and using a good or service

Databases and modeling tools from such vendors as Acxiom, Claritas, and Equifax have gone beyond providing basic geodemographic information for market identification and analysis. These sources and others offer detailed psychographic profiles that provide insight into what makes customers tick. Lillian Vernon, the Rye, New York-based cataloger of gifts, home goods, and children's products, outsource the information-gathering and assessment responsibility. They add lifestyle, attitudinal, and behavioral information to their own customer transaction data from past and current customers to gain a sophisticated look at new and existing market opportunities. In the brave new world of multichannel marketing, vendor programs such as Mapinfo's PSYTE U.S. Advantage can identify customers and prospects who prefer buying online, ordering via phone, or shopping in a store. These tools and others are vital approaches not only in market segmentation and selection but also in developing contact strategy.[2]

Having gone to all of the work of collecting and analyzing market data and using it to discover and comprehend the mysteries of selected market segments, you now need to employ some guidelines that will assist you in selecting one or more segments that suit your particular situation. Consider these questions:

- How accessible is your chosen market segment? Is your market reachable using the firm's current communication and distribution channels? What marketing program changes will be required to access each consumer segment?

- Is your chosen market segment large enough to be profitable? What is the current and future sales potential? Are the financial rewards sufficient to warrant the development of a special marketing effort?

- How compatible are the needs and expectations of the chosen segments to your business mission and marketing objectives? Are the operational and marketing requirements for serving the selected market segments consistent with the resources and capabilities of your firm?

- Will the market segment respond favorably to your special offers that have been designed to meet their individual needs? Are you capable of developing a marketing program that is unique enough to capture the loyalty of these selected target customers?

- What relative advantages do you have in serving this market segment relative to the strengths of competitors? Do you have sufficient competencies to defend and grow your competitive position?

The final step in conducting a market analysis involves positioning all of your marketing efforts in the minds of your customers in a fashion that clearly distinguishes it from those of its competitors. Market positioning is one of the marketing strategies that we will explore in the next section.

PHASE 3: STRATEGIC MARKETING

Marketing Strategies

The purpose behind a well-conceived database marketing effort is its generation of intangible value that is created by being "in the know." This intangible asset (information) is a major source of wealth in the knowledge/experience/service economy of today. Marketing strategy is the force that drives this value creation process. A well-articulated marketing strategy is a vital integrative tool for connecting the realities of the marketplace with the practicalities of a strong marketing effort. Good strategy can provide direction and focus to each marketing program, give meaning to the marketing effort by creating a unique identity, reduce ambiguity and inconsistency in decision making and action taking, align and integrate vertical and horizontal marketing operations, create value for all of the firm's stakeholders, and assist the firm in gaining a sustainable competitive advantage by finding the right strategic fit between the internal organizational capabilities of the firm and the marketplace possibilities of the external environment. There are several categories of marketing strategy; let's talk about the more well-known categories—reference and growth.

Reference Strategies

A reference strategy is one in which you make direct and indirect comparisons between your market offering and those of your competitors. Customers tend to think in relative terms when organizing their thoughts and assessing their choices. Consumers make assessments in terms of a good or service being better, faster, cheaper, or cooler than someone else's good or service. When developing a market offering for specific target markets, it is important not only to be different but also to establish a unique mind-set about the firm and its offerings. Differentiation is the marketing strategy of developing a set of unique and meaningful differences that will distinguish the firm's marketing programs from themselves and from the offering of competitors. You need to continuously ask yourself, what are my "points of difference" and are they important to my target consumer groups? The consumer buying process starts with buyer awareness and interests; having a differentiated offering is one of the best ways to build recognition and appreciation for it. Differentiation distinguishes your market offering from the sea of alternatives that make up the marketplace. Goods are differentiated by functional and aesthetic features and psychological benefits. Service differentiation is achieved by offering more service extras in a more consumer-friendly manner (the way customers are treated, assisted, and served). Better value, greater convenience, and lower prices are three additional approaches used to create a difference.

Positioning carries the competitive referencing strategy to the next level. By employing the positioning marketing strategy, you are attempting to establish a distinctive and consequential consumer mind-set with respect to your firm and its offering. While being different is important, positioning goes beyond this basic concept. Positioning is all about being more appropriate, more consistent, more personal, more relevant, and more desirable when compared to what has been tendered by competitors. Depending on the situation, positioning strategies can be either creative or adaptive. Creative positioning seeks to fashion a new and distinctive perception of the firm and its marketing programs in order to improve the likelihood that chosen market segments will judge the offering to be superior to competitive deals. Adaptive positioning focuses on altering how consumers think about the firm's current offerings. The goal of a repositioning strategy is to change consumer mind-sets in such a fashion that the firm's modified offering is viewed in a more favorable light than its past position and the new positions of its competitors.

Growth Strategies

Finding new and exploiting existing market opportunities is the core growth goal to be achieved through the implementation of market penetration, marketing development, and product development strategies. Long-term survival requires that you be able to redirect your efforts in response to environmental changes, and to increase your organization's resources by identifying and pursuing profitable growth opportunities. Essentially, growth strategies address the question of "what should our business be?" Growth opportunities and the means available for harvesting new market prospects include intensive, integrated, and diversified marketing strategies.

Opportunities found within the organization's current portfolio of businesses are referred to as *intensive growth opportunities*—occasions when current products and current markets have potential for generating incremental sales volumes. Your firm may be able to realize considerable growth potential by more aggressively marketing current products to existing markets (*market penetration*), by introducing current products to new markets (*market development*) and by developing new products for existing markets (*product development*).

Integrated growth opportunities are those that occur within the organization's current industry. Integration involves those occasions in which an organization establishes a strong position or a leadership role within a given industry by gaining greater control over its marketing channels of distribution or competitive business enterprises. By vertically integrating one or more levels of a distribution channel, marketers expect that resulting efficiencies will help them to increase sales revenues. A *vertically integrated marketing channel* is one in which a single channel member at one level controls and manages all or most of the functions performed by all channel members in all levels of the distribution system. Gaining control of competitors who operate at the same level (e.g., retail level) within the same channel is the marketing strategy known as *horizontal integration*.

If you elect to add attractive businesses whose business nature and format are dissimilar to current business concepts, you are pursuing diversified growth opportunities. *Diversified growth* is achieved by entering new markets with new products. The important question to answer in chasing this type of growth chance is "how new and different" should proposed products and markets be from our current business operations? You can elect to add new businesses and markets that are similar to and have numerous synergies with existing businesses and markets or you can venture into entirely new business concepts and hitherto unexplored markets. The further you get from you core businesses and markets, the more difficult it gets to develop the necessary expertise for successfully running the business.

Marketing Offers

To interact with consumers, there must be some basis for that interaction; that basis is your market offer. As a multichannel marketer you must recognize that you cannot be all things to all customers. Successful marketing in the future will require a unique set of value propositions to a select group of customers. To implement an effective differentiating and positioning strategy, create a persuasive offer that speaks to the consumer's inner mind-set. Customer are more cynical, doubtful, and dubious about offers that do not grab them with something that they value; they want you to clearly communicate to them how the attributes and benefits of your offer represent a good "return on their investment" of time, money, and effort when buying, using, and/or possessing your product.

An *offer* is the total attributes and benefits package that you present to the customer as an exchange proposal. It is the deal, contract, arrangement, proposal, or proposition that you develop in hopes of soliciting a favorable response. In traditional marketing vernacular, it represents three of the four Ps of marketing; it is a unique combination of products, prices, and promotions. From the consumer's perspective, the offer communicates what the customer gets and what they have to do in order to get it. A good offer provides the prospective customer with a good rationale for accepting it.

So, what constitutes a good offer? One that gets the right response. You can ensure a better offer response rate if you follow some simple guidelines. First, clearly articulate and communicate the importance of those attributes and benefits deemed essential by prospective buyers. Second, make sure that you have one or more "points of difference" that will attract attention and promote reaction. Third, your offer's affordability needs to match your customer segment's ability to buy. Fourth, be sure one or more of the attributes or benefits contained within the order is viewed as being superior to those offered by competitors. The fifth guideline suggests that you work hard to ensure that your offer is hard to duplicate—your offer should contain aspects that make it difficult for competitors to duplicate. Making your offer compelling is the sixth guideline to successful offers. Does your offer contain sufficient benefits and attributes to motivate the customer to respond now? If customers can see, feel, taste, hear, or smell an offer, they are better able to judge its merits. More tangible offers are usually more effective than offers based on fewer sensory cues. Finally, there is no purpose in creating an offer that will not generate a fair return on the effort. Profitability is the concluding guideline to more successful offers.

Marketing Channels

In recent years, as markets have fragmented and competition intensified, the role of the marketing channel has become an increasingly important and vital element in the success of any marketing program. The concept of a marketing channel is thought of in broader terms today than in the past. The old view of marketing channels focuses on developing a physical distribution network that is capable of moving goods from producers to consumers in the most cost-efficient manner possible. Marketing channels were viewed as physical logistical challenges associated with moving products. As shown in Figure 9.4, the more current view of marketing channels is that they are a collection of inbound and

Figure 9.4
Multichannel Marketing Model

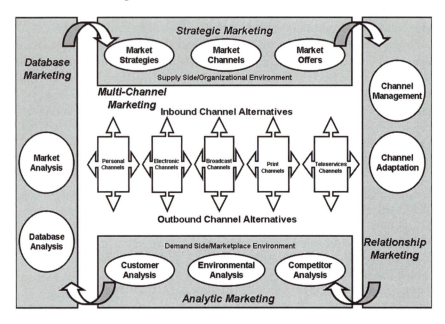

outbound channel alternatives that serve as connecting pathways between supply side elements of the organization's operational environment and the demand side dynamics that characterize the marketplace environment. Designing the architectural structure of your marketing channel involves identifying and selecting your "go-to-market" strategies and tactics. Channels are the vehicles that promote two-way (outbound marketing and inbound response) exchanges between the marketer and selected consumer groups.

There is no doubt that marketers are doing the right thing in offering their customers more ways to buy their products and services. One estimate is that customers of multichannel marketers spend considerably more (upwards to 30%) than those who pursue a single-channel source approach. Proliferation of avenues for reaching and serving customers have created new and promising opportunities for market growth; increased use of mobile phones, growth of wireless networks, and 4G video calling all provide for new contact strategies. Imagine the impact on personal financial services business if the customer could have a face-to-face conversation with the bank official using 4G video technologies. Some studies suggest that clients would be more inclined to engage in complicated transactions if they could use this form of personal channel.[3]

Marketing channels are viewed as operating systems because their architecture structures and designs satisfy system requirements of sequential linkages, nonrandom organizations, and goal orientation. Marketing channel links are comprised of a wide variety of participating partners organized to perform certain marketing, distributive, and operating functions at certain times and places. The marketing channel is typically viewed as two subsystems—the industrial (organizational) channel level and the consumer (final) channel. Industrial channels originate with the raw-resource producer, proceed through various jobbers, semiprocessors, and industrial distributors, and terminate with the final manufacturer. Consumer channels are the communication and exchange pathways between the final manufacturer and the final consumer; wholesalers and retailers bridge the gap between consumer channel origins and destinations.

Successful "go-to-market" strategies of the future will require marketing channels designed as "borderless marketing systems" that incorporate the best collection of channel alternates that are capable of delivering a comprehensive marketing effort. The unbound nature of future channel structures is a logical outcome of the borderless consumer who uses different marketing channels to meet her or his needs at different stages of the buying process. A shopper may discover a new product by browsing through a magazine at a Barnes & Noble bookstore, search for additional information about the product on the Internet, and place an order through an inbound teleservices channel. Being less mindful of channel boundaries, consumers are migrating from one channel to another in search of an acceptable combination that is best suited to his or her particular needs at any given point in time. Channel choices range from the traditional marketing channel designed as a single pathway between marketer and responder, to a multiple-channel structure where several channel alternatives are available as independent and separate avenues to the market, and finally to hybrid multichannel marketing networks where an appropriate collection of channels are vertically and horizontally integrated to provide customers with their preferred choice of a channel alternative for supplying a particular task.

PHASE 4: MULTICHANNEL MARKETING

In traditional marketing channel architectures, channel members (jobbers, distributors, manufacturers, wholesalers, and retailers) operated in a self-serving fashion by jockeying for power and control of channel operations and market access. The limitation on vertical integration (between various levels of the channel) and the total absence of horizontal integration (between different types of channels) hindered most efforts at establishing a cooperative and coordinated channel effort. As suggested above, the dawn of a new era of multichannel marketing will require most businesses to pursue a strategy in which they use several different channel alternatives that are both vertically and horizontality integrated. What are those channel alternatives? Your choices include personal, electronic, broadcast, print, and teleservices channels. Let's briefly examine each of these channel alternatives.

Do you prefer "face-to-face" communications and interactions? Personal channels feature one-on-one explanations and demonstrations of the attributes and benefits of an offer. Brick-and-mortar retailers and direct personal selling are the two most common forms of face-to-face personal channels. Electronic channels utilize the Internet for communicating and interacting globally. By using text, pictures, sound, and video, electronic channel marketers use the World Wide Web and e-mail to contact prospects and customers. Radio and television constitute the primary forms of broadcast channels. Because broadcast channels have traditionally been limited to outbound communication with little or no inbound interaction capabilities, they are poorly configured for direct customer response. However, as part of a multichannel strategy, broadcast channels play a vital role in a multidimensional marketing network. Print channels rely on words and visuals (pictures, tables, and graphics) to extend and accept offers. Direct-mail packages, magazines, and newspapers are the principal print medium for generating customer interest and response. The final channel alternative is teleservices channels. The telephone is a convenient and effective two-way communication tool; as such, you can use it to contact and interact with prospects and customers (outbound telemarketing) or have customers contact and interact with you (inbound telemarketing).

PHASE 5: RELATIONSHIP MARKETING

What kind of relationship do you have with your channel stakeholders (customers, stockholders, employees, communities, business partners, competitors, and managers)? Relationship marketing is the channel philosophy that all channel activities be directed at establishing, nurturing, and building successful relationships with customers and additional stakeholders with a vested interest in the channel's success. While relationship marketing has historically been viewed as the partnership between the firm and its customers, multichannel marketers must take a broader view, including the creation of win-win relational exchanges between the firm and all of its strategic partners (stakeholders). In this final phase of the multichannel marketing process, we will look at the issues inherent in managing channel operations and adapting those operations to new environmental conditions.

Channel Management

In the normal course of marketing channel operations, a large number of different types of interactions among different channel levels and between different channels types are necessary if the entire marketing effort is to be completed in an efficient and effective manner. Buying, selling, stocking, informing, financing, transporting, transferring, and promoting are the more common interactions that need to be managed.

A channel manager will be charged with the responsibility of managing the entire set of channel flows (activities and movements among channel members). Channel movements and activities are two-way (inbound and outbound) interactions. The more complex nature of multichannel structures greatly complicates channel architecture. All channel partners with a multichannel structure must deal with both inbound and outbound channel flows within and between channels. Communication flows must deal with both the inbound and outbound movement of information (informative facts and figures) and promotions (persuasive appeals and creatives) from one channel level to another within the same vertical marketing channel as well as horizontally between various channel partners at different channel levels within different channel networks. The difficulties of managing all of these vertical and horizontal lines of communication are more than compensated for by the enhanced marketing capabilities and expanded market opportunities. Equally complex are the vertical and horizontal interaction flows of negotiations (offer propositions and responses), transactions (order placement and fulfillment), and relations service features and actions. Each of these will be discussed more fully in chapters to come.

Marketing channels can be characterized by a number of different structural designs. Channel structure describes the arrangement or positioning of channel partners within the marketing channel network. Channel structure is a function of channel length, width, direction, and multiplicity.

The length of the channel is the vertical dimension of its distribution network. Long channels are indirect structures that have several independent intermediaries (e.g., wholesalers and retailers) between the channel origin (e.g., producer) and the destination (e.g., consumer). Short channels are direct pathways to the marketplace containing few if any middlemen. Shorter channels tend to be more vertically integrated than their longer counterparts. The operational efficiency and the marketing effectiveness of shorter channels offer competitive advantages that are superior to long, indirect structures.

Decisions regarding channel width are based on the intensity of market coverage the channel architect deems necessary to gain the needed exposure and degree of availability of your marketing program. Channel designers can plan market coverage densities that range from intensive distribution (readily available in as many outlets as possible), to selective distribution (available in limited number of outlets), to a very restrictive and exclusive distributive network (one outlet per market area).

Channel multiplicity relates to the practice of developing several channel alternatives in an effort to reach the same or different market segments. As discussed

delivered and responded to via several different marketing channels (multichannel marketing) in order to build and nurture mutually beneficial relationships with your customers and channel stakeholders. Concluding the multichannel marketing process is the need to adapt channel operations through continuous and dynamic improvement efforts.

NOTES

1. Ray Schultz, "Three's Company," *Direct* 16, no. 9 (July 1, 2004).

2. Ann Meyer, "Homing In," *Catalog Age* 21, no. 5 (May 1, 2004).

3. "Digital Demands Multimedia Tack," *Precision Marketing*, October 7, 2005, 12.

4. Robert Fuchs, "Mobile Marketing Has Its Advantages," *Marketing News*, October 1, 2006, 21.

CHAPTER 10

BUSINESS-TO-BUSINESS INTEGRATED MARKETING

Nadji Tehrani

DON'T PUT ALL YOUR EGGS IN ONE BASKET: USE INTEGRATED MARKETING!

Every so often, marketing reinvents itself. A French philosopher once said, "The more things change, the more they stay the same." However, when it comes to marketing, that is only 50 percent true. The method of marketing changes but the marketing principles stay the same. Because of this ever-changing nature of marketing, there will always be a great challenge in figuring out what the formula for success today versus yesterday is.

Putting all of the above together, it becomes clear that marketing is often like shooting at a moving target; that is why it is the most challenging and most complex part of any corporation. Ironically very few, if any, companies pay enough attention to this vital art and science.

As I travel around the country visiting companies, I continuously find that a certain number of blunders continue in many companies. Here are a few examples:

1. Some companies hire a complete marketing staff, but they give them no budget to market anything! I hope this makes sense to somebody!

2. Other companies want to get by with public relations (PR) only. In other words, they give only lip service to marketing by trying to get something for nothing. Obviously, that kind of marketing will never succeed, and the companies that believe in that philosophy will flounder until they lose their competitive advantage.

3. Other companies commit even greater sins by spending millions of dollars developing a product or group of products, and then they say there is no money left for

marketing! To me, this is completely backward! Many companies successfully do it the other way around. They do not have much of a product, but they market the hell out of it, and as unlikely as it may seem, those are the companies that come up with the biggest market share!

Not long ago, I visited a company that offers one of the best, if not the best, speech product in the industry. We met with the CEO and asked about his company and his marketing plans. The answer was something like this: "We have invested 35 years in building this product line and we have no money to market it." I will never understand this kind of logic. This company will also flounder until someone else comes along with an inferior product and markets the hell out of it and eats his lunch. It seems like many companies simply choose to ignore marketing. These companies fail to realize that companies exist for two and only two reasons, namely, marketing and innovation. Without these, no company would get anywhere.

WHAT IS INTEGRATED MARKETING?

When newspapers were invented, they gradually became an important tool for marketers. When radio was invented, some uninformed marketers said, "Well, that's the end of newspapers." That was nearly 60-plus years ago. When TV was invented, the same people said, "That's the end of newspapers and radio"—and so on! Today, we know that those misguided comments were nothing more than hogwash. Yes, newspapers, radio, TV, and the Web are still around and they are all serving an important function in marketing. To the extent that people have different tastes, some prefer print, some prefer the Web, some prefer the mail, etc.; conventional wisdom dictates that if you want to reach your total market, you have ONE AND ONLY ONE SOLUTION and that is integrated marketing, encompassing ALL of the above components. As Reed Business Information states: "Understand that one advertising medium can't do it all. An integrated approach of print and online initiatives will allow you to better accomplish your goals and objectives. To reach their goals, marketers need to piece together their own custom Integrated Marketing Solution."

Today's business-to-business (B-to-B) marketer has a plethora of tools to use in his or her toolbox. Among these are: newspaper, radio, TV, Internet, direct mail, target marketing, database marketing, PR, custom portals, telemarketing, print advertising, trade show marketing, relationship marketing, e-mail marketing, and search engine marketing. What is important to remember here is that you must identify the right combination of these tools and decide how to use them in your campaign. In some cases a number of these tools will be used simultaneously, while in others the tools will be sequenced so that one directly enhances the other. For the B-to-B marketer, the science is understanding how these tools work independently and together, and the art is being able to extract the best from the tools to have a successful campaign.

The business universe gets more competitive and more demanding every minute. Both the pace of business as well as the number of participants are continuously increasing. What does that mean for marketers? It means that they are battling for attention against an ever-shrinking time frame in an ever-more crowded arena.

B-to-B advertising eliminates many of the obstacles. In a high-attention venue, with an involved and deeply interested audience, advertisers have the time, the attention, and most of all, the interest of audience members. That is why it makes good business sense to extend the advertising impact by taking advantage of the multiplicity of media platforms B-to-B vehicles offer. A combination of print advertising, website presence, trade show appearances, and conference sponsorships means an advertiser's impact on the audience is magnified geometrically.

THE MISSING LINK IN MARKETING: DIFFERENTIATION AND POSITIONING

Your customers must have a reason to buy from you and that reason comes from positioning and differentiation. In order to better understand the purpose of positioning and differentiation, which, in my opinion, are the most crucial parts of marketing strategy, let's refer to the *American Heritage Dictionary* for the definition of differentiation and positioning. Although they do not have a direct definition for differentiation and positioning in marketing, if you look at the definitions for differentiate and position, one will arrive at the same conclusion, as follows. *American Heritage* defines "differentiate" as: (1) to constitute the distinction between or (2) to perceive or show difference in or between; and discriminate.

It describes "position" as:

- The right or appropriate place
- The way in which something or someone is placed
- The act or process of positioning
- To place in proper position; last but not least, an advantageous place or location

Looking at the above definitions, one can clearly conclude that to effectively market, any product or service must be differentiated from its competition, thereby giving the potential buyer a reason to purchase the product or service in question. As for positioning, the definition clearly points out that it is crucial for any product to be positioned in an appropriate place or, preferably, advantageous location.

Over the years, I have learned that if you do not position yourself advantageously, your competition will position you and your product in the most disadvantageous way. Having said that, one must clearly explain that positioning is not a part-time job by any stretch of the imagination. Positioning and differentiation, like marketing itself, are not part-time jobs. In fact, to do it right, they are more than full-time jobs. That means you must market every day, you must position every day, and you must differentiate every day—365 days a year, 24 hours a day, 7 days a week. In short, marketing, positioning, and differentiation are 24/7 jobs, period, end of story.

POSITIONING AND DIFFERENTIATING ARE VITAL TO THE SUCCESS OF ANY MARKETING CAMPAIGN

With so much global competition, customers need a reason to buy from you, and that reason comes from your positioning and differentiation, which explains to your customer or potential customer what sets you apart or what sets your product or service apart. Without that, no one has any reason to buy your product or service as opposed to your competitors'.

In an ultra-fast-moving and rapidly changing environment, one can practically assume that market conditions also change month to month, maybe even day to day, as opposed to 25 years ago when things changed more slowly. Consequently, one must always remain 100 percent focused on the marketplace as well as on the validity of positioning vis-à-vis the current conditions of the marketplace. It would be a disaster if one were to lose sight of adjusting one's positioning to reflect the changing marketplace requirements. The next important item is that when companies fail to change their positioning, they lose market share and lose considerable revenue. In fact, such companies may not even survive when markets change so rapidly.

In today's extremely complex, information-jammed world, we are exposed to thousands of advertisements and promotions of various kinds, and in short, we are inundated with an information explosion. It has been said that in the last 30 years, more information has been produced than in the previous 5,000 years. The emergence of the Internet has added ultrasonic speed to the growth of information available. Therefore to make your products and services stand out in the marketplace, you must do a superb job of positioning, differentiation, marketing, and advertising.

The first law of positioning states that it is better to be first than to be better. Who was the first man who flew over the Atlantic? Obviously, it was Charles Lindbergh. Who was the second person to fly over the Atlantic? Answer: nobody knows and nobody cares. What was the name of the horse that won the Triple Crown in 1973 and broke practically all racetrack speed records? The answer: Secretariat. What was the name of the horse that came in the number 2 position right behind Secretariat in all three races? The answer, no one remembers and no one cares about number 2. Only horse-racing fans would remember that the name of the second-place horse was Sham. The bottom line: the first law is true, and if you really want to be a market leader, you must position yourself as such every minute, every hour, every day, every month, 365 days a year and 24/7.

ONLINE MARKETING COMES OF AGE

Everyone knows that the latest evolution in marketing focuses on online marketing. Every time a new marketing concept comes along, people say, "This is the answer to all marketing needs. We are going to cancel everything else and jump on the online bandwagon!" Years ago, when we launched *Telemarketing* magazine in a pioneering act to lay the foundation for what is now the multibillion-dollar contact center/CRM and call center industry, most people said the same thing about telemarketing. I heard people dropping direct mail or print advertising in favor of telemarketing. This was not the right thing to do because no one buys anything from a company they have never heard of. When the marketers came to their senses in the early 1980s, they learned that in order to get the best results from telemarketing, they must combine it with direct mail, trade show marketing, and personal visits (for high-value products) in order to get maximum results. In other words, we learned back then that the only way to market effectively is through integrated marketing. Stated differently, the more things change, the more they stay the same. Today, integrated marketing is also the only way to go. One cannot cancel all other marketing plans in favor of online marketing only. There is no disputing the fact that a well-designed print ad will stand out in a publication just as a well-designed online ad will be noticed on a website. And standing out in a crowd ensures that your brand is recognized and your marketing message conveyed.

More and more companies today are leaning toward online marketing. Many are making the mistake of stopping everything else and putting all of their marketing eggs in the online basket. This is, in my opinion, completely unwise because other forms of marketing such as print, trade shows, exhibition, etc., create the perception of stability, dedication, longevity, awareness, and commitment of the company, not to mention brand recognition and marketing through education, which are vital in the marketing process. As stated above, no one buys anything significant from a company they have never heard of. Here are some guidelines for online marketing and beyond:

1. When thinking of doing online marketing, do not forget other forms of marketing.

2. Check the reputation of the company behind the website on which you would like to do your online marketing.

3. More importantly, check the Alexa (http://www.alexa.com) ranking of the website on which you plan to advertise. This step is by far the most important part of selecting a suitable online marketing vehicle that has proper Web traffic. Alexa.com is a division of Amazon.com, and specializes in auditing Web traffic of ALL websites regardless of

the type of website. When looking at Alexa.com rankings, it is vital to remember that the lower the ranking number, the greater the website traffic in terms of bringing the necessary eyeballs to that website. In other words, you do not want to choose websites that have higher ranking numbers than 4,000 on Alexa.com. As an example, the Alexa ranking of TMCnet.com is approximately 3,000, plus or minus. As such, TMCnet.com is ranked by Alexa.com as being in the top 3,000 websites in the world! Websites with much higher numbers simply do not have the traffic, and it could lead to a waste of your marketing dollars.

4. Compare the Alexa ranking charts directly with competing websites by superimposing all of the competing websites along with your preferred website on which you would like to advertise. This will give you an idea of the suitability of your chosen website. Once again, these charts are vitally important to help you judiciously select and eliminate the sites with extremely poor traffic.

5. Check the quality of the content. Quality editorial matter brings quality readers, and quality readers become quality sales leads for your products and services.

6. Investigate the WebTrends rankings of your chosen site versus competition.

7. Check the relevant term ranking on the leading search engine sites before you select your final website for your marketing purposes. For example, TMCnet.com ranks as number one in over 40 relevant terms on Google. We are not aware of any other site in the telecom industry that even comes close. If your chosen site cannot match this type of prominence, it simply does not deserve your advertisement.

8. ALWAYS remember that on Alexa.com, the lower the number, the better the traffic.

9. Look at your chosen site's value proposition. How does it compare your value proposition with competing sites?

10. Investigate the "renewal rate" of other online advertisers on your chosen website. If the renewal rate is less than 90 percent, do not waste your money advertising on that website. As a point of reference, the marketing channel renewal rate on TMCnet.com is 99 percent.

11. Does your chosen website offer guaranteed lead generation? If not, forget it.

12. Remember that only outstanding content delivers quality sales leads. Therefore place maximum emphasis on the integrity and longevity and reputation of your chosen website.

THE MOST EFFECTIVE WAY TO GENERATE LEADS

Integrated marketing and/or multimedia programs are effective ways to market and generate sales leads. In today's world, customers tend to react to advertising and marketing materials in different ways. In other words, some prefer voice (radio or telephone), others television, others magazine, others print advertising, others channel marketing, and others Internet advertising of several forms. To conduct full-court marketing or a winning marketing program, you must consider integrated marketing as the vital point of your marketing program. Indeed, nearly 10 years ago, the tagline of *Customer Inter@ction Solutions* was "The Magazine of

Integrated Marketing." That was a decade ago when we came to the realization that someday we must all consider integrated marketing because "one size fits all" does not work in marketing.

There has been an evolution in the nature of incoming leads. Having gone through direct mail via coupons, postcards, regular mail, and bingo cards, the nature of incoming leads upgraded to telephone plus mail then to 80 percent via toll-free 800 numbers in the '80s and '90s. No matter where you advertise, nowadays over 90 percent of the leads are coming via your website and the rest via toll-free inbound 800 numbers or regular phone.

Even if you conduct integrated marketing and generate the most qualified sales leads, placed in the hands of an unproven salesperson, no sales will result. In other words, if you do not keep in mind all of the above guidelines, such as appropriate integrated marketing, etc., you still may hit a point where your marketing campaign is not producing desired results. In that case, we suggest you keep in mind all of the above guidelines and develop a checklist to determine where there is a shortfall and misconnection in your marketing campaign and fix it.

If you follow the anatomy of a healthy organization, you will find that without exception, no company can exist without new business, and simply stated, no company can remain in business without sales. It follows, therefore, that to generate sales one must have sales leads because "all sales begin with sales leads." As vital as lead generation is, it is mind-boggling that so many companies ignore this phenomenally important part of business and simply give it casual attention, if any at all.

Leads can be generated from any or all of the following:

1. Trade shows
2. Print advertising
3. Telemarketing
4. Channel marketing
5. Web advertising
6. Direct mail
7. Integrated marketing (which is regarded as the most powerful method)
8. Effective response-driven campaigns (which begin with response-driven advertising)
9. Effective positioning (no marketing campaign could be functional without it)
10. Differentiation (again, no marketing campaign could be functional without it)
11. PR

THE ROLE OF CRM

Next comes the job of CRM (customer relationship management), the objective of which is to keep the customer satisfied by developing a strong relationship with the customer. In short, the job of advertising is to generate sales leads, and the job of salespeople is to close the sales and turn the leads into customers. The job of CRM is to keep the customers.

One of the original purposes of CRM has been to develop a technique that will help companies improve customer retention, customer satisfaction, and customer loyalty. However, if you truly analyze your relationship with your vendors, or many companies' relationships with their vendors, you will find that in most cases, customers are taken for granted and therein lies the root of the problem. I learned a long time ago that if you do not nurture your relationship with your customer on a weekly or monthly basis, it is only a matter of time before you will lose that customer. And yet, many companies totally ignore their major customers, and that is a violation of all the commandments of good CRM!

For example, how many of you have heard from your car manufacturers after you have purchased a car? Did anyone call to see if you were satisfied? Do they call you every month or every six months or every year? Most importantly, did anyone call you a month or two prior to when your lease terminated to try to sell you a new car? In my experience, the answer to all of the above is a resounding no!

I chose car manufacturers as an example because a car is a very expensive item and it can range anywhere from $20,000 to $60,000 or more per customer. To me, that is a significant purchase, and manufacturers must communicate regularly with customers, not only to find out if they are satisfied but also to encourage them to buy their next car from that particular company. At the moment, none of the above is taking place and that is why practically all of the car manufacturers are losing customers left and right to their competitors!

When a vendor fails to contact its customers frequently, no relationship is built. As a result, the customer has no reason to be loyal to that vendor. If you ignore your customers and do not show appreciation and care, the customers have no reason to remain loyal to you. I realize that most companies are unintentionally committing the above mistakes, but in this day and age when the customers have many choices, it is the violation of all the commandments of business, not to mention CRM, to ignore customers and not try to show appreciation and care in order to keep that customer loyal!

On the other hand, to go to the next level in building customer loyalty and conducting true CRM, you need to find out what it takes to help your customers acquire new customers and keep them. If you can achieve this, then you will have a customer for life. But then again, how many companies are doing this? I would guess less than 1 percent, and therefore there is no customer loyalty and retention, and billions of dollars of losses in business are the result every year because of the above problems.

If you are really and truly committed to positioning your company for maximum market share and profitability, here are a few suggested steps for you to take:

1. The Role of CRM: You must genuinely try to keep most, if not all, of your existing customers through implementation of a truly functional and sensible CRM and e-CRM program.

2. The Case for Marketing Frequency: Position and differentiate your company 24/7/365 in an advantageous way and remember that aggressive marketing, advertising, and promotion are NOT part-time jobs. A true leader does not claim leadership for one week, disappear for six weeks, place a couple of ads, and then disappear again for six months. Those types of leaders will not be leaders for long. In fact, they will become followers and in some cases go out of business.

3. On Positioning and Differentiation: Through your clever positioning and differentiation tactics, be very specific communicating to the marketplace what sets your product or service apart from your competition. This is vitally important because it gives your customers and your prospects a reason to buy from you rather than from your competition.

4. Remember, if you do not position yourself 24/7/365, your competition will position you in the most disadvantageous way.

5. Market Aggressively: Maintain the most powerful, aggressive marketing campaign that includes a clever marketing strategy, truly effective advertising, and targeted vertical trade show participation. Remember that there is no shortcut to marketing domination, the greatest market share, and success.

In my opinion, the above guidelines are a few of the most vital points you need to keep in mind. Focus on them 100 percent and implement them around the clock, 365 days a year if you are to gain the lion's share of the market and leapfrog your competition. And remember that this economy is truly on your side to help you gain your dream market share, so make the most of it.

OLD-FASHIONED MARKETING HABITS CONTINUE

During my daily association with various CEOs and marketing executives, I find that many are committed to direct mail only or trade show only or e-mail only as the sole marketing vehicle for their companies. They act as if they have never heard of integrated marketing. Indeed, I have seen many companies that waste thousands of dollars on one or two media and ignore the rest. Obviously, these companies will never gain the full benefit of their marketing dollars.

I recently investigated such a company and discovered that in spite of the fact that thousands of dollars were spent on one or two media, the company did not commit to integrated marketing, and that company's name did not appear in the appropriate categories in any of the major search engines. The bottom line is that the successful marketers of today are those that use integrated marketing, and anything less will not do. In previous editorials, I have frequently mentioned that marketing is not a part-time job and there is no shortcut in marketing. And yet, many marketers are ignoring the above facts, and their companies are losing millions of dollars in new business.

One of the most prevalent problems I have recently found with many marketers is that they are ignoring print, trade show, telephone, and channel marketing. In my opinion, there is no greater disaster that can result from ignoring these vital components of "integrated marketing." And yet, the mediocrity continues, and many companies are completely oblivious to these facts and foundations of modern marketing.

Advertising blunders also continue. Indeed, many advertisements that I find in a variety of publications are guilty of the following problems. First, they are not communicating the benefits of the products or of doing business with that company. Second, they are not differentiating themselves from the competition. Third, they have not positioned themselves effectively. Fourth, they are too busy or they do not say anything. Fifth, they are poorly designed and are using colors that turn off readers. Sixth, and last but not least, many of them do not even have a powerful benefit-driven headline. To make matters worse, 70 percent of the sales leads generated from advertising are not followed up!

If the above is the case, one has to wonder, what is the purpose of advertising if you do not give the customer a reason to do business with you? And again, Corporate America seems to be oblivious. The lousy ads appear in many publications and newspapers without having any effect whatsoever! How do you solve the problem? The client must do a much better job of informing the ad agency about the benefits of the product and, most importantly, what differentiates that product from the competition.

As stupid and ill-advised as this may sound, believe it or not, a few marketing/PR people go out of their way to destroy relationships with the most powerful media companies in their industries! To me, this is like someone developing a new Bible for Catholics and, as the first order of business, they decide to break all relationships with the pope! I know this sounds stupid, but it is also sad and it is happening! Unfortunately, this is also a true story. Who is to blame? Of course, top management for hiring and keeping such idiots on the payroll!

In any business, every now and then one encounters an entrepreneur who has no experience in marketing who likes to take on the role of a marketing manager, or one meets a marketing director who simply speaks at the direction of the entrepreneur who has no experience in marketing. Unfortunately, often in these cases if they market and do not sell something for a short period, they cancel all of their marketing without investigating why they did not sell anything. Such people should know that only properly prepared marketing messages that speak to the audience in a benefit-driven manner, and that are properly placed in a magazine (or other media) that targets their audience, are the ones that will generate sales leads. In addition, unlike the common belief that all leads will turn into sales, sales leads, no matter how qualified, are worthless if you place them in the hands of unproven salespeople. In other words, a response-driven campaign that is properly developed, speaks to the audience with something to offer, and is placed in an appropriate, targeted publication will generate leads and only sales leads, but no sales by itself. Consequently, sales leads should first be qualified and then must be placed in the hands of a good salesperson with appropriate closing techniques to sell the product/service and convert the sales leads into customers.

THE BIGGEST MISTAKES OF ALL

In my judgment, two of the biggest blunders made by businesses are as follows:

1. The greatest mistake made by downsizing is laying off the core people who are the foundation of your business success. Let it be known that categorically I truly hate to lay off anyone solely because of economic conditions.

2. Many ill-advised senior managers also authorize drastic cuts in advertising, marketing, and trade show participation. As far as I am concerned, these people are making the greatest possible mistake and thereby inflicting the greatest possible damage to their corporations. Here is why: In a slow economy such as the one we are now experiencing, every corporation loses anywhere between 50 and 70 percent of its current customers. We also know that all sales begin with a sales lead. Furthermore, the sole purpose of marketing, advertising, and trade show participation is to generate qualified sales leads, which, when handled properly by the sales department, will become new customers. However, when you cut all marketing, advertising, and trade show budgets, and you lose 50 to 70 percent of your customers, how then can you replace the lost customers and still remain in business? To me, this is a very simple principle of business, and yet in every recession, the majority of corporate leaders still make the mistake of eliminating their marketing, advertising, and trade show budgets. In my judgment, this explains why so many companies go under at such times! It is like cutting off your nose to spite your face!

WHY SOME COMPANIES FAIL

Based on my years of experience watching businesses develop, grow, and then decline, I offer the following lessons or examples of the most common failures.

Lesson #1: Ignorance Is the Entrepreneur's Best Friend

I am a firm believer that ignorance is truly the entrepreneur's best friend. I once read a study made by a reliable research organization that stated that 90 percent of entrepreneurs are between the ages of 30 and 38, because that is a period in life when people do not know an excessive amount about business, but they do know some things for real. Consequently, entrepreneurs in that age bracket are more likely to take a plunge, and once they are in the water, they know that they have to sink or swim. That element alone leads the entrepreneurs to become successful.

Lesson #2: Why Do Some Companies with Poor Products Succeed and Others with Very Good Products Fail?

Believe it or not, this was precisely the case for a pair of companies, one with a great product and the other with a mediocre product. Ironically, the former (the company with a great product) nearly went bankrupt, while the company with the mediocre product maintained better than 80 percent market share! If you asked me to explain why this was so in one word, I would say "marketing." If you allowed me three words, I would say "lack of marketing," and if I could use two more words, I would say "lousy marketing." Believe it or not, this is a true story, and I admired the company with the highest market share simply because the CEO of that company was a master marketer, while the CEO of the failing company considered marketing to be a necessary evil, and he gave it only lip service. The ironic thing, in this case, is that the above scenario occurred with not only many high-technology companies but also several teleservices companies.

Lesson #3: The Case for the Teleservices Companies

Company A and Company B ranked #48 and #49 in the Top 50 Teleservices Agencies ranking as selected by the editors of *Customer Inter@ction Solutions* magazine. The CEO of Company A was a master marketer and frequently consulted with TMC. He followed practically every suggestion that we gave him. He was also an excellent manager and had very talented and hardworking employees. As a result, the company rose from #48 to #2 in the Top 50 rankings (over a five-year period), and thanks to the tremendous business savvy of the CEO of Company A, the company went public in the mid-1990s at about $15 a share. Subsequently, the price rose to $80 per share. Later on, there was a two-for-one split, and the split stocks also rose to $80 per share. The bottom line is that the CEO and founder of Company A cashed in an estimated $600 million worth of stock, and through exceptional investing, he has now become a billionaire. Company B did nothing: no marketing, no promotions, no advertising, and therefore the company went nowhere. Again, this is a true story.

Lesson #4: Having a Marketing VP with No Budget

Believe it or not, some companies are shortsighted enough to have a marketing vice president, but no budget. They try to rely completely on word-of-mouth marketing. Even if these companies have not gone out of business over the last 25 years, they have not made much progress either. To me, it is incomprehensible for any company to have a director or vice president of marketing, but no budget for promotion or advertising.

Lesson #5: Rush to Market

Back in 1990, a leading company in our industry came up with a product that was supposed to be all things to all people. For political and personal reasons, this product was marketed long before it was ready. The powerful marketing and previously existing respect for this company in the industry led many innocent call center executives to adopt that technology, only to find out that it was completely nonfunctional and, in fact, that it was nothing more than a major headache. As a result, the company lost major market share and still has not recovered from that disaster.

Lesson #6: Suing Your Influential Customers

Another idiotic and totally incomprehensible action that a few CEOs have taken in the recent past was actually threatening to bring a lawsuit against their leading customers. The reason? The customer refused to renew its contract with Company A because of Company A's obsolete product and unreliable technical service. The shortsighted CEO of Company A was blinded by his ego and did not realize that the contact center industry, like many other industries, is an extremely well-connected group. In other words, when somebody screws up a great company by offering lousy service, yet does not allow customers to go elsewhere by virtue of threatening lawsuits, that CEO has no reason to exist, in my opinion. Fortunately, one such CEO was let go just before the company went under. This was not the first time I had witnessed such an illogical and idiotic action of bringing a lawsuit against a prestigious customer. Back in my chemistry days, the CEO of a chemical adhesives company where I was employed submitted a completely defective product to the company's leading customer. When the customer refused to pay, the ill-advised CEO brought a lawsuit against the customer. That ill-advised action took the chemical company, which had heretofore been the #1 supplier to the industry, to last place. Eventually, the company was sold for practically a song to a leading competitor. One wonders how the board of directors of any responsible company could put up with this kind of stupidity— instead of providing maximum care for their leading customers, they actually brought a lawsuit against them. Yes, it sounds utterly stupid, but it has happened and I have witnessed it.

Lesson #7: The Demise of Horizontal Trade Shows

Once upon a time, the granddaddy of all technology shows, COMDEX, featured exhibitors who offered soup to nuts in terms of products. Suddenly, there was a shift in the marketplace from exhibiting at horizontal shows in favor of exhibiting at small but highly focused and targeted trade shows. As a result, COMDEX no longer exists. What made matters worse in COMDEX's case were ill-advised managers who treated every exhibitor like dirt and dictated to those exhibitors that if they wanted a particular space the next year, exhibitors must increase their booth size by 20 to 50 percent. The rule was, "Take it or leave it." Eventually, exhibitors who were not getting much business out of COMDEX anyway declined to continue exhibiting, and COMDEX is now history.

Lesson #8: The CEOs Blinded by Ego

As I have indicated in many of my previous editorials, a CEO can be a double-edged sword. On the positive side, a CEO with the right frame of mind and the proper attitude can enhance the revenues of his or her company tremendously. The right CEO will actually build and reinforce relationships with all customers, or as many of his or her customers as possible, and, in fact, will play the role of ambassador for the company. Alternatively, many CEOs would prefer to deal only with other CEOs. In such cases, the wrong CEO (who is rude and has a huge ego problem) would spell disaster. I know one CEO who inherited a company with about 80 percent market share. That market share was largely the result of an outstanding CEO who had run the company previously. The new CEO, a person with horrible interpersonal skills, came in and started to break most, if not all, of the company's relationships one by one! As a matter of fact, I became so disgusted with that particular company that I wrote an editorial about how lousy some companies are in treating both their customers and the leading media in their industry. One analysis that I used was that the company acted as if the world owes them everything and they owe nothing in return. Needless to say, that particular CEO was let go, and the rest of the company was extremely happy for that.

Lesson #9: Build Great Products and Keep Them a Secret!

Another great lesson that we continuously learned from mistakes made by small to medium-size companies is as follows: the tendency of technology companies has often been to build a better mousetrap only to find that the mouse died 15 years ago! Believe it or not, as funny as this may seem this is still the case in 80 percent of technology companies. Recall the CEO of a speech technology company that I told you about earlier in the chapter, who had invested many years of his life and all his money in developing his product, but insisted that he had no money for marketing. Can you believe he actually said something so idiotic? We have stated in these editorials many times that "if you don't market, you don't exist." In fact, in previous editorials I updated that comment by saying, "If you're not on the first page of Google and/or Yahoo search results for your industry, you don't exist." Nevertheless, high-tech companies continue to ignore the rules of marketing and they give only lip service to it. Ironically, the few companies that do market seem to have one or more of the following problems:

- The marketing pieces and advertising are not benefits-driven.
- There is no differentiation statement.
- There is no positioning statement.
- There is a wrong message to the wrong audience.
- There is no call to action!

With that many problems, it is no wonder that many who do a lousy job of marketing do not blame their lack of knowledge about effective marketing; they say marketing does not work or advertising does not work, whereas in reality their poor marketing message has all of the above problems, and in most cases, their messages have no call to action. That should explain the reason for unusually high rates of failure within the technology companies—they typically spend 95 percent of their budgets on research and development of new products and next to nothing on marketing. Today, no company prospers without the implementation of well-strategized integrated marketing.

Lesson #10: Do Not Hang Your Hat on PR Alone

Many times, I have witnessed CEOs and vice presidents of many technology companies go on media tours with the PR staff. The companies visit both the leading publications as well as the industry analysts. Oftentimes, they feel that their visit will lead to press via PR, and thereby they feel that their marketing job is done. Many CEOs, while visiting the leading media providers, rarely ask "How do you think I should market my product?" And that is the source of the problem, because a leading publisher who really understands the industry can offer practical solutions and suggestions for effective marketing strategies at no charge. Yet many companies are not receptive to it, and they feel that PR alone is going to do the job. In my humble opinion, that will never happen, and it is only wishful thinking.

Lesson #11: M&A Blunders

In the mid-1990s, when the contact center industry was flourishing and growing at literally 50 to 100 percent a year, Wall Street became extremely interested in the contact center industry, specifically in teleservices. Investment bankers started calling me and asking me what I thought about this company or that company. It looked as if there was a feeding frenzy or, more specifically, an acquisition frenzy going on. Every week or every month, I would hear of a new acquisition. I was concerned about this activity—not because I did not feel that consolidation would be good, but because many of the acquirers were financial buyers, which means they were strictly interested in making a profit and they were clueless about the many, many details that need to be considered in order to effectively run and manage a call center. I recall talking to such a financial buyer who used to be a waiter in a restaurant; he then purchased the restaurant and subsequently went into the real estate business and made a ton of money. At that time, he discovered the rapid growth of call centers. As a result, he borrowed millions and acquired half a dozen incompatible and subpar companies. Before too long, as expected he ran into major problems. I recall receiving a call from that person asking me what he had done wrong. Unfortunately, it was too late. If he had called me prior to the acquisitions, I would have told him that his particular combination of incompatible companies would never have become a unified profit center. As a result, millions of dollars were wasted.

Lesson #12: The Unlikely and Unfortunate Story

A few years ago, a poorly funded company (Company X) claimed to have developed a new technology that raised the eyebrows of all technology-savvy people. The company made every claim known to humankind, and they made many, many promises. While no one was taking them seriously, they decided to manipulate an analyst to state that upon evaluation of all products in this category, the analyst found Company X's product to rank at #1. Obviously, some monetary rewards must have changed hands, otherwise such nonsense never would have been presented. The industry was up in arms. All manufacturers were against this action, and they spent a considerable amount of time informing the rest of the industry to beware of Company X's questionable practices. To make a very long story short, eventually Company X went out of business.

I have always wondered what is in the minds of the people who continue to make mistake after mistake and misleading statement after misleading statement, getting involved in all of the problems that I have outlined above. I once explained some of these problems to a highly respected CEO of our industry who, in my judgment, was one of the most, if not the most, knowledgeable CEOs in our industry. I shared with him some of the errors that were being committed. I asked him what he thought about the issue. His answer was, "If this industry wasn't so good, many of those CEOs would be pumping gas!" The more I thought about it, the more I realized he was right. Obviously, the purpose of this editorial is not to embarrass anyone or badmouth any individual or any company; rather, the main objective of this editorial is to learn from some of the mistakes made in the last 25 years. If I can prevent anyone from making any of the above mistakes, I think I have accomplished what I set out to do!

MARKETING THROUGH EDUCATION: THE ONLY WAY TO GO

It has been proven that the only way to market high-technology products is through education. There is simply no other way. One of the best ways to address this is to come up with unique and innovative editorial/marketing strategies to get your message across convincingly. The key to successful marketing must include the following, at a minimum:

1. Think out of the box and think integrated marketing.
2. Be innovative.
3. Remember the top three rules of marketing and advertising, which are benefits, benefits, and benefits. If your marketing message does not have a powerful, benefit-driven message, do not expect any results.
4. Positioning. Nothing is more important than all of the above, plus positioning.
5. And . . . differentiation.
6. Last, but not least, please note that without question, an integrated print, online, and trade show campaign is much more effective than focusing on only one or the other exclusively.

The combination of positioning and differentiation is what gives your customers a reason to buy your product as opposed to your competitor's product.

To be successful, you need to follow the above guidelines to avoid wasteful spending and costly mistakes and, above all, do not put all of your eggs in the same basket. Online can be extremely rewarding if you follow the above guidelines. That is, integrated marketing should be the foundation of your marketing program to include online, print, trade shows, etc., to bring appropriate brand recognition and marketing through education in order to help you maximize your marketing ROI.

CHAPTER 11

Nostradamus Knows Direct Interactive Marketing: Direct Marketers as 21st-Century Trend Messengers

William J. Hauser

INTRODUCTION

During the 16th century, Michel de Nostredame (Nostradamus), a French physician, gazed into his crystal ball and made predictions that are debated and, in some cases, anxiously awaited almost four centuries later. Written in the form of rather obscure four-line poems, or quatrains, Nostradamus and his work remains relevant today. Actually, one might look at the continued popularity of Nostradamus's work as an extremely successful direct multichannel marketing campaign.

The predictions written as quatrains have made and still make excellent copy. Because they are obscure, often written in a combination of languages, the reader is required to reread and study their contents many times over (stickiness). This obscurity also makes them adaptable to just about any recent historical time frame (relevance). Over the epochs the predictions (product) have remained the same; it is the delivery channels that have changed. Originally marketed by word of mouth and in limited print, Nostradamus's quatrains are universally marketed today via the Internet, books, television, movies, and other channels. Interestingly, unless some of Dr. Nostradamus's more dramatic doomsday predictions happen in the near future, there is no end in sight for this product. Think about it. A marketing campaign that has lasted for almost 400 years and is still going strong. I think we all might love being the account executive on this campaign!

As technology continues to breathe new life into marketing, especially direct interactive marketing, it might prove profitable to conjure up Nostradamus and his crystal ball to observe where direct interactive multichannel marketing is headed in the first quarter of the 21st century. However, as with Nostradamus's earlier predictions, a caveat is offered here.

> Nostradamus's predictions come true
> As history allows them to.
> But a crystal ball's view clouded
> Makes predictions in uncertainty shrouded.

The following article will view direct interactive marketers as the trend messengers of the 21st century. It will then borrow Nostradamus's crystal ball to look first at 21st-century consumers. Next, it will envision the role of technology and its future impact on interactive multichannel marketing. From this, we will delve deeper into the all-seeing orb in an attempt to predict the consumers' responses to it and any potential obstacles in the prediction.

The Macroscopic Millennium

A few years ago, you went to bed at night in one millennium and woke up the next morning in a new one. While this may not sound like it is a big deal, think about what was occurring. You were born into a century of rapid technological and social change. The 1900s were full of events that were unimaginable a century before. How many people in the 1800s even knew what an atom was, much less understand what it means to split it or make it a weapon of mass destruction? Similarly, how many 19th-century thinkers would have ever fantasized that they could speak into a little mouthpiece and be able to communicate to anyone, anywhere in the world?

Where the 20th century has brought sweeping macroscopic innovations, the 21st century will foster in a trend toward understanding everything to the nth degree. Technology will continue to advance at even more accelerated speeds than it did in the past. With these advances our capacity to gather information and understand the environment around us will continue to grow and expand. Where we were once satisfied with a broad explanation, we will expect and demand the most minute of details. As we become inundated in our "intelligence society," even the simplest of relationships or transactions will become complex, characterized by the need to have all the information available, even if it is just buying a gallon of milk.

In order to obtain this information, new tools will be developed that are beyond our dreams. Those bulky objects we call personal computers today will soon be museum pieces. Books, as we know them today, may become obsolete and exist only as antiques or collector's items. The communicative capacity of the Internet will be viewed by the late 21st-century thinker in the same way that we currently view the technological advances of two cans and a waxed string.

These sweeping changes will be exciting for the direct marketer to identify and follow. The marketer will have new-millennium tools available to track trends, understand messages, and ascertain the impact of these innovations on business and culture. More importantly, the marketer will thrive in an environment of rapid social and technological change that he or she can convert into actionable policies and actions. The direct marketers of the 21st century will also serve as the trend leaders for many of the new trends. Because of the plethora of information available to everyone, the marketers will want to take the time to thoroughly investigate and understand the short-term and long-term impacts of a myriad of trends. Because they are the ones with this information, they will become valued as the trend messengers.

DIRECT MARKETERS AS TREND MESSENGERS

Trend Messengers

Since trends are an integral part of a culture, the direct marketer can use the trends to define the likes/dislikes, current interests, "hot buttons," and general whims of the group. By definition trends are ideas, attitudes, or behaviors that reflect a current style or pattern of behavior within a group or culture. These trends reflect social conditions and demonstrate a direction in which these conditions are moving. Trends influence and are influenced by a number of groups in the culture or society. Finally, trends are time based and dynamically change within those time parameters.

The information given off by the trends is what is called trend messages. Like all messages, there is a sender and a receiver. The message must be communicated from the sender to the receiver in such a way that there is a shared understanding of the contents. If the receiver does not understand the message or translates it differently than the intended meaning, confusion arises.

Trends are complex messages and are subject to a wide variety of interpretations. This is why the direct marketer should not accept a trend message at its face value. A successful trend analyst will look at each trend from a number of different perspectives. This process, called triangulation, allows the analyst to understand the causes or conditions that helped the trend to emerge, the climate in which the trend exists, how individuals are responding to the trend, and most importantly, the trajectory or path the trend is expected to take over the next few years or months.

The intricacy of trend networks and the multiple messages generated from these networks further complicate the direct marketer's work. Since different groups and individuals will interpret trend messages differently, it is imperative that each meaning be placed in its own social context. Understanding the social context and the receiver's motivations/needs is as important as understanding the trend message itself.

In 21st-century society and business, the individual who can identify trends and successfully convert the messages into programs and products is an extremely valuable asset. This person has the ability to define and shape the direction of the culture, group, and, especially, the business world. These individuals are called trend messengers. Trend messengers will take the multitude of messages given off by a trend, develop actionable interpretations of the messages, and then help others to develop successful responses to them.

Trend messengers play different roles at the different levels of society or business. At the national level, news commentators identify and define those macroscopic trends affecting the rest of us. Because their audience is so large, their interpretation of the trend is quickly shared by the group listening to them. Remember that the messenger's interpretation is not necessarily value-free or unbiased. The messenger's political, social, and religious background will help to shape his or her interpretation of the messages. Due to the near universal reach of the media, today's national trend messenger wields a great deal of power. Political officeholders and their opponents spend great amounts of time and money trying to persuade the public that their interpretation of the trend is the only right way to view it. At the local level, similar trend messengers exist to help shape the opinions of the individuals who live or work in the area. While these individuals may not have the reach or power of the national players, they are still able to exert substantial influence in people's daily lives.

At the individual business level, trend messengers are essential. Most businesses work in an environment shaped by a large number of trends. These trends can be both beneficial or harmful to the business. Anyone can say that they have identified a trend and this is what it means. However, without understanding the numerous components of the trend, its networks, and its implications, the response may be wrong or, at the worst, damaging to the company. Business trend messengers develop a knack for identifying and interpreting trends. It becomes almost second nature to place trends in their social context and then apply their findings to program and product development. This second nature, however, comes from experience; that is, the expertise to identify, analyze, and interpret trend messages and translate this process into actionable responses. So, trend messengers rely on a blending of the art of trend identification and the science of trend analysis and interpretation.

Becoming a trend messenger and successfully interpreting trend messages is exciting and fun, and can be profitable for both the individual and the company. Trends and their messages are everywhere. The successful trend messengers will be the ones who can quickly and accurately turn trend messages into profit for their companies.

Trend Evolution

Today's trends are tomorrow's reality! Tomorrow's trends provide the material for today's science fiction writers. In the early 1900s airplanes and automobiles were considered fads that would surely pass quickly into oblivion. As each of the decades of the first half of that century passed, older generations must have marveled at how dramatically things had changed in just the past 10 years. It had become a way of life in American society. Not only did the automobile evolve through a number of its own trends (e.g., convertibles, large engines, rumble seats, tail fins, whitewall tires), it also served as the incubator for a number of other related trends. Where would fast-food restaurants, gasoline stations, drive-in movies, 24-hour shopping, ATM banking, weekend trips, and even the suburbs be if the automobile had remained a fad?

Airplanes have followed a similar evolutionary trend trajectory. Orville and Wilbur Wright's first excursion must have seemed very strange to those who observed it or heard about it for the first time. But within a few short years, this futuristic phenomenon became interwoven into the fabric of our culture. All of a sudden airplanes were being used for entertainment, travel, and warfare. As the airplane's trend messages were heeded, the trend accelerated at lightning speeds. In less than 30 years after the Wright brothers, planes could cross the country and, eventually, the oceans. People could travel distances in a day that used to take a week or more. But this was not enough. By the late 1940s, words such as "jet" airplanes and "rocket-powered" crafts began to enter our vocabulary. By the end of the 1990s, even the youngest pilot-in-waiting knows that you can now fly to Europe in about three hours and to the moon in a couple of days.

Studying the evolution of major trends is like studying the history of a culture. As the trends evolved to new forms, so has culture's reaction to them. Today's trends, as advanced as we may think they are, are only reflections of our culture at a given point in time. As time changes so does this reflection. What will our trend reflections look like 50 or 100 years from now? Will trips to other parts of the world be in our own family "astromobile"? Will trips to the moon or other nearby stars become commonplace? If this sounds farfetched, look at the turn of the 21st century through the same glasses that your ancestors viewed the new 20th century. To the direct marketer in 2099 we may look as simple and unsophisticated as the horse and buggy.

Trend Messengers or New-Age Prophets

The role of the trend messenger is still in its embryonic stage, but it will grow exponentially into the next century. Direct marketers must be prepared to take the lead in information gathering, trend tracking, and, most importantly, converting trend messages into actionable solutions to business needs. The role of trend messenger will become essential in those businesses where innovation and staying in touch with the consumer is important to their success. Understanding trends and how individuals and groups respond to them will be a skill that will be in great demand in the future.

Since the beginnings of the human race, individuals have been trying to predict the future. Whether it was reading tea leaves, tarot cards, or crystal balls, our forefathers conjured up ways to try to figure out was going to happen next in their lives. Even if they were right a fraction of the time, they gained the reputation as being a seer of the future. Today, we still attempt to gaze into the future but in a more scientific way. Computers have replaced tarot cards, and telecommunications has replaced the crystal ball. But today's direct-marketing trend messengers are not all that different from their ancient ancestors. They are expected to give meaning to events and actions and to use the resources at hand to "show others the way."

The tools that future generations of direct marketers will have available can only boggle our minds today. Millions of pieces of information will be collated, analyzed, and interpreted within a matter of seconds. Decisions will be intelligence based, and their outcomes will be evaluated at different times in different settings. The status of the future trend messenger will be elevated, and the role will become a prized asset for trend-centered companies.

THROUGH THE CRYSTAL BALL

The 21st-Century Consumer

The year is 2011. The oldest baby boomer is 66, and the youngest boomer is 48 years old. Less than a century ago, people in this group (if they lived that long) would have been considered elderly. Now, 10 plus years into the 21st century, the majority of these individuals live healthy, active lives and few people would consider them "over the hill." These charter members of the new-millennium club are still the largest and most powerful consumer group. However, their offspring have caught up. The children and grandchildren of the baby boomers have become adults and have emerged as very powerful consumer segments.

These two groups are integrally linked. The mature consumers have taught the younger consumers how to select the "best value" products and how to be brand loyal. Since both groups share information and opinions, they greatly influence each other's product awareness and purchase decisions. Thus, while these segments are major forces by themselves, together they form a strong network. Within this network the diversified consumer groups reside at different points on both the lifestyle and life cycle continuum. More importantly, they provide different perspectives and strongly influence each other's decisions.

The key difference between the mature and young (45 and under) consumers is their different positions on the life cycle continuum. Mature baby boomers are looking for products and services that help them maintain and enhance their lifestyles. Their key focus is convenience. Time is a precious resource, and anything that can be done to allow them to use this time to their advantage is appreciated and rewarded. The mature boomers are in the process of reengineering their nests. They are renovating their current living quarters or moving to smaller ones. At the same time, they are downsizing their possessions and reorganizing their lives to meet their current lifestyle needs. Most importantly, this mature consumer group spends a good deal of its time helping others, especially family members. The "peace, love, and happiness" philosophy of the 1960s, while somewhat subdued by the conservatism of age, has been firmly ingrained in their psyche. This feeling, coupled with the family focus of the late 1990s, has led the group to be very supportive of significant others in the form of financial assistance, gifts, and advice to family members. Like their parents and grandparents, the mature baby boomers relish the opportunity to give of themselves (emotionally and financially) to their children and grandchildren.

As the younger consumer groups (i.e., Generation X and the Echo Boomer Generation) have grown in size, the pendulum is gradually swinging back toward youth. Like their parents, these groups have their unique needs and lifestyles. While they appreciate the values taught them by their parents, they want to be different. This is reflected in the products and services they want and purchase. At the same time, these emerging groups are in the process of creating and feathering their own nests. In most cases these are their first homes, and coupled with the growth of their families is the need to make the nests meet their lifestyles. Because of their growing families and the resources they need to get started and maintain their lifestyles, this group relies on their parents and grandparents for help, support, and advice. It is here that brand support and loyalty are enhanced. The younger consumers' familiarity with products and services is reinforced by the wisdom they receive from their "trusted" elders.

The living environment in 2012 is similar for all the consumer segments. The pessimism toward government, politics, and business that was planted in the 1960s and germinated throughout the rest of the century remains strong in 2012. Highly active, highly stressed living environments are the norm. The average age of most houses is over 50 years, and many dwellings are in need of substantial renovation. More people are living alone due to the growth of baby boom widows and widowers, the growth of single-parent families in the late 20th century, and a trend toward singles living alone or in alternative arrangements. Not unlike in the late 1990s, consumers in 2012 are fearful of victimization. Aging neighborhoods, aging consumers, and the uncertainty of random crimes keep the new-millennium consumer on guard for his or her well-being and protection. Environmental awareness and activity are a normal part of the behavior, having been internalized into the culture by the youth who learned it in school and practiced it into adulthood.

Consumers Define Value

Each consumer in the 21st century is driven by his or her own definition of "value." These definitions are learned from others and based on individual experience and attitudes as the consumers attempt to deal with the world around them. Because their social environment constantly changes, their definitions of value are also subject to change. The notion of value is centered around the psychological feeling of making the "best deal." Delighted consumers are those who feel satisfied that they are the winners in the transaction they just completed. While price is important, it is but one of a constellation of factors that make up the value equation.

Because of their busy lifestyles, new-millennium consumers value superior solutions to their needs and problems. They have high expectations for product innovation, quality, and service. While switching costs (especially time and convenience) are high for most consumers, they will change to someone who they perceive is providing them a better solution. However, these consumers will support brands that continuously meet and surpass their expectations. The brands that have become a part of the consumer's family are the ones that will thrive and enhance consumer loyalty throughout the 21st century.

The new-millennium consumer is actually an extension of the late 20th-century consumer. They continue to demand more for less. They want more value and satisfaction for less for less time, effort, and money. They do their homework and demand to be treated as an intelligent partner looking for the best solutions. While they remain critical and somewhat pessimistic, they expect companies to create solutions for "just my needs." Businesses that are able to do this on an ongoing basis will be richly rewarded.

The Power of Communications

The 21st century is the century of mass communications. Information is spread almost instantaneously from individual to individual, house to house, community to community, nation to nation. Information that took weeks and, in many cases, months to get from one point to another now can be received as quickly as it is transmitted. An individual can pick up his or her telephone and speak to a friend or colleague in China and another one in Argentina. Not only can that individual talk with each one, the system is configured to enable the three of them can carry on one conversation. Similarly, the Internet is currently at about one-tenth of its full potential. Its capacity to store and disseminate information will grow exponentially as the new technologies, markets, and needs continue to demand more of it.

If one thinks about it, the trajectory of the communication trend has accelerated almost exponentially during the past 50 years. Imagine living in the 1940s. Television was a novelty, telephones were rotary with party lines of many users hooked into one system, and radios and newspapers were the chief sources for information. Events were at least a week old before you saw them on the newsreels at your local theater. But keep in mind that all of these forms of communication were light-years ahead of the technology even 50 years earlier.

Now look at the world almost 80 years later. Television is no longer a novelty and may even be considered a necessity in many parts of the world. Instead of one or two channels on a very small and fuzzy screen, you now have a choice of hundreds of channels on a large screen with a deciphonic sound system. Current events are transmitted "live" into your living room. Telephones have advanced to the stage where you can make calls, fax information, text message, take pictures, and link directly into your home computer. Telephones are no longer constrained to walls or booths; they are portable and cellular and can be taken anywhere you go.

Now look ahead to the year 2040. If the communication trend continues to follow its astronomical growth trajectory, one can only imagine what communication devices and media will be commonplace then. Futurists tell us that by this time everyone will have his or her own personal identification number. The number will be uniquely yours, and no matter where you go in the world, people will be able to communicate with you by just dialing the number. Along with this personal identifier will be personal communication devices that will go everywhere you do. These devices will be very small and powerful and may even become a part of your wristwatch.

This communication trend is important to direct marketers for a number of reasons. First, it is the medium by which information is spread. Small, isolated events that in the past would have not moved any farther than 50 miles from the point of origin now achieve global impact within a matter of minutes. Second, because of the large audiences that receive the messages, the role of the direct marketer becomes extremely important. No longer is the messenger's sphere of influence small. Instead, the messenger may now be putting his or her "twist" on a message that is being received by millions of people. In today's environment, the messenger has the power to change the definition, interpretation, and direction of a trend in a matter of seconds. Third, the speed at which messages are communicated to the masses accelerates the life cycle of a message. With instantaneous communications the message has a very short incubation period. It also becomes subject to different interpretations quicker and therefore is more likely to be adapted to individual, group, or cultural needs.

All of this makes the marketer's job more difficult. There is little time to analyze the message and project its future. Decisions are made based on available information. However, most of this information will be outdated within a matter of days or weeks. Also, because of the size and diversity of the audience, the direct marketer must be prepared to examine the message from a number of individual and cultural perspectives. This can become a task of major proportions.

Thus the 21st-century telecommunication trend is integrally linked to most other trends. It affects how these trends are defined, grow, and are supported. Changes in the telecommunication field not only affect the acceleration of the trend trajectory, they also influence how the trend will be viewed and followed. As such, the telecommunication trend is and will continue to be one of the most powerful macroscopic trends in existence.

The Age of Aging

In 1945 millions of jubilant soldiers returned home to their loved ones and had babies. From 1946 to 1964, these babies came in record numbers. Little did anyone know at the time that this group would someday be the largest age cohort in American history. Not only is it the largest group numerically, it is also the most educated and the most powerful age cohort, both politically and economically. This group of "baby boomers" has influenced all aspects of American society and continues to do so well into the first quarter of the 21st century.

As the age structure of the population has continued to change, so has culture's view of it. Advertising, once focused on the young, upwardly mobile individual, is now oriented toward the middle-aged consumer. While this shift has gradually evolved, businesses have been slow to understand and respond to the trend. This response is only now occurring, in earnest, with most companies. Perceptions are changing from viewing the "mature" consumer as a small niche group that has outgrown its need for most products to an ever-growing, powerful and affluent group of consumers who may be looking for new products and services or may be purchasing products as gifts to help and assist others, such as their children or grandchildren.

The mature market has traditionally been viewed by the business world as a group of individuals who have accumulated all the material possessions they need and therefore are a less than viable market. Many businesses have erroneously labeled this group as "old" and view the mature segment as not being interested in or physically capable of using their products. Businesses have also assumed that this group of consumers do not have the financial wherewithal to purchase their products or services. This could not be further from the truth.

In 1996, the baby boomers began to cross the threshold into the 50 age bracket. As this group approached this benchmark age, the messages also changed. The new business mentality is to view the mature consumer of the early 21st century as a very important and influential segment. Today's mature consumers are looking for products and services that preserve and enhance their active lifestyles. This group no longer stops being active because "you're too old to do that"; nor do they mind "looking their age" because they are interested in looking and feeling their best no matter what the physical age may be. Thus marketing messages concerning youthfulness are being redefined from the traditional life cycle definitions to also include lifestyle definitions.

Mature consumers of the 21st century have more disposable income than the other consumer segments. More importantly, they have high levels of discretionary time. They gather information, study it, and then make informed decisions before they purchase the product. Probably the area most overlooked with this group is that of customer loyalty. While most businesses have long realized that established, satisfied consumers are the foundation of brand loyalty, they have neglected the loyalty of some of their most faithful and enduring supporters. Not only are older consumers among the most loyal, they are the key agents of socialization for other consumers. Social scientists have long demonstrated the importance of this intergenerational learning process, which can be parent to child, older adult to younger adult, or vice versa. Direct marketers need to use this interaction to better understand how consumers learn about products and become brand loyal. Older consumers are very influential in making younger consumers aware of products and services: either by using the product as the child grows up or by explaining the advantages of one product over another.

Thus the macroscopic aging trend is affecting business attitudes toward older consumer groups. Marketers are beginning to realize the vast amount of power the aging consumer has. Mature consumers have a great deal of purchasing power; that is, they have the financial ability to buy products that they feel meet their expectations, needs, and lifestyles. Aging consumers also have immense amounts of influencing power. They can influence businesses in the short run through their purchases and investments in the company. More importantly, they also have the ability to exert long-term influence over the company as they teach other generations of consumers about the "value" of the products.

But What about Generation X?

With the dawning of the 21st century comes the realization that Generation Xers have become middle-aged. This group of individuals, also is known as the baby busters, was born between 1965 and 1986. Currently this cohort accounts for 17 percent of the total U.S. population and approximately 46 million individuals. While about one-half the size of the baby boomer (1946–64) cohort, one must still remember that the 46 million individuals, if taken as a group, comprise a larger population than over three-quarters of the world's nations. In fact, this group actually would be the 24th-largest country in the world.

For better or worse, Generation Xers are the by-products of their parents' generation. A number of factors influencing their parents in the 1960s and 1970s helped to shape the way this group thinks and acts. As the first group to live through the baby boomer trends, the Xers are faced with the dilemma of dealing with their parents' youthful idealism turning to mature conservatism (i.e., "do as I say, not as I did"). In a dialectical sense, the X Generation is the logical synthesis of the baby boomer philosophical and ideological struggles with the previous generation (Xers' grandparents).

Numerous factors happened in the 1960s and 1970s that directly impacted the Generation X phenomena. First of all, this era led toward an awareness among women that more options were available to them. This, in turn, led to both legislative and attitudinal changes in equality. Concurrently, men were beginning to have a general attitudinal shift that enabled them to support these changes. The overall effect of this was to change perceptions of traditional family roles, thereby changing the structure of the American family.

Related to the dynamic changes in social and political factors were changes in the educational institution. The '60s and '70s witnessed the highest proportion of women attending college ever in history. This movement toward educational advancement had a number of direct effects on baby boomer women. First, the university setting and the advanced education opened up new avenues and options for additional opportunities. This is an extremely important factor. Attending colleges and universities meant obtaining new perspectives on attitudes and values. At the same time, the educational environment presented a forum where the time-honored ways of doing things could be debated. It is important to remember, however, that new learning goes both ways. Men attending college also had their eyes opened to the disparities in existing norms and traditions and gained the realization that changes in these traditional behaviors and attitudes were necessary and forthcoming.

A dramatic outcome of the growth in female educational advancement was the trend toward delayed childbearing. Not only was childbearing delayed due to the completion of undergraduate and graduate degrees, it was also delayed as women entered into the labor force and pursued career opportunities. This delay was one of the contributing factors for the lower number of births during this time frame. Three other factors are directly related. One factor was the introduction and mass usage of the birth control pill. Not only did it reduce unwanted pregnancies, it gave women new freedom in relationships and competition with men. More importantly, it allowed them to have better control over the planning of their lives (i.e., school, career, parenthood). A second factor was the legalization of abortion in 1972. Like the pill, it presented women with alternatives to childbearing and helped to affect the smaller size of the succeeding generation. A third trend was with the liberalized divorce laws of the '60s and '70s. These laws allowed women additional freedoms and opportunities that did not exist under the traditional patriarchal system of the past. At one point during this time, 40 percent of all U.S. marriages ended in divorce. This trend was to directly affect the Generation Xers in that they became the products of broken homes and dissolved marriages. As a matter of fact, approximately 50 percent of all Xers spent at least one year in a single-parent household before reaching the age of 18.

Finally, the above factors probably would not have occurred to the extent they did if economic trends had not been conducive to all of these changes. The expanded economies of the '60s and '70s provided more jobs and opportunities and enabled more women to pursue careers. In the 1980s the economy continued to affect women's growing entry into the labor force, but for different reasons. The prolonged recession during this period caused more women to enter the labor force to supplement family incomes. At the same time, the dissolution of many families created a large group of sole breadwinners. In this case, women's entry into the labor force became essential as they increasingly took on the single-parent, head-of-household role.

It is very important to remember that all of these factors are interrelated. Each was and is dependent on the others. Together they helped to shape not just the baby boomer generation but also their offspring. However, the offspring (Generation Xers), unlike their parents, had little to do with the development of these factors, but were required to face the consequences of them.

Among the consequences, Generation Xers were really the first latchkey generation. Growing up in families with working mothers and, in many cases, absent fathers, members of this generation learned quickly how to take care of themselves and their siblings. This meant preparing their own meals and finding entertainment around the house. The Xers were weaned on the personal computer and arcade games. For the most part these skills were self-taught, and members of this group do not have the computer phobia prevalent among older generations. Television and VCR growth was a direct result of the need to find entertainment for latchkey kids while their parents were away from the house. When the parents were available, the kids' days were overly busy being chauffeured from one organized activity to another.

Generation Xers were also the first mall generation. Malls became the "in place" for meeting friends, eating, attending movies, browsing, and shopping. This was usually done without being chaperoned by the parents. Thus Xers became very independent, experienced, and educated shoppers. Since work meant getting money to purchase things, most Xers worked during their school years. Parents, out of a combination of wanting to give their kids more than they had and guilt, created a generation of entrepreneurs, capitalists, and brand-conscious consumers. As the baby boomer parents moved away from the "five & dime" mentality of the 1950s, they became more brand conscious. While purchasing name brands for themselves, they also lavished their kids with "designer" products. This brand awareness was socialized into the Xers and then enhanced by them.

Finally, Xers, more than any other generation, have worked in ethnically and racially integrated and diverse settings. As a group they are more tolerant of and comfortable with differences and are more likely to have friends outside their racial group. Demographically, as a group the Xers are more racially/ethnically diverse than the overall population.

America: Melting Pot or Stew Pot?

As many of us were growing up it was common for us to hear that the United States was the great cultural "melting pot." That is, the best ideas, values, and attitudes from each culture are mixed into one assimilated blend that we call the United States of America. Recently, sociologists have changed this analogy from a melting pot to a stew pot. In the stew pot analogy, each culture adds its unique flavor to the American blend. Like a good stew, however, each cultural ingredient maintains its own identity. To someone visiting this country in the first decade of the 21st century we are all considered Americans; but among each other we are very conscious of our ethnic backgrounds or heritage. Thus it is probably more accurate to view ethnic diversity in the United States as accommodation (stew pot) than assimilation (melting pot).

The United States' history is one of ethnic diversity. Since our beginnings, the trajectory has swung back and forth between assimilation, distrust, and accommodation. In the early 2000s, the trend appears to be heading in the direction of accommodation. This is being brought on by changing attitudes and shifting demographics. Since the 1960s it appears that this culture has witnessed, to varying degrees, an attitudinal shift in favor of ethnic diversity. While this shift may not always be evidenced in relations between ethnic groups, it has surfaced in more subtle ways such as trends in ethnic foods and ethnic color and fashion motifs.

Demographically, over the last couple of decades the major growth in the population in the United States has been among ethnic populations. Demographic projections indicate that the white population growth in the first few decades of the 21st century will continue to remain relatively flat. However, major ethnic populations such African American, Hispanic, and Asian will grow at a relatively accelerated pace. Of these three, the Hispanic segment is expected to grow the fastest.

With the increased growth in population also comes an increased growth in social and economic power. Ethnic populations will continue to grow politically and, at the same time, wield more economic power. As this economic power is converted into purchase behavior, it will be even more imperative for direct marketers to understand the nuances in attitudinal, behavioral, and cultural differences in each of these ethnic groups. For example, it would be quite erroneous to view an ethnic group, such as Hispanics, as one group. Mexican culture differs from Central and South American cultures, which differ from a Puerto Rican culture, which is different from a Cuban one. Similarly, there is no one Asian or African American ethnic culture. As the ethnic groups differ from the dominant culture on the macroscopic level, so then do they differ from each other on the microscopic level.

In the 21st century ethnic diversity will continue to grow and manifest itself. The challenge that marketers face is to decide when to emphasize the cultural stew or when to emphasize the individual ingredients. Do the various ethnic groups desire culturally specific products or do they want mainstream products? Conversely, how much ethnic flavor will spill over to the overall culture? For example, Spanish-American colors are prevalent in the southwestern part of the United States. It is possible that this ethnic color palette has become the dominant color preference for most individuals living in the Southwest, regardless of ethnicity.

In order to successfully compete in the 21st century, marketers will need to understand each ethnic group's unique cultural heritage, values, and customs. To do so, they will have to understand the unique trend messages and interpretations associated with each culture and ethnicity. At the same time, they will need to be acutely aware of how the unique ethnic messages apply to the overall society.

We Have Got the Whole World in Our Hands

The 21st century will continue to manifest an ever-changing world. How many of us had heard of Bosnia or Herzegovina before 1990? What about Afghanistan, Darfur, and other trouble spots in the first decade of the new millennium? As you watch television or read your daily newspaper, you are observing changes on a daily basis that were unimaginable even a decade ago.

For the direct marketer the 1990s evidenced the opening of the global market arena. More appropriately, however, we should call it the global *markets* arena. With the formation of the European Economic Union, the opening of the Eastern European and former Soviet markets, the strong advances of the Pacific Rim nations, the North American Free Trade Agreement, and the advancements in the standards of living in the developing nations of Central and South America, new and profitable markets are available to those companies that take the time and effort to understand them.

Even with the advent of major trading blocks, it is important for marketers to remember that they are really dealing with a multitude of cultures that are very different from their own culture and, also, from each other. Consumers in Mexico City may be dramatically different in their lifestyles and consumption behavior than people living in the United States and even from those consumers in other parts of Mexico or in neighboring Latin America countries.

Similarly, products and services that meet consumer needs in the United States may have to be adapted to meet the needs of other cultures. For example, many of the products used in U.S. households would be considered too large for most households around the world. Similarly, eating habits, food preparation techniques, and food storage requirements differ significantly from China to Ireland to Brazil.

Shakespeare once said that "the whole world is a stage." We are actors on that stage. Kind of overwhelming, isn't it? How do you influence events in Japan, Germany, or Argentina? It may be more accurate, however, to view the world not as one all-encompassing stage, but as a series of "sets" at different "locations." For you, the direct marketer, this may even be more bewildering. You can no longer evaluate just one role; you must learn to analyze a number of roles and, also, understand how the same role is played a number of ways on a number of different stages in order to achieve a great performance.

Our Children's World

What about the environment in the 21st century? While we have heard much recently about how nearly everyone considers him or herself an environmentalist, the trend toward environmental concern and awareness in the early 21st century is still at an embryonic stage. Individuals are becoming more aware of environmental issues and concerns as they read and hear about them in the media. However, this awareness has still not been converted to real large-scale action. Numerous national studies have continued to show that over 70 percent of people in this country are aware of environmental concerns, but less than 15 to 20 percent actively do something (i.e., recycle, drive less, consume less) to remedy environmental problems.

The movement toward environmentalism is an excellent example of trend lag. Most individuals in the United States support the notion that environmental problems are serious and must be dealt with. However, when it comes to actually getting involved with the trend, the number of "doers" decreases immensely. There are a number of reasons why this discrepancy or lag occurs. First, messages are confusing. Individuals are confused as to the breadth and scope of environmental problems (i.e., ozone depletion vs. solid waste vs. water pollution vs. air pollution), confused as to what is being done about the problems, and confused as to what they personally should be doing. These feelings of confusion are coupled with a notion that the environment is an abstract "public issue" that does not affect the individual as a "personal problem" and therefore they need do little or nothing about resolving it.

Other factors directly influence the environmental trend. First is the need for convenience. Individuals living in a fast-paced, stress-filled world are looking for ways to make their life easier. From this need for convenience, a number of products and services have emerged. The use of prepared, fast foods and disposable paper products does make life a little easier for the active individual who has little time to shop, prepare meals, and wash dishes. However, this convenience comes at an environmental cost. All of these convenience items are made for a onetime usage and quickly end up in the trash, thereby adding to the solid waste problem.

Another way the drive toward convenience has affected the environmental trend is in the perception held that environmental behavior is time consuming and inconvenient. For example, people in this society are accustomed to throwing trash into a container with very little thought about what they are doing or what will happen to it. When asked to begin separating this trash into recyclable and nonrecyclable items, the process becomes inconvenient and a waste of precious time. It is as if individuals assume that once trash is collected, someone else will do the environmental chores for them.

Ironically, another positive trend, consumers in search of "value," has had a negative effect on the environmental movement. Consumers in search for the best deal or value are willing to travel from store to store to find it. In doing so, they are using up diminishing resources and adding pollution to the atmosphere.

Barring unforeseen ecological disasters, current attitudes toward the environmental trend will remain constant throughout the first quarter of this century. Small changes in consumer attitudes and behavior will gradually occur over time. However, these changes will be more concrete and enduring than the faddish behavior of the early 1990s, such as "green marketing." It is interesting that the long-term adherence to the trend will come from a nontraditional direction. Children, as part of their educational process, are being taught about the environment and how to become good environmental stewards. As they internalize the attitudes and practice the behaviors, the trend will become institutionalized in American society. These attitudes and behaviors will become part of normal daily living and environmental sensitivity and activity will evolve to another level.

Thus our children have become the environmental trend messengers. They bring home the information they learned in school and share it with members of their family. At the same time, they take on the role of monitor by influencing both the family's attitudes and environmental behavior. Children, as we know, can exert pressure and influence to do what they want or think is correct

21st-CENTURY ADVANCES IN DIRECT MARKETING

Multichannel Marketing

Next, let's gaze into Nostradamus's crystal ball to see what the world of direct marketing will be like in the 21st century. Multichannel marketing, a "new" idea at the end of the 20th century, will quickly become the standard-bearer for marketing in the 21st century. Customers no longer accept limited channels for both marketing and distribution. Instead they expect the direct marketer to "read their minds." That is, customers do not want to select between a number of alternative channels; they will expect the marketer to present them with the channel that best fits their needs and convenience.

This will be done by creating analytical profiles of the customers based on at least three integrated factors. The optimal profiling scheme will utilize a balanced combination of demographic, attitudinal, and behavioral factors. This will be necessary to obtain a well-rounded or triangulated view of the customer. It is essential to remember that these factors are interconnected. Demographic factors influence attitudinal factors and both, in turn, affect the customer's behavior. This is why it is limiting and, in many cases, misleading to use only one or two of the factors and not all three.

One of the best ways of looking at this combination of elements is to think of a three-dimensional chessboard. Make the top layer the customer's demographics, the middle layer the customer's attitudes, and the bottom layer the customer's purchase behavior. Not only do the unique elements move across each of the layers or boards; they also move up and down. Thus an element may indicate that certain customers with comparable demographic characteristics may share similar attitudes and acquire similar products. Conversely, even customers with similar demographic characteristics may have different attitudes and these, in turn, will drive their behavior in different directions. For example, a 50-year-old may be interested in retirement planning. This individual may not have much knowledge of financial planning, not be actively involved in personal financial matters, be leery of advice, and not be open to taking much risk. The constellation of these factors would lead us to create a program or campaign specifically oriented to this cluster. On the other hand, if that same 50-year-old perceives him or herself to be somewhat knowledgeable of finances, willing to seek and use advice, and willing to take some risks, another strategy would prove to be more effective.

Because the elements that go into a customer profile are subject to change, the overall profile must be viewed as a dynamic process. As the customer's lifestyles and life cycle changes and as the demographic, attitudinal, and behavioral factors change, the overall scheme will need to be flexible enough to adapt to it. Static schemes will lose their robustness after a short period of time. Actually, the best schemes are boxes within boxes, that is, larger schemes that can be reconfigured into a number of smaller schemes and/or vice-versa. This enables us to maintain the structure of the larger foundation profile while being able to cluster and analyze the smaller pieces of intelligence to better understand and service the customer's needs. In this way, the profile becomes the easel on which we paint a number of unique customer pictures.

The multidimensional profiling, coupled with the ever-improving technological advances, will empower the direct marketer to create true 1:1 marketing with their customers. Because they will know what the customer's needs and preferences are, the marketer will be able to quickly customize the message and delivery channels in a way that the customers feel that they are understood and the company is looking out for them. Not only will this build a sense of trust, it will generate additional business from those customers and, most importantly, motivate the delighted customers to refer others to that business.

Of course the obvious concern here is to the amount and scope of customer information. What will be the tipping point at which the customer begins to feel that his or her privacy is being invaded and that the information is actually working against them? By the second decade of the 21st century, information technology will have alleviated the vast majority of information theft occurring during the first few years of the century. At the same time, information gatherers and users will treat the handling of personal information as a sacred bond between the customer and the company. During the latter part of the first decade of the century, these attitudes and behaviors will change due to strong sanctions (fines) against the offending companies and even stronger sanctions (fines, imprisonment) against individuals who do not treat the information as part and parcel of another individual.

With these changes in place, 21st-century customers will be more willing to share personal information, because they know that it is secure and being collected in their best interest. The 20th-century attitude of "who are you going to sell my information to" will be replaced by a new attitude of the best way to help to direct marketer to help me is to provide him or her with useful and accurate information about myself. As a customer, therefore, I will be receiving a profitable return on my information investment.

Life in the Information Cyber-Maze

From a technological standpoint, we are only beginning to scratch the surface of the information technology in the early part of the 21st century. It is not too hard to imagine a time where you will have immediate, real-time access to every major global information base just by talking into your wristwatch. Think what you will be able to do with that power! Decisions will be made on the spot with accurate and timely information. Whether you are in the process of buying a new car or a loaf of bread, you will be able to scan current product and price information and negotiate your best deal in a matter of minutes. Businesses will be able to identify new markets and consumer segments and, given the breadth of data available, will be able to develop a profile of the market, evaluate how other companies have fared in the market, and develop a strategic market plan to successfully enter and grow that market. The wealth of information may actually make it possible for the market analyst to correlate all of the data and come up with projections that will indicate, with a high degree of accuracy, how successful the business will be.

While this sounds exciting, it is not without its pitfalls. Having all of this information available may actually create a trend away from information usage.

Individuals, overloaded with data, may begin to feel trapped within their own networks. The information cybernet will then become the cyber-maze. Once inside the maze, the individual may spend the majority of his or her time just trying to navigate or survive the maze. As tidal wave after tidal wave of new information continuously bombards the net, the individual may find that the overload is too much. When this happens, the trend trajectory may move away from information-based behavior to a more primitive instinctual behavior. New groups will surface with a "know nothing" philosophy of life. As this anti-information sentiment grows, a new trend will evolve. While the laws of *Fahrenheit 451* may be a little too dramatic, expect changes to range from "clear-mind" coffee klatches to "no net" protests to wide-scale information sabotage.

Global Customer Relationship Management

By the end of the first decade of the 21st century, customer relationship management (CRM) is no longer a new concept, it is a way of life. Whether called customer lifetime value, 1:1 marketing, permission marketing, or mass customization, CRM has one underlying theme: the customer rules. Actually, CRM is much more than a theme, it is a philosophy or way of thinking that must permeate through all levels of the corporate culture and processes. If not followed thoroughly and comprehensively across all aspects of an organization, it stands a very good chance for failure and, even worse, can be very unprofitable for a company.

Realizing that CRM is a strategic vision and not just a set of tools or processes has required a dramatic philosophical shift from how companies traditionally thought about and carried out their business. For many in the last part of the 20th century, CRM was thought to simply be the cross-selling of products and services. However, direct marketers today realize that this is only a small part, or actually the outcome, of a successful CRM philosophy. That is, in the course of knowing, understanding, and servicing customers, you must be able to provide them additional products/services or unique combinations of the two that are "right" for them and profitable for your company. This profit is immediate in the sense of incremental products and services sold and, more importantly, is long term in the additional loyalty and business received from the customer over a sustained period of time.

In a nutshell, CRM can be defined as growing deep and enduring relationships with your profitable customers. In breaking down this definition into its component parts, one quickly sees that CRM needs to be a strategic vision and plan and not simply a set of processes or programs. At the heart of this definition is the customer. A customer-centric philosophy is exactly what it states. The customer is the center of attention, and everything done is centered around meeting and exceeding the customer's needs and expectations. During the 1990s retailer and manufacturer CRM programs focused on delighting the customer. By going past a product/service mentality and offering customers unique solutions that meet their needs and solve their problems, a company offers more than what is expected and therefore delights them. A delighted customer is a satisfied customer. A satisfied customer is more likely to acquire additional products/services and therefore become a more profitable customer. The satisfied customer is also more likely to maintain and grow his or her relationship over an extended period of time. Most importantly, the satisfied, delighted customer will become a loyal supporter and advocate, thereby bringing other customers to us.

The key term in the above definition is deep relationships. This means going past the list of products/services currently owned by the customer and understanding his or her aspirations, preferences, lifestyles, and life cycle stages. It also means understanding their current needs, anticipating their future needs, and then communicating solutions to them in a nonthreatening, trusted-advisor manner—that is, offering them the products/services that they will find the most personally useful via the channels they prefer to use.

By definition, deep customer relationships should be long-term growth relationships. As customers experience continued delight with your solutions, they will continue to increase their level of comfort that you are providing them with the best solutions. The cumulative effect of these positive experiences will further solidify the relationship and, more importantly, allow it to grow. It is extremely important to remember here that good relationships are a reciprocal process. As you provide customers with profitable solutions that meet and exceed their expectations, they become more comfortable with the idea that you are looking out for their best interests. As this comfort level builds, customers will be more likely to allow you to provide them the expert advice that they have now come to expect. The unique blending and cross-selling of products, programs, and services becomes the logical outcome of this process. As with any type of relationship, the continuous meeting of expectations and the growth of trust will continue to deepen and strengthen it. In the end, these delighted customers are (and/or become) your most profitable customers.

Direct interactive marketing fits all of the above criteria for providing the customer with an optimal experience. By its nature, direct marketing is one-to-one marketing focusing on a unique customer wants and needs. Direct marketers in the 21st century want to thoroughly understand their customers, anticipate their needs, exceed their expectations, and, most importantly, gain their trust. Due to exponential advances in telecommunications, the CRM program of the 21st century will be global. By the second decade of this century, direct marketers will have mastered all of the problems and pitfalls of marketing and fulfillment. This will be in the form of global partnerships, which by design "market globally, but fulfill locally." At the same time, the best direct marketers will have developed new strategies that will enable them to profitably compete against a global cacophony of competition. Direct interactive marketers will quickly become the trend messengers for the 21st-century global CRM trend. Customers will come to expect a seamless process from beginning to end. Those companies slow to catch on to this established way of life will not be around by the end of the first quarter of the century.

NOSTRADAMUS: FULL CIRCLE

The year is 2107. Much has changed in the last 100 years. Advances in health care have caused the average individual to live to a young 104 years of age. Ironically, changing trends in the last 100 years have caused men to live longer than women. Lifestyle (e.g., smoking) and employment (e.g., stress) trends have actually lowered the life expectancy rates for women. It is now commonplace for four to five generations of family members to be alive and functioning within the family unit. Thus the nuclear family of the 20th century has become the extended family of the late 21st century.

The fuel-burning automobile can only be found in a museum. Environmental trends that started in the late 1900s and blossomed in the 2020s caused this form of transportation to be outlawed. The death of the car really passed unnoticed since most people found it more convenient and cost-efficient to use mass transportation. Specially designed units made it possible for each family to have their own private vehicle that links to a worldwide transportation grid, making it possible to go to grandma's across town in seconds and to Europe in a matter of a couple hours. All of this is done without the family leaving the comfort of the vehicle.

All houses are now made out of stone. Researchers have observed a pattern where new homes moved from towering castles to ground-hugging cave-like dwellings made from natural materials. Not only are these dwellings easier to maintain, they provide natural warmth and cooling, making them very fuel and cost efficient. Instead of adding floors on top of each other, the new avant-garde houses now add floors below each other.

After years of searching for the ideal convenience foods, scientists finally came up with water-soluble food strips that are added to your favorite beverage. The water supply, once a problem area in the past century, is now treated with vitamin supplements, so that by drinking the water everyone is assured of receiving their optimum amount of required vitamins and nutriments.

What Would Nostradamus Think?

While digging through the basement of an obscure little bookstore in a tiny little alley in Paris, we come across some heretofore unknown manuscripts written by Nostradamus. As we begin to translate and interpret the quatrains, we quickly see that Nostradamus has predicted what direct interactive marketing will be like at the end of the 21st century. First, he tells us that by the end of the 21st century, all marketing will be direct and all marketing will be interactive. He also suggests that the tools direct marketers will have available then are unfathomable by today's standards. Technology- and intelligence-based decision making is as commonplace as putting on one's shoes. Global fulfillment issues have long been resolved due to global alliances, and he even hints at products being beamed around the world.

However, Nostradamus offers a few words of caution to the 21st-century direct marketer. His crystal ball foresees a period of time in the 21st century where consumers revolt against technology totally intruding into all aspects of their lives. "Big Brother" notions of the 20th century have become the paranoia of the late 21st century. Only those companies that have truly built a strong bond of loyalty and trust with their customers will survive. Direct marketers will do well to heed this cautionary glimpse into the future for, as Nostradamus says:

As the new millennial century wanes
And the machine's iron fist does life permeate,
Only those in trust bonded
Shall the dawn of the new day see.

Part IV

GLOBAL MARKETING: NEW CHALLENGES AND OPPORTUNITIES

CHAPTER 12

THE NEW GLOBAL MARKETING REALITIES

Gary A. Knight

INTRODUCTION

Today, business operates in a fiercely competitive, borderless world in which customers access products and services from everywhere, and their expectations regarding value and quality have grown apace. Increasingly, international marketing capabilities honed on global experience are minimal requirements to participate in the global marketplace. Spectacular growth in technology, a consequent revolution in the telecommunications industry, and a broad-based spread of e-commerce have shifted the ways organizations manage themselves. The emergence of an inextricably linked international marketplace for goods, services, capital, and investment contributes to complexity and competition in a global market that is growing in magnitude and scope.

Perhaps the most important trend of the last few decades is globalization, which reflects the growing interconnectedness of national economies and interdependence of consumers, producers, suppliers, and governments in different countries. It reflects the production and marketing of products and brands worldwide by firms located across the globe. Combined with declining trade barriers and the increasing ease with which international business takes place, the activities of these firms are leading to gradual integration of the economies of most nations in the world.

Globalization is a revolution-in-progress, the central story line of the 21st century, with major consequences within as well as between nations. Globalization is a powerful and positive force that stimulates economic growth, creates jobs, raises incomes, expands both choice and competition, improves product quality, and lowers prices. The fact that virtually all the world's nations willingly participate in some form of international free trade is evidence that they see it in their own best interest. Indeed, it is a lack of trade, investment, and freedom that keeps the world's poorest economies in poverty and environmental degradation.

Business leaders must confront the key future challenges of international marketing. In this chapter, I review key trends and realities that confront the contemporary international marketer. Let's first review the critical role of information and communications technologies.

INFORMATION AND COMMUNICATIONS TECHNOLOGIES

While globalization makes going global an imperative, advances in information and communications technologies (ICTs) provide the means for taking business operations abroad. ICTs make the cost of international operations affordable for all types of companies, explaining why so many small and medium enterprises (SMEs; defined here as firms with less than 500 employees) have entered the international arena.

Communications technology is critical. It took five months for Spain's Queen Isabella to learn about Columbus's voyage, two weeks for Europe to learn of President Lincoln's assassination, and 1.5 seconds for the world to witness the collapse of New York's World Trade Center. The most profound technological advances have occurred in the area of communications, especially telecommunications, satellites, optical fiber, wireless technology, and of course, the Internet. These developments are revolutionary and similar in their effects to the commercialization of the printing press in Europe in the 15th century. The resultant widespread dissemination of information and knowledge gave rise to a giant leap in human activity.[1]

More than 500 million people worldwide already have access to the Internet. It has become the information backbone of the global economy, allowing for voice, data, and real-time video communication, as well as facilitating cross-border business transactions. A wide range of goods and services—from auto parts to bank loans—are marketed online. South Korea, where Internet access is nearly 100 percent, is leading the way. South Korea's broadband networks for home use are much faster than European and U.S. systems. Korean schoolchildren use their cell phones to get homework from their teachers and play games online with gamers worldwide. Adults use their phones to pay bills, do banking, buy lottery tickets, and check traffic conditions. South Korea is becoming the dominant global player in high-tech industries such as mobile communications, digital robotics, and various software categories.[2]

Widespread diffusion of the Internet and e-mail makes company internationalization extremely cost-effective. The Internet provides cheap and ready access to information and opens up the global marketplace to companies that would normally not have the resources to do international business, including countless SMEs and born-global firms. Such companies often succeed by entering "virtual alliances" with partners in key markets and locations overseas. The Internet has fostered an ongoing revolution in the way firms acquire and use information vital to conducting international market research. Search engines, databases, reference guides, and countless government and private support systems assist managers to maximize knowledge and skills for international business success.

The Internet also facilitates international marketing activities, particularly by smaller firms. By establishing a website, even tiny companies take the first step in becoming multinational firms. Today, many firms leverage the Internet to engage in direct marketing, the selling of goods or services directly to end users, bypassing traditional intermediaries. Some direct marketers engage in catalog sales, in which catalogs of the firm's offerings are mailed to potential customers. For instance, Eddie Bauer does a thriving catalog business with customers in Asia, Europe, and North America. More and more firms use the Internet to provide detailed product information and the means for foreigners to purchase offerings. Some are entirely Internet based, with no retail stores at all, such as Amazon.com. On the other hand, more than one-third of traditional retailers (e.g., Kohls, Tesco, Walmart, Zellers) now employ some type of Internet-based marketing.[3]

The Internet also facilitates consolidation and increased efficiency of the global supply chain and international distribution channels. It facilitates efficient outsourcing, which allows firms to concentrate on their core competencies. With real-time information sharing, manufacturers and distributors optimize cross-national communications and consequent international operations. SMEs benefit through the ability to project the image of being larger firms, cut international operations costs, and provide products through virtual warehouses. The time from ordering to receipt can be greatly reduced, allowing smaller firms to compete internationally.

But while many direct marketers have flourished on the Internet, others have floundered. Skillful supply chain management based on brick-and-mortar facilities still provides the backbone for global sales. However, the Internet holds great promise, and its role in direct international marketing will likely increase over time.

GLOBALIZATION

Globalization is of course a key international marketing reality. Cross-national merchandise trade has increased dramatically since the 1980s. By the early 2000s, the total of merchandise exports and imports represented more than 40 percent of world GDP. Globalization and technological advances permit more and more firms to target billions of consumers and industrial buyers worldwide. Highly international firms source input goods from suppliers worldwide and sell their products and services in hundreds of foreign markets. Growth in world trade is presenting much greater choice in products and services to consumers worldwide. The competitive and value-adding activities of globally active firms are pushing down prices and contributing to higher living standards worldwide.[4]

The most salient feature of globalization is growing integration and interdependence of national economies. Global companies devise extensive multicountry operations via investments aimed at production and marketing activities. The aggregate activities of these firms give rise to economic integration.

Globalization also means convergence of buyer lifestyles and needs. Today, people in Tokyo, New York, and Paris can buy the same household goods, clothing, automobiles, and consumer electronics. The same pattern is observable in industrial markets as well, where the raw materials, parts, and components that professional buyers source from suppliers worldwide are increasingly standardized, that is, similar or uniform in design. As income levels rise, demand preferences are converging for both industrial and consumer goods and services. More than 90 percent of movies shown in Canada are made abroad, primarily in the United States. The movie market in Europe and Japan is dominated by popular Hollywood films. Media contribute to the homogenization of world consumer preferences, in part by emphasizing a particular lifestyle dominated by the United States. Increasingly, this trend is spreading to the developing countries as well. Converging tastes and global production platforms facilitate the launch and marketing of highly standardized products to buyers around the world.

Intense global competition is forcing firms to reduce the costs of production and marketing. Global corporations strive to drive down prices via economies of scale and by standardizing what they sell. Today, globalization of markets is transforming the world into a global village, where companies undertake international marketing activities in a giant global marketplace. In their own way, globalization and technological advances are resulting in the "death of distance."[5] That is, the geographic and, to some extent, cultural distance, that separates nations is shrinking.

THE RISE OF TERRORISM

One of the negative manifestations of globalization is the rise of global terrorism. Terrorism is the threat or actual use of force or violence to attain a political goal via fear or intimidation. Large-scale terrorist attacks have proven capable of stimulating declines in the global economy. Terrorism is similar to natural disasters, wars, political crises, and other "supply chain shocks" that occasionally threaten international firms. The main threat of terrorism and other shocks results from *indirect* effects. These include the decline in buyer demand, unpredictable global supply chain shifts or interruptions, and government policies and laws enacted to deal with terrorism. Such outcomes decrease revenues, increase costs, and generally increase the complexity of international marketing. Among all the business functions, sales, marketing, and the global supply chain are among the most affected.[6]

Perhaps the greatest threat from terrorism is the resultant psychological response leading to substantial declines in consumption and other shifts in people's behavior. For instance, following the September 11, 2001, attacks, there emerged a short-term flight from the dollar, and Swiss banks recorded a sharp increase in inquiries about their special accounts for foreigners. The indirect effects of terrorism can also trigger shortages of externally sourced critical inputs, especially for multinational firms—be it due to production or to delivery constraints. Attempts to recoup decreasing sales via increased advertising and other promotional activities lead to unplanned expenses. The cost of protecting against such events will increase as insurance providers put up premiums to account for increased risk.

But managers can take proactive steps to deal with indirect effects. Emphasizing strong brands and superior product quality helps companies deal more effectively with declines in buyer demand following disasters. Marketing communications and public relations are potentially important "recovery marketing" tools to help maintain demand. Regular scanning and forecasting about emergent business conditions are critical for firms that rely heavily on foreign-sourced input goods. Global supply chains benefit from "scenario planning," in which specific strategies and tactics are developed around possible terrorism-related scenarios.

Managers may need to consider the potential role of terrorism when evaluating foreign countries, both as markets and as potential sites for foreign direct investment (FDI). The issue of terrorism will be progressively more used as a segmentation variable in the evaluation and selection of markets. This is bad news for those countries and regions that experience regular or particularly severe terrorism. Colombia and India are especially vulnerable, followed by countries in the Middle East, Latin America, and Asia. Terrorism is most likely to occur in those regions where it has tended to occur historically, that is, in non-Western or less-developed countries. These areas will also tend to be most vulnerable to economic and consumption downturns in the wake of terrorist events.

As firms face increasing regulations, policies, and other imperfections imposed by national and supranational governments, distribution and logistics are particularly affected. Shipments are delayed and shortages occur. Thus some firms will tend produce more essential inputs themselves, as opposed to buying them from suppliers. Or they will acquire needed inputs from a broader range of suppliers, from sources located in a broader range of locations, or from sources that are more familiar in order to reduce their vulnerability. For example, Compaq Computer has established secondary suppliers for all of its critical input components. The firm owns assembly operations in various locations worldwide. Management can quickly shift production from one locale to another in the event of a crisis. Jabil Circuit, a manufacturer of high-tech electronics, requires suppliers to be able to boost deliveries by 25 percent with a week's notice, and by 100 percent with four weeks' notice.[7]

Some firms will increase their inventories of essential inputs, as a cushion against terrorism's effects. Inventory stocks are more vulnerable the greater the firm's reliance on international supply sources. Careful supply chain management is critical to ensure a proper balance between customer service and the inventory costs of growing safety stocks.[8]

EMERGING MARKETS

One of the most exciting new realities for international marketers is the rise of emerging markets. These fast-growth, modernizing countries are responsible for the much of the explosion in world trade and investment over the past two decades. The *Economist* (http://www.economist.com) tracks the progress of emerging markets, including countries such as China, India, South Korea, Thailand, Argentina, Brazil, Chile, Mexico, South Africa, Turkey, Czech Republic, Hungary, Poland, and Russia. In the mid-2000s, the top 25 emerging market countries together sustained average annual GDP growth rates of nearly 7 percent. They have been growing much faster than those of the advanced economies, which suggests that several emerging markets will join the group of wealthy nations in the not-too-distant future. Most importantly, they have engaged in substantial privatization, modernization, and industrialization. Significantly, they have growing middle classes that can afford to participate in the market for a broad variety of goods and services.

China and India together represent about one-third of the world's population. China is the biggest emerging market, and its role in international business is rapidly expanding. With a population of 1.3 billion people (one-fifth of the world total), China is the world's second-largest economy in purchasing power parity terms. The Chinese economy continues to grow at the astonishing annual rate of nearly 10 percent. During the past decade, the number of Global 500 firms headquartered in China has risen from 3 to 15 and will expand further. Leading exemplars include Shanghai Automotive (China's top automaker), Sinopec (a large oil company), and Shanghai Baosteel (a steel manufacturer).

Emerging markets are increasingly important target markets, that is, buyers of goods and services. They enjoy strong growth rates and prospects for market expansion. Accelerating demand growth will soon make the 25 emerging markets larger and more attractive than the countries of Europe and Japan combined. Consumer expectations are rising as local governments open markets to international competition. Infrastructural investments are improving the climate for business. These trends greatly improve the prospects for global business success, especially among multinational corporations that collaborate closely with local intermediaries. Instead of dismissing emerging markets, international marketers now see them as important target markets. Despite widespread poverty, most have high-income segments that represent attractive markets. For instance, China has some 300 million consumers, and India has roughly 200 million consumers with significant purchasing power. Roughly one-quarter of Mexico's 100 million people enjoy affluence equivalent to many in the United States.

Emerging markets are excellent targets for sales of raw materials, parts, machinery, and other industrial goods used in the manufacture of finished goods. Most specialize in particular industries that create focused product demand, such as the textile machinery industry in India. They also house a range of niche markets.

Finally, governments and state enterprises are major target markets for sales of, especially, infrastructure-related goods and services. The government and industrial segments are promising targets for capital equipment, machinery, power transmission equipment, transportation equipment, high-technology products, and other goods typically needed by countries in the middle stage of development.

But multinational corporations (MNCs) must be mindful of risks in emerging markets. Legal frameworks are often inadequate, existing laws are insufficiently enforced, or judicial systems may be slow, corrupt, or subject to manipulation. Intellectual property protections for new technologies, brand names, logos, and manufacturing processes are often inadequate. Piracy and other intellectual property violations are commonplace in some emerging markets. Political instability is an important, potentially inhibiting factor. Protectionism may take the form of special loans, subsidies, or tax incentives for home-grown firms, and high market entry barriers for foreign competitors. Infrastructure is often inferior in emerging markets in areas such as energy systems, transportation, and communications.

Many emerging markets are characterized by family conglomerates (FCs), large, highly diversified holding companies that have been around for some time. FCs are dominant players in emerging economies such as South Korea where they are known as *chaebols*, India where they are called business houses, Mexico where they are termed *groupos*, Turkey where they are known as *holding companies*, and various other Asian and Latin American countries. Many are well-known international firms—Daewoo, Hyundai, Koc, Reliance, San Miguel, Samsung, Tata—that seek partnerships with foreign firms because of the opportunity to gain new technical know-how, strong brands, and intellectual property.

CHINA AND INDIA AS SOURCING PLATFORMS

Along with the growth of emerging markets, China and India are playing a growing role in international trade. Offshoring (also known as "global sourcing") is a key new reality. It reflects the tendency of firms to establish value-adding operations in advantageous locations abroad. Offshoring offers economies of scale, access to specialist knowledge, and the ability to subcontract critical organizational processes. China and India have grown in popularity as offshoring destinations because their cost of labor is substantially lower than in the advanced world, and because they possess large pools of knowledge workers. For example, the cost of hiring a software code writer in India is typically one-fifth that of the United States.[9]

Information and communications technology mean that the output of design and research jobs can be transferred around the globe at the touch of a button. For example, Massachusetts General Hospital has its CT scans and X-rays interpreted by radiologists in India. At present about 40 percent of world software is written in India. Information technology firms, from Intel to Microsoft, are moving their programming activities to Bangalore, India.

The lower costs of upstream activities that MNCs enjoy by offshoring are passed on to consumers. This translates into lower prices at JC Penney, Marks & Spencer, WalMmart, and other firms that outsource extensively from the developing world. Lower prices across a whole range of retailers and other businesses provide for much higher standards of living by allowing people to keep more of their money.[10]

INTERNATIONAL SERVICES MARKETING

A critical but often overlooked reality is the growing international marketing of services. Services are deeds, performances, or efforts performed directly by people working in banks, hotels, airlines, construction companies, repair shops, retailers, and countless other firms in the services sector. The production of services represents about 80 percent of U.S. GDP and two-thirds or more of the annual GDP in nearly all other developed countries. Thus services are extraordinarily important in the world economy and global trade. In the United States and several European countries, travel and tourism are now the number one source of revenue from foreigners. Because services has become the biggest part of the economy of nearly all countries, global trade in services is growing dramatically. In recent years services trade has been growing faster than products trade. In total, world exports of commercial services (i.e., excluding government services) amounted to nearly $1.6 trillion in 2002, about 20 percent of total world trade.

But most services cannot be exported and are normally offered abroad by establishing "brick-and-mortar" facilities via FDI.[11] Banks often expand internationally by forming strategic alliances with foreign correspondent banks. They use multibank alliances to provide automatic teller machine access in many locations for their clients. Partly because services comprise nearly 70 percent of GDP in developed nations and approximately 50 percent of GDP in most other countries, the internationalization of services is growing rapidly. Indeed, in recent years internationalization of services has been growing faster than that of products.

FDI in services has grown enormously in recently years. Among the reasons for this trend is the innovative application of product design and engineering, advanced production processes, marketing and distribution, customization, outsourcing, and globalization strategies as critical factors to the international success of manufacturing firms. Finance, telecommunications, insurance, transportation, distribution, and information services are the focal key support activities that underpin international trade and facilitate international marketing activities.[12]

But marketing services abroad is challenging. While the cost of establishing services operations abroad tends to be less capital-intensive than for products-producing firms, operating services firms internationally can be costly. This results in part because services production does not benefit to the same degree as products production from economies of scale. To serve customers, the service MNC must establish a full-service operation in each location where it operates, so it must replicate the existing structure in each affiliate. This presents challenges for finding qualified personnel to staff each operation, to maintain quality control, and to standardize services cross-nationally.

Knowledge is important to all firms, but particularly to services providers. A key issue for these firms internationally, therefore, is protecting critical knowledge that provides the basis for the firm's competitive advantages. Much knowledge in services firms is relatively tacit and is therefore embedded in the firms' personnel. Knowledge that is transferred via more traditional means—manuals, training programs, and various telecommunications vehicles—is harder to protect. Internationally, services firms that rely heavily on such knowledge, particularly in countries with weak intellectual property laws, are relatively vulnerable.[13]

A key knowledge-related source of competitive advantage is often relationships with customers. This knowledge includes knowledge of key individuals and historical knowledge of the relationship as it has evolved over time. Grosse (2000) suggests that this type of knowledge can be protected if it is retained within multi-person teams, as opposed to individual employees. In this way, if an employee leaves, the knowledge still remains with the team. The international marketing of services implies a strong role for customer relationship management.

BORN GLOBALS AND INTERNATIONAL SMEs

Another new reality is the rise of the international SMEs. SMEs make up over 95 percent of all companies and create about 50 percent of total value-added worldwide. They have far fewer financial, human, and tangible resources than the large multinational corporations that have traditionally plied the waters of global trade. Historically, international business was beyond the reach of most SMEs. However, technological advances and globalization have created a business environment in which young, smaller firms can market their offerings around the world. As a result, companies that internationalize at or near their founding, *born-global firms*, have sprung up rapidly.[14]

Despite the scarce resources that characterize most SMEs, born-global managers see the world as their marketplace, from or near the firm's inception. The period from domestic establishment to initial foreign market entry is often three or fewer years. By internationalizing as early and rapidly as they do, they develop a "borderless" corporate culture. Born globals typically target their products and services to a dozen or more countries. Smaller size confers much flexibility for succeeding abroad. Born globals usually internationalize via exporting and leverage relationships with strong foreign distributors who provide key local advantages related not only to downstream international business activities but also to gathering market intelligence, forging links with key foreign contacts, deepening relations within extant markets, and cultivating new buyer segments.[15]

These young entrepreneurial firms internationalize early for various reasons. Management may perceive big demand for the firm's products abroad—"export pull." Management may possess a strong international orientation, pushing the organization into foreign markets—"export push." Occasionally, the firm specializes in a particular product category for which demand in the home market is too small, pushing management to seek growth abroad. Often, born globals enjoy relationships with foreign facilitators and customers who pave the way for international expansion.[16]

The emergence of born globals has given rise to the field of *international entrepreneurship*. Entrepreneurship is the process of creating or seizing opportunities and pursuing them even in the face of limited company resources. Management at entrepreneurial firms is typically innovative, proactive, and risk seeking. When a firm exhibits these characteristics in cross-border business, they are engaged in international entrepreneurship.[17] International entrepreneurship involves the firm in new and innovative activities in the pursuit of business activities across national borders. Managers with an entrepreneurial orientation have an obsession for opportunity. They are comfortable dealing with uncertainty and have the flexibility to make course changes to company strategies as the need arises. In international business, the entrepreneurial manager is creative, is innovative, has a strong feel for the firm's business environment, and is ready to pursue new opportunities. They are capable of anticipating the future. Such behaviors can be found in any company, but today they are particularly salient in born globals and other smaller international firms.[18]

International entrepreneurship is an exciting trend because it implies that *any* firm, regardless of size, age, or resource base, can participate actively in global markets. The traditional view of the large multinational corporation as the dominant player in international business is evolving. Youth and lack of experience, as well as limited financial resources, are no longer major impediments to the large-scale internationalization and global success of the firm. Countless SMEs are internationalizing at or near their founding, and succeeding in international markets. Younger, smaller firms are playing a substantially greater role in international marketing than ever before.

COLLABORATIVE APPROACHES

Collaborative ventures have been around for many years, but they continue to contribute much to firms' international marketing performance. While collaboration can take place at similar or different levels of the value chain, most ventures focus on research and development (R&D), production, or marketing. Collaboration makes possible the achievement of projects that exceed the capabilities of the individual enterprise. Groups of firms sometimes form strategic alliances to accomplish large-scale goals such as development of new technologies, or the construction of major projects, such as building power plants. They draw on a range of complementary technologies, accessible only from other firms, to innovate and develop new products. The advantages of collaboration help explain why the volume of such partnerships has grown substantially in the last few decades.[19]

Firms are more likely to collaborate if, relative to other international entry modes, collaboration reduces the partners' *transaction costs*, that is, the general costs of doing business. Firms also enter collaborative arrangements for strategic reasons. That is, they transact internationally by whichever mode helps them achieve strategic objectives, leading to long-term profit maximization. Consistent with *organizational learning theory*, firms may also collaborate in order to share organizationally embedded knowledge or technology that is not easily conveyed in written or explicit form.[20]

Philips and AT&T formed a joint venture to develop central-office switching devices for the telecommunications industry. Nabisco entered a joint venture with a Japanese firm, Yamazaki, to market its snack products in Japan. The host country partner contributes knowledge of the local language and culture, market navigation know-how, and useful connections to the host country government. Western firms often seek joint ventures to access markets in Asia. The partnership allows the foreign firm to access key market knowledge and gain immediate access to a distribution system and customers.

Project-based, nonequity alliances are increasingly common in international business. They involve pooling resources and capabilities among firms in order to pursue a well-defined project in a finite period. Once the venture bears fruit, the partners may shift their approaches and compete in more traditional ways.

For example, IBM and NTT formed a strategic partnership for a limited period. Under the arrangement, IBM provides outsourcing services to NTT, Japan's dominant telecommunications carrier, and in turn, NTT provides outsourcing services and contacts for computer services sales to customers in Japan.[21] Companies also increasingly form consortia, large-scale partnerships that involve more than two firms for handling very large projects. For example, Boeing, Fuji, Kawasaki, and Mitsubishi joined forces to design and manufacture major components of the Boeing 767 aircraft.

The firm enters a collaborative venture when it ascertains that a necessary link in its value chain is somehow weak or inadequate. If this is the case, it then chooses a partner that can replace the function of the weak link. In this way, the firm can meet its growth and other strategic objectives faster or more effectively. More specifically, firms enter collaborative arrangements in order to gain access to new markets or opportunities, reduce the costs and risks of international business, gain access to knowledge or other assets, create synergies for innovative activities, placate government authorities or access protected markets, and prevent or reduce competition.[22]

About half of all collaborative ventures fail within their first five years of operation. The majority fall short of partners' expectations.[23] International ventures are especially problematic because in addition to involving complex business issues, they also entail the additional burden of dealing across culture and language, as well as differences in political, legal, and economic systems.[24]

International collaborative ventures sometimes break down due to cultural differences. The partners may never arrive at a common set of values and organizational routines. The undertaking is especially complex when the parties are from very distinct cultures. For example, European and North American firms face considerable challenges in managing joint ventures with partners in China. Another challenge in international collaborations is the risk of creating a competitor. Collaboration takes place between firms that are current or potential competitors. Accordingly, the partners must walk the line between cooperation and competition. For example, for several years, Volkswagen and General Motors succeeded in China by partnering with the Chinese firm Shanghai Automotive Industry Corp. (SAIC). The Western firms transferred much technology and know-how to the Chinese partner. Having learned much from Volkswagen and General Motors, SAIC is now poised to become a major player in the global automobile industry and competitor to its old partners.[25]

CONTEMPORARY APPROACHES TO INTERNATIONAL MARKETING

Market Orientation

In order to respond optimally to differing conditions abroad, contemporary firms develop a market orientation. Having a market orientation means that the firm attempts to ascertain the needs and wants of the buyers in a market and then creates products and services that specifically fit those needs and wants. It is realized by conducting market research to ascertain market characteristics and the needs of buyers, by disseminating the research findings throughout the firm, and by responding to the findings by creating products and services that specifically address buyer needs and wants. Typically, a strong market orientation translates into substantial adaptation of products and services to suit the needs and tastes of foreign customers.

For example, when targeting China and other Asian markets, dairy producer New Zealand Milk adds ginger and papaya flavoring to its milk products, to suit the tastes of people in Asia.[26] When Procter & Gamble (P&G) introduced Oil of Olay skin moisturizer into Taiwan, it reformulated the product to suit the preferences of Taiwanese women after market research revealed that they prefer less moisturizer.[27] Hollywood movies must be dubbed or translated into the language of target markets. Packaged foods in Europe are often labeled in four different languages.

Customer Relationship Management (CRM)

International firms also increasingly strive to develop strong relations with their foreign customers via CRM. It involves collecting, storing, and analyzing customer data to develop and maintain two-way communication between the firm and its key customers. By leveraging information technology, international firms like Credit Suisse and HP identify their most valuable buyers and then tailor product and service offerings to closely match their needs. In this way, the firm develops "customer equity."[28] The ultimate goal is to maximize value propositions to the firm's most important customers, so that they remain customers indefinitely. For most firms, keeping good customers is more profitable than finding new customers.

Global Marketing Strategy

When the firm extensively standardizes a product for foreign markets, it is following a global strategy. It involves creating a relatively standardized marketing mix, targeted to all countries or, at minimum, major world regions. It is based on identifying and targeting cross-cultural similarities. The firm applies the same or similar approach or content for one or more elements of the marketing mix across as many markets as possible. Citibank, Nestlé, HP, and Xerox are examples of MNCs that use global strategy to great success.

The viability of global marketing strategy varies across industries and product categories. For example, commodities, industrial, and high-technology products lend themselves to a global approach, while many consumer goods require greater adaptation. P&G applies a global strategy for its international marketing of disposable diapers, a commodity. But its line of laundry detergents is more adapted to local markets, because cleaning methods and washing machines vary significantly across countries.

Product Innovation

Product innovation is also critically important to the success of international firms. Many product innovations originate from firsthand knowledge of dealing with the needs of individual foreign markets. Various new ideas about how to improve products emerge from dealing in the extreme conditions often found abroad. Some MNCs have globalized R&D by locating development laboratories in different countries and then coordinating R&D activities to leverage the technical resources of the firm's worldwide operations.

R&D intensity, that is, total R&D expenditures as a percentage of total sales, has increased in many industries such as chemicals, electronics, pharmaceuticals, and medical equipment. This has resulted because firms increasingly recognize that technology is a major source of global competitive advantage. Innovative processes are needed to develop global products and stay abreast of growing global competitive pressures. The growth of information and communications technologies facilitates low-cost coordination of global R&D activities. More than 12 percent of total R&D spending is performed by firms' foreign affiliates (http://www .oecd.org). One disadvantage of performing R&D activities abroad, however, is the risk of dissipating proprietary knowledge to foreign partners or competitors, particularly in countries with lax intellectual property laws.

The ability to innovate depends on the availability of knowledge workers and university graduates trained in the sciences and high-technology areas. Accordingly, countries such as Australia, Canada, Finland, France, Germany, India, Japan, South Korea, the UK, and the United States enjoy particular advantages in innovation and the development of new technologies. Many firms leverage links with universities. For instance, Rolls-Royce co-opts research with academic technology centers, such as Loughborough University in the UK, to develop new technologies for the firm's jet engines.

Innovation leads to new product development. Before 1980, product development and design was a sequential process, usually based in a single country.

Engineers and marketing people agreed on a set of technical specifications, and a product was developed and sent to the factory for manufacturing. However, because the product was developed in a single national environment, it required substantial adaptation for selling abroad.

Global Products

Today, many more firms develop global products, which are adapted for world markets from scratch. The primary impetus is to capture economies of scale in R&D, product development, production, and marketing. Growth in R&D parallels the emergence of demanding global customers with increasingly similar needs and tastes. P&G developed Pringles potato chips as a standardized global product. Worldwide it is produced and promoted as one product, one process, one package, and one marketing campaign. The savings for P&G have been enormous.[29]

Global firms increasingly employ cross-national teams from the firm's major subsidiaries and functional areas to design new products. The team approach requires substantial cross-national coordination. But when skillfully managed, it results in products that are both cost-effective and relatively customized to individual markets. It reduces development time and costs. Companies make their suppliers partners in the design process to optimize sourcing and production. Product development is no longer a sequential process; rather, design and development occur simultaneously, and all major players are co-opted from the beginning.[30]

For developing global products, the team leverages computer-aided design (CAD), which facilitates three-dimensional design on compatible computer systems that accommodate contributions by design team members from around the world. Sophisticated software allows the team to pilot various configurations of the product at virtually no cost. Rapid prototyping means that new designs can be quickly tested on global customers and modified based on resulting market research. Savings result from a single, unified design effort.[31] The Boeing 777 was developed by design teams composed of members from Europe, Japan, and the United States. The jet was broken down into tail, fuselage, wings, and other modular sections. Each section was designed and developed by a global team.

In developing global products, leading MNCs focus on the commonalities among countries rather than the differences.[32] The team develops a basic product or product platform into which variations for individual markets can be incorporated inexpensively. Development of a basic product platform appropriate for all markets allows the firm to capture economies of scale for producing most of the product. For example, personal computers are now designed so that the expensive hardware is virtually the same everywhere, but the software is changed to accommodate local languages. While the basic computers that Dell sells worldwide are essentially identical, the letters on its keyboards and the languages used in its software are unique to countries or major regions. Roughly speaking, the balance is about 80/20. That is, about 80 percent of each Dell computer sold worldwide is identical, and about 20 percent is adapted for each local market as a function of differing languages.

Many products are designed using modular architecture, a collection of standardized components and subsystems that can be rapidly assembled in various configurations to suit the needs of individual markets. For example, global cars like the Ford Mondeo or the Honda Accord are designed around a standardized platform to which modular components, parts, and features are added to suit specific needs and tastes.

Global Branding

The worldwide standardization of positioning, advertising strategies, personality, look, and feel characterize a global brand. Management seeks to achieve a clear and consistent identity with its target market regardless of geographic location. Developing and maintaining a global brand name is the most effective way to build global recognition and maximize the international marketing program.[33] For example, the Eveready Battery Co. consolidated its various national brand names—such as Ucar, Wonder, and Mazda—into one global name, Energizer, in order to build a consistent image and global brand name. While most brands are conceived on a national level and then internationalized, the best approach is to build a global brand from scratch. Several firms have done this, choosing brand names and images that can be easily recognized and pronounced worldwide. An example is Japan's Sony Corporation.[34]

Strong global brands have the following attributes:

- Brand development is based on understanding customers via market research; managers understand the brand's meaning for each target audience.
- The brand delivers the benefits that customers seek. It is based on a targeted and compelling concept that provides superior value, a solid "value proposition."
- The brand is both consistent and relevant.
- The firm employs a full range of marketing communications activities to deliver the desired customer experience and build brand equity.
- Brand equity is continuously monitored.
- The firm commits sufficient financial and other support to maintain the brand over time.[35]

The most successful brands are positioned around a strong psychological proposition. For example, research revealed that consumers in China value products that give them a sense of "well-being," "self-indulgence," and "harmony." Volkswagen and Vidal Sassoon attempt to incorporate these values into their brands when marketing to the Chinese.[36]

THE MANAGERIAL IMPERATIVE FOR INTERNATIONAL MARKETERS

The centers of economic activity are shifting profoundly. Today, Asia (excluding Japan) accounts for 13 percent of world GDP, while Western Europe accounts for more than 30 percent. Within the next 20 years the two will nearly converge. In coming years, the United States will continue to dominate much of international trade, but China and India will become the most important new international players in the near term. Partly due to the rise of China and India, the consumer landscape will change and expand substantially. Almost a billion new consumers will enter the global marketplace by 2015 as economic growth in emerging markets pushes them beyond the threshold level of $5,000 in annual household income—a point when people begin to spend on discretionary goods. Through 2015, consumer spending power in emerging markets will increase from $4 trillion to more than $9 trillion—almost the present spending power of Western Europe. The elderly market segment will balloon, and firms will need to develop products and services for this key market. In the United States, the Hispanic population will expand dramatically.[37]

Technological connectivity is transforming the way people live and interact. We are still at the early stage of this revolution. Firms are learning how to make the best use of information technology in designing processes and in developing and accessing knowledge. New developments in fields such as biotechnology, laser technology, and nanotechnology are moving well beyond the realm of products and services. More transformational than technology itself is the shift in behavior that it enables. Increasingly, people work not just globally but also instantaneously. They are forming communities and relationships in new ways. More than 2 billion people now use cell phones. They send 9 trillion e-mails a year and enter a billion Google searches a day. For perhaps the first time in history, geography is not the primary constraint on the limits of international marketing and other global activities.[38]

A purely domestic focus is no longer viable for most firms, particularly product manufacturers. In order to remain competitive, domestic management must develop a greater understanding and knowledge of international marketing. Managers must adopt a global rather than a local focus. The most sophisticated firms will deliberately seek simultaneous presence in all of the world's major trading regions. A global approach is critical to gain and maintain competitive advantage and ensure long-term performance. Companies must locate their value chain activities in those countries and in markets where they can derive maximal competitive advantages.

Having a global presence is not limited to large MNCs. Smaller firms are also increasingly global, often pursuing global niche strategies by targeting specialized foreign markets. Trade liberalization implies greater competitive rivalry from global firms. In order to meet globalization's growing competitive challenges, companies are increasing the level of their offshore investment and overseas sourcing. Suppliers are following their internationalizing customers abroad.

Managers must strike some ideal balance between global control of the organization and decentralized decision making at the level of individual countries. This implies striking the right balance in standardizing and adapting products, services, and marketing itself. Managers must leverage technology, especially in information and communications, to manage their international marketing activities. To achieve economies of scale, companies will emphasize standardization of products and marketing and centralization of production activities in fewer locations. By the same token, global competition pressures firms to be entrepreneurial and flexible in their pursuit of new or latent opportunities and the resolution of current problems and future threats.

NOTES

1. "The Net Imperative: A Survey of Business and the Internet," *The Economist*, June 26, 1999, B5–B7.

2. "Broadband Wonderland," *Fortune*, September 20, 2004, 191–98.

3. "Clicks, Bricks and Bargains," *The Economist*, December 3, 2005, 57–58.

4. Thomas L. Friedman, "It's a Flat World, After All," *The New York Times Magazine*, April 3, 2005, 33–37.

5. "The Death of Distance: A Survey of Telecommunications," *The Economist*, September 30, 1995.

6. Michael Czinkota, Gary Knight, and Peter Liesch, "Terrorism and International Business: Conceptual Foundations," in *Terrorism and the International Business Environment: The Security-Business Nexus*, ed. Gabriele Suder, 43–57 (Cheltenham, England: Edward Elgar, 2004).

7. Yossi Sheffi, *The Resilient Enterprise: Overcoming Vulnerability for Competitive Advantage* (Cambridge, MA: MIT Press, 2005).

8. M. Czinkota and G. A. Knight, "Managing the Terrorist Threat," *European Business Forum* 20 (Winter 2005): 42–45.

9. "A World of Work: A Survey of Outsourcing," *The Economist*, November 13, 2004, special section.

10. Jagdish Bhagwati, Arvind Panagariya, and T. Srinivasan, "The Muddles over Outsourcing," *Journal of Economic Perspectives* 18, no. 4 (Fall 2004): 93–114.

11. M. K. Erramilli and C. P. Rao. "Service Firms' International Entry-Mode Choice: A Modified Transaction-Cost Analysis Approach." *Journal of Marketing* 57 (July 1993): 19–38.

12. G. Feketekuty, "Keynote Address: A Framework for Global Trade in Services," in *Proceedings of the Services 2000*, ed. I. T. Administration (Washington, DC: U.S. Department of Commerce, 1999).

13. Grosse, Robert, "Knowledge Creation and Transfer in Global Service Firms," in *Globalization of Services*, ed. Y. Aharoni and L. Nachum, 217–32 (London: Routledge, 2000).

14. Gary Knight, "Entrepreneurship and Marketing Strategy: The SME under Globalization," *Journal of International Marketing* 8, no. 2 (2000): 12–32.

15. Gary A. Knight and S. Tamer Cavusgil, "Innovation, Organizational Capabilities, and the Born-Global Firm," *Journal of International Business Studies* 35, no. 2 (2004): 124–41.

16. Ibid.

17. Patricia McDougall and Benjamin Oviatt, "International Entrepreneurship: The Intersection of Two Research Paths," *Academy of Management Journal* 43, no. 5 (2000): 902–6.

18. Knight and Cavusgil, "Innovation."

19. Masaaki Kotabe, Hildy Teegen, Preet Aulakh, Maria Cecilia Coutinho de Arruda, Roberto Santillan-Salgado, and Walter Greene, "Strategic Alliances in Emerging Latin American: A View from Brazilian, Chilean, and Mexican Companies," *Journal of World Business* 35, no. 2 (2000): 114–32.

20. Bruce Kogut, "Joint Ventures: Theoretical and Empirical Perspectives," *Strategic Management Journal* 9 (1988): 319–32.

21. Robert Guth, "IBM Announces Deal with Japan's NTT," *Wall Street Journal*, November 1, 2000, 23.

22. Vern Terpstra and Bernard Simonin, "Strategic Alliances in the Triad," *Journal of International Marketing* 1, no. 1 (1993): 4–25.

23. Yves Doz, "The Evolution of Cooperation in Strategic Alliances: Initial Conditions or Learning Processes," *Strategic Management Journal* 17 (Summer 1996): 55–85.

24. Sing Keow Hoon-Halbauer, "Managing Relationships within Sino-Foreign Joint Ventures," *Journal of World Business* 34, no. 4 (1999): 334–70.

25. Alex Taylor III, "Shanghai Auto Wants to Be the World's Next Great Car Company," *Fortune*, October 4, 2004, 103–10.

26. Cris Prystay, "Milk Industry's Pitch in Asia: Try the Ginger or Rose Flavor," *Wall Street Journal*, August 9, 2005, B1.

27. Roger Calantone, S. Tamer Cavusgil, Jeffrey Schmidt, and Geon-Cheol Shin, "Internationalization and the Dynamics of Product Adaptation: An Empirical Investigation," *Journal of Product Innovation Management* 21 (2004): 185–98.

28. Katherine Lemon, Roland Rust, and Valarie Zeithaml, "What Drives Customer Equity," *Marketing Management* 10, no. 1 (2001): 20–26.

29. Jay Galbraith, *Designing the Global Corporation* (San Francisco: Jossey-Bass, 2000).

30. Ibid.

31. Ibid.

32. George Yip, *Total Global Strategy II* (Upper Saddle River, NJ: Prentice Hall, 2003).

33. David A. Aaker, *Managing Brand Equity* (New York: The Free Press, 1991).

34. Yip, *Total Global Strategy II*.

35. James Gregory and Jack Wiechmann, *Branding across Borders* (Chicago: McGraw-Hill, 2002).

36. Gilbert Lee and Nic Hall, "Brand Strategy Briefing: The 15 Global Hot Buttons," *Brand Strategy*, June 2004, 58.

37. "The U.S. Hispanic Market: Wearing the American Dream," *Financial Times*, June 5, 2006.

38. Ibid.

CHAPTER 13

CULTURE AND INTERNATIONAL MARKETING

Vern Terpstra

INTRODUCTION

What is culture? The simplest definition is that culture is the distinctive way of life of a group or nation of people. A dictionary puts it in more detail. It is "the totality of socially transmitted behavior patterns, arts, beliefs, institutions, and all other products of human work and thought characteristic of a community or population." Culture is also learned behavior. It depends on the environment, not heredity; it is not biologically transmitted.

In other words, culture is a very complex phenomenon and a challenge to firms who wish to market internationally. How does the firm's product or service fit in with the foreign market's culture? How must it be adapted to fit? Every firm must make its own adjustment and adaptation to satisfy foreign customers. We shall look at various dimensions of culture and their significance for international marketing. A very simple illustration of cultural differences was used by Hong Kong Shanghai Bank in advertising on an international airport poster. They showed an image of a grasshopper and the following message:

USA – Pest

China – Pet

Northern Thailand – Appetizer

LANGUAGE

Language is the most obvious difference between cultures. Inextricably linked with all other aspects of a culture, language reflects the nature and values of that culture. For example, the English language has a rich vocabulary for commercial and industrial activities, reflecting the progressive nature of the English and U.S. societies. Many less industrialized societies have only limited vocabularies for those activities, but richer vocabularies for matters important to their culture.

Because language is such an obvious cultural difference, everyone recognizes that it must be dealt with. It is said that anyone planning a career in international business should learn a foreign language. Certainly, if a person's career involves dealing with a particular country, he or she will find learning the country's language to be very useful. Because it is usually impossible to predict to which countries a career will lead, it is best to study a language spoken by many people (e.g., Mandarin Chinese) or a language that is commonly used as a first or second language in many nations (e.g., English, French, or Spanish). Whether or not it is a primary language of the parties involved, English is frequently used in negotiations, legal documents, and business transactions.

This does not mean, however, that American firms can bask in their knowledge and use of English. Language still provides a challenge to international marketing. Frequently, translation will be needed, and translation can be expensive. The WTO spends over one-fifth of its budget translating its documents. The European Union spends over $1 billion for translators and interpreters, and that is just for EU members, not the rest of the world.

It is said that a language defines a cultural group, that nothing distinguishes one culture from another more than language. What does it mean, though, when the same language is used in different countries? French, for example, is the mother tongue not only for the French but also for many Belgians and Swiss. Spanish plays a similar role in Latin America. The anthropologist, however, stresses the spoken language as the cultural distinction. The spoken language changes more quickly than the written language and reflects the culture more directly. Although England, the United States, and Ireland use the same written English, they speak somewhat different dialects. These three cultures are separate yet related, as are the Spanish-speaking cultures of Latin America.

Even where a common language is spoken, different words signifying the same meaning are occasionally used, as are different pronunciations. In England, people say "lorry," "petrol," and "biscuits"; in the United Sates, people say "truck," "gasoline," and "cookies." Incidentally, even within one country—for example, the United States, where almost everyone speaks "American" English—there are different cultural groups, or subcultures, among which the spoken language varies.

Language as a Problem

Activities such as advertising, branding, packaging, personal selling, and marketing research are highly dependent upon communication. If management is not speaking the same language as its various audiences, it is not going to enjoy much success. In each of its foreign markets, a company must communicate with several audiences: its workers, its managers, its customers, its suppliers, and the government. Each of these audiences may have a distinctive communication style within the common language.

Language diversity in world markets could be an insurmountable problem if managers had to master the languages of all their markets. Fortunately, that is not the case. To be effective, any person assigned to a foreign operation for a period of a year or more should learn the local language. However, cultural bridges are available in many markets. For example, in countries where a firm is operating through a distributor, the distributor may act as the bridge between the firm and its local market. In advertising, a firm may be able to rely on a local advertising agency. Agency personnel, like the distributor, probably speak the advertising manager's language—especially if the firm communicates principally in English.

SOCIAL ORGANIZATION

The social organization of a group of people helps define their roles and the expectations they place upon themselves and others in the group. Concepts such as family vary from group to group, which becomes evident when talking about these concepts to people from other cultures. The nature of people's friendships with others—how quickly the relationships develop, how the friendships are nurtured, and how long they last—also reflect on the social organization within the culture or group. Social organization is formally defined in the government and the laws that proscribe certain behavior among people. The nature of social organization and the impact on business is discussed next.

Kinship

Kinship includes the social organization or structure of a group: the way people relate to other people. This differs somewhat from society to society. The primary kind of social organization is based on kinship. In the United States, the key unit is the family, which traditionally included only the father, the mother, and the unmarried children in the household. Of course, the definition is changing, as is reflected in each census. The family unit elsewhere is often larger, including more relatives. A large extended family is common in many less developed nations.

Those who call themselves brothers in Congo, for example, include cousins and uncles.

In developing countries, the extended family fulfills several social and economic roles. The family unit is not prescribed or defined by a specific religious restriction, as does the *baradari* of Hinduism. The extended family provides mutual protection, psychological support, and economic insurance or social security for its members. In a world of tribal warfare and primitive agriculture, this support was invaluable. The extended family, still significant in many parts of the world, means that consumption decision making takes place in a larger unit and in different ways. Pooled resources, for instance, may allow larger purchases; for this reason, per capita income may be a misleading guide of market potential. The researcher may find it difficult to determine the relevant consuming unit for some goods. Is it a household or a family? How many members are there?

Common Territory

In the United States, common territory can be a neighborhood, a suburb, or a city. In many countries of Asia and Africa, common territory is the tribal grouping. In many countries, the tribe is often the largest effective unit because the various tribes do not voluntarily recognize the central government. Unfortunately, nationalism has not generally replaced tribalism. Tribalism and religious or ethnic divisions often lead to bloody conflict, as in Congo, Ireland, Israel and Palestine, Pakistan, the Philippines, Rwanda, and Sudan. Even in Europe, the Scots and the Welsh are not happy about being under British rule. For businesses, in many countries, groupings based on common territory may be a clue to market segmentation.

Special Interest Group

A third kind of social grouping, the special interest group or association, may be religious, occupational, recreational, or political. Special interest groups can also be useful in identifying different market segments. For example, in the United States the American Association of Retired Persons (AARP), the Sierra Club, and the National Rifle Association (NRA) represent market segments for some firms.

Other Kinds of Social Organization

Some kinds of social organization cut across the categories just discussed. One is the caste system or class groupings. These may be detailed and rigid, as in the Hindu caste system; or they may be loose and flexible, as in U.S. social classes.

The United States has a relatively open society, but there is still concern about social standing and status symbols. While social class is more (or less) important and rigid in comparing countries, each country has its own social and ethnic groupings that are important for its society and the economy. These groupings usually mean that some groups are discriminated against and others are favored. Different groups may require different marketing strategies.

Other groupings based on age occur, especially in affluent industrialized nations. For example, senior citizens usually live as separate economic unit with their own needs and motivations. Age groupings are a major market segment in industrialized countries. As noted in the discussion of the extended family, much less separation between age groups exists in less developed areas. Generally, strong family integration occurs at all age levels, as well as a preponderant influence of age and seniority, which is in contrast to the youth motif prevalent in the United States. Of course, Generation X and baby boomers are important age groupings in the United States.

A final aspect of social organization concerns the role of women in the economy. Women seldom enjoy parity with men as participants in the economy; and their participation is related to the economic development of nations—the poorer the nation, the fewer women seen in jobs outside the home. The extent to which women participate in the money economy affects their role as consumers and consumption influencers. Even developed countries exhibit differences in attitudes toward female employment.

TECHNOLOGY AND MATERIAL CULTURE

Material culture includes the tools and artifacts—the material or physical things—in a society, excluding those physical things found in nature unless they undergo some technological transformation. For example, a tree as such is not part of a culture, but the Christmas tree is. Technology refers to the techniques or methods of making and using that which surrounds us. Technology and material culture are related to the way a society organizes its economic activities. The term "technology gap" refers to differences in the ability of two societies to create, design, and use that which exists in nature or to use that which has been transformed in some way.

When referring to industrialized nations, developing nations, the nuclear age, or the space age, one is referring to different technologies and material cultures. One can also speak of societies being in the age of the automobile, the bicycle, or foot transportation—or in the age of the computer, the abacus, or pencil-and-paper calculation. The relationships between technology, material culture, and the other aspects of life are profound but not easily recognized because people are the products of their own culture. It is primarily as people travel abroad that they perceive such relationships.

In discussing this topic, Karl Marx went so far as to say that the economic organization of a society shapes and determines its political, legal, and social organization. His view was termed "economic determinism," his materialist interpretation of history. Few people today would take such a strong position, but they may recognize many examples of the impact of tools, techniques, and economic organization on the nature of life in society. For example, people's behavior as workers and consumers is greatly influenced by the technology and material culture.

The way people work and how effectively they work is determined in large part by their technology and material culture. Henry Ford's assembly line revolutionized U.S. productivity and, ultimately, the standard of living. U.S. farmers' use of equipment and technology has made them the world's most productive agriculturalists. Ironically, agriculture is one of the most capital- and technology-intensive industries in the United States. The farmer does not do the research and development, however, but land-grant universities, equipment manufacturers, and chemical companies do. The computer, as one of the newer artifacts, affects the way people work, the kind of work they can do, and even where they work. If you consider the nature of the factory and agricultural methods and the role of the computer in an African nation, you can see technology and material culture as a constraint on work and productivity in a culture.

One of the most striking examples of the potential impact of technology is India. In the 20th century, India was almost a third-world country. In the 21st century, India is a world leader in computer and information technology and sells its services to the United States and other first-world countries. Most of the world's poorest countries are not able to imitate India's success, but technology can help them also.

In 2005, the United Nations launched a "Digital Solidarity Fund" to finance projects that address "the uneven distribution and use of new information and communication technologies" and that will "enable excluded people and countries to enter the new era of the information society."

One of the simpler new technologies, the mobile phone, is having the greatest impact on economic development. The world's poorest are rushing to embrace mobile phones because of their benefits. They can be used by illiterates and do not depend on a permanent electricity supply. They are shared and rented out by the call. Farmers and small businesses can shop around for the best place for supplies and equipment, as well as the market with the best price for their products, reducing the need for travel.[1]

How people consume and what people consume are also heavily influenced by the technology and material culture. For example, the car has helped to create the conditions that made suburban living possible, with the accompanying lifestyle and consumption patterns. Television has a wide-ranging impact on consumer and voter behavior. The microwave oven influences not only the preparation of food but also the nature of the food consumed. Considering artifacts such as the digital camera and the cellular telephone, one can imagine further ramifications of each new project on the life of the consumer. Knowing the impact of these products in the U.S. culture, one can conjecture how consumer behavior might be different in countries with much lighter penetration of such products.

Material Culture as a Constraint

Managers need to develop insight into how material culture in foreign markets affects their operations abroad. In manufacturing, foreign production by a firm may represent an attempt to introduce a new material culture into the host economy. This is usually the case when a firm builds a plant in a less developed country. The firm generally checks carefully on the necessary economic prerequisites for such a plant: for example, raw-material supply, power, transportation, and financing. Frequently overlooked, however, are the other cultural preconditions for the plant.

Before making foreign production decisions, a firm must evaluate the material culture in the host country. One aspect is the economic infrastructure—that is, transportation, power, and communications. Other questions are these: Do production processes need to be adapted to fit the local economy? Will the plant be more labor-intensive than plants at home? The manager discovers that production of the same goods may require a different production function in different countries.

In large diversified markets such as the United States, almost any industrialized product can find a market. In developing nations, however, firms that make industrial goods find increasingly limited markets in which they can sell only part, or perhaps none, of their product line. The better the picture of the material culture in world markets, the more able a firm is to identify the best prospects. The prospects in countries where the principal agricultural implement is the machete differ from those in countries where farmers use tractors.

Firms that manufacture consumer goods are also concerned with the material culture in foreign markets. Simple considerations such as electrical voltages and use of the metric system must be taken into account. Product adaptations may also be necessitated by the material culture of the family unit. Does the family have a car to transport purchases? Does the family have a stove to prepare foods or a refrigerator in which to store foods? If electrical power is not available, electrical appliances will not be marketable unless they are battery powered. To those people who wash clothes by a stream or lake, detergents and packaged soaps are not useful; the market is for bar soaps only.

Large multinational companies are learning from entrepreneurs in developing countries that the key to success in markets where income is low is to sell products that come in small sizes, are relatively cheap, and are easy to use. Unilever packages its shampoo in single-use sizes, selling it for a few cents in India. Other examples include three-inch-square packages of margarine in Nigeria that do not need refrigeration, and an 8¢ tube of Close-Up with enough toothpaste for about 20 brushings. Unilever expects that developing markets will account for 50 percent of all sales by 2010, up from 32 percent in 2005. Freeplay Energy in London designed and sold 3 million hand crank radios. Since many people in developing countries have no electricity and cannot afford to purchase batteries, these units are popular for listening to farm and health reports. Phillips Electronics of the Netherlands has developed its own version, which the firm is now selling in India for around $20. Indian firms located in Madras and Bangalore are developing wireless kiosks that allow users to access the Internet for as little as 3¢ an hour, and computers with voice recognition software, which is aimed at users who cannot read.

Marketing strategy is influenced by the material culture. For instance, the promotional program is constrained by the kinds of media available. The advertiser wants to know the availability of television, radio, magazines, and newspapers. How good is the reproduction process in newspapers and magazines? Are there advertising and research agencies to support the advertising program? The size of retail outlets affects the use of point-of-purchase displays. The nature of travel and the highway system affects the use of outdoor advertising.

Modification in distribution may also be necessary. These changes must be made based on the alternatives offered by the country's commercial infrastructure. What wholesale and retail patterns exist? What warehouse or storage facilities are available? Is refrigerated storage possible? What is the nature of the transport system—road, rail, river, or air? What area does it cover? Firms that use direct channels in the United States, with large-scale retailers and chain-store operations, may have to use indirect channels with a multitude of small independent retailers. These small retailers may be relatively inaccessible if they are widely dispersed and transportation is inadequate.

If local storage facilities are insufficient, a firm may have to supply its own packaging or provide special packaging to offer extra protection. Whereas highways and railroads are most important in moving goods in the United States, river transport is a major means in other countries. And in still other countries, air is the principal means of transport. Thus, in numerous ways, management is concerned with the material culture in foreign markets.

Perhaps the subtlest role of international business is that of the agent of cultural change. When a firm introduces new products into a market, it is, in effect, seeking to change the country's material culture. The change may be modest, such as a new food product, or it may be more dramatic, such as a machine that revolutionizes agriculture or industrial technology in the host country. The product of the international firm is alien in the sense that it did not originate in the host country. The firm must consider carefully the legitimacy of its role as an agent of change.

It must be sure that any changes it introduces are in accordance with the interests of the host country. When the product is coming from a developed nation and sold in developing countries without modification, people may resent the firm's product as a form of "neo-colonialism," "Westernization," or "imperialism." Along this line, someone coined the term "cocoa colonization" concerning U.S. cocoa business abroad.

EDUCATION

In developed nations, education usually means formal training in school. In this sense, those people without access to schools are not educated; that is, they have never been to school. However, this formal definition is too restrictive. Education includes the process of transmitting skills, ideas, and attitudes, as well as training, in particular disciplines. Even so-called "primitive" peoples have been educated in this broader sense. For example, regardless of formal schooling, the Bushmen of South Africa are well educated in relation to the culture in which they live.

One function of education is to transmit the existing culture and traditions to the new generation. Education plays an important role in cultural change in the United States, as it does elsewhere. For example, in the past, developing nations' educational campaigns were carried out with the specific intent of improving techniques used in farming and in reducing the population explosion. In Britain, business schools were originally established to improve the performance of the economy. Some attribute the rapid economic development of Singapore to formal apprenticeship programs.

International Differences in Education

When looking at education in foreign markets, the observer is limited primarily to information about the formal process, that is, education in schools. This is the only area for which the United Nations Educational, Scientific and Cultural Organization (UNESCO), the World Bank, and others have been able to gather data. Traditionally, literacy rates have been used to describe educational achievement; recently, however, international agencies have been measuring inputs as well as educational system outputs other than literacy. For example, the World Bank still includes adult and youth illiteracy rates in its reports. Now it has begun measuring participation in education, which includes enrollment ratios in primary, secondary, and tertiary levels of education, and educational efficiency, which includes completion rates at different levels of education and average number of years in school. In addition, the World Bank also reports on inputs such as expenditures per student, teachers' compensation, number of faculty with appropriate qualifications, and pupil-teacher ratios. Perhaps most importantly, the goals of the World Bank have changed from activities aimed merely at increasing literacy rates to measures designed to ensure that "all children complete a full course of primary education," a target it hopes is achieved by 2015.

The education information available on world markets refers primarily to national enrollments in the various levels of education—primary, secondary, and college or university. This information can give an international marketer insight into the sophistication of consumers in different countries. There is also a strong correlation between educational attainment and economic development.

One could argue that qualitative measures such as math and science scores on international achievement tests should also be used as indicators of human capital development and long-term economic prospects. Because U.S. students consistently score lower on these exams than students in other countries, some fear that the United States may lose its technological edge in the future.

Because only quantitative data are available, there is a danger that the qualitative aspects of education might be overlooked. Furthermore, in addition to the limitations inherent in international statistics, the problem exists of interpreting them in terms of business needs. For example, a firm's needs for technicians, marketing personnel, managers, distributors, and sales forces must be met largely from the educated population in the local economy. When hiring people, the firm is concerned not only with the level but also with the nature of the applicants' education.

Training in law, literature, or political science is probably not the most suitable education for business needs. Yet in many nations, such studies are emphasized almost to the exclusion of others more relevant to commercial and economic growth. Too often, primary education is preparation for secondary, secondary education is preparation for university, and university education is not designed to meet the needs of the economy. In many nations, university education is largely preparation for the traditional prestige occupations. Although a nation needs lawyers and philosophers, it also needs agricultural experts, engineers, managers, and technicians. The degree to which the educational system provides for these needs is a critical determinant of the nation's ability to develop economically.

Education and International Marketing

The international marketer must also be something of an educator. The products and techniques a firm brings into a market are generally new to that market. The firm must educate consumers about the uses and benefits. Although a firm may not make use of a formal educational system, its success is constrained by that system because its ability to communicate depends in part on the educational level of its market. An international marketer is further concerned about the educational situation because it is a key determinant of the nature of the consumer market and the kinds of marketing personnel available. Some implications for businesses include the following:

- When consumers are largely illiterate, existing advertising programs, package labels, instructions, and warranties need to be adapted to include fewer words and more graphics and pictures.

- When women are largely excluded from formal education, marketing programs may differ from those aimed at female segments in developed nations. When a firm is targeting women audiences with less education, messages need to be simple, perhaps with less text and more graphics.

- Conducting marketing research can be difficult, both in communicating with consumers and in getting qualified researchers. If few people are able to read, written surveys would be an ineffective tool in gathering data. Personal interviews, although more costly, would tend to increase response rates and accuracy.

- Cooperation from the distribution channels depends partly on the educational attainments of members in the channel. When overall levels of education are low, finding local qualified marketing employees for certain service or managerial positions may be difficult and very competitive. Long-term training programs and commitments to employee education may raise local operating costs.

RELIGION

If you are to gain a full understanding of a culture, you must become familiar with the internal behavior that gives rise to the external manifestations. Generally, it is the religion of a culture that provides the best insights into this behavior. Therefore, although an international company is interested primarily in knowing *how* people behave as consumers or workers, management's task will be aided by an understanding of *why* people behave as they do.

Numerous religions exist in the world. This section presents brief overviews of animism, Hinduism, Buddhism, Islam, Shinto, Confucianism, and Christianity. These religions were selected based on their importance in terms of numbers of adherents and their impact on the economic behavior of their followers. Adherents to these religious beliefs account for over three-fourths of the world's population. The animists alone have a reported number of adherents varying from 100 million to 245 million.

Animism or Nonliterate Religion

"Animism" is the term used to describe the religion of indigenous peoples. It is often defined as spirit worship, as distinguished from the worship of God or gods.

Animistic beliefs have been found in all parts of the world. With the exception of revealed religion, some form of animism has preceded all historical religions. In many less developed parts of the world today, animistic ideas affect cognitive behavior.

Magic, a key element of animism, is the attempt to achieve results through the manipulation of the spirit world. It represents an unscientific approach to the physical world. When cause-and-effect relationships are not known, magic is given credit for the results. The same attitude prevails toward many modern-day products and techniques.

For example, during the author's years in Congo, he had an opportunity to see reactions to European products and practices that were often based on a magical interpretation. In one instance, a number of Africans affected the wearing of glasses, believing the glasses would enhance the intelligence of the wearer. Some firms that manufacture consumer goods in Africa have not hesitated to imply that their products have magical qualities. Of course, the same is sometimes true of firms elsewhere.

Other aspects of animism include ancestor worship, taboos, and fatalism. All of them tend to promote a traditionalist, status quo, backward-looking society. Because such societies are more interested in protecting their traditions than in accepting change, companies face problems when introducing new products, ideas, or methods. A firm's success in bringing change depends on how well it understands and relates to the culture and its animistic foundation.

Hinduism

There are over 900 million Hindus in the world, most of them in India. In a broad sense, about 80 percent of India's population is Hindu; but in the sense of strict adherence to the tenets of Hinduism, the number of followers is smaller. A common dictum is that Hinduism is not a religion, but a way of life. Its origins go back approximately 3,500 years. It is an ethnic, noncreedal religion. A Hindu is born, not made, so a person cannot become a Hindu or convert to Hinduism, although he or she may become a Buddhist, for example. Modern Hinduism is a combination of ancient philosophies and customs, animistic beliefs, legends, and more recently, Western influences, including Christianity. A strength of Hinduism has been its ability to absorb ideas from outside; Hinduism tends to assimilate rather than exclude.

Despite this openness, many in India are unhappy about marriages between Christians or Muslims and Hindus because it is viewed as a threat or dilution of Hindutva (Hindu-ness) of the culture. Much violence has occurred between the Hindu and Muslim populations, with one instance of over 500 people killed in Gujarat in early 2002. Because Hinduism is an ethnic religion, many of its doctrines apply only to the Indian situation. However, they are crucial in understanding India and its people.

Sikhism is a religion also practiced in India that represents a combined form of Hinduism and Islam, featuring a much-debated aspect, the caste system. While the Indian government officially abolished it over a half century ago and instituted quotas and job-preferment policies, there are still examples of separate *gurdwarars* (houses of worship) for Sikhs and the *Dalit*, or Scheduled Caste (formerly called "untouchables"), some of whom are converting to Buddhism, Christianity, and Islam to escape the caste system.

Another element and strength of Hinduism is *baradari*, or the "joint family." After marriage, the bride goes to the groom's home. After several marriages in the family, there is a large joint family for which the father or grandfather is chief authority. In turn, the older women have power over the younger. The elders give advice and consent in family council. The Indian grows up thinking and acting in terms of the joint family. If a member goes abroad to a university, the joint family may raise the funds. In turn, that member is expected to remember the family if he or she is successful. *Baradari* is aimed at preserving the family.

Nirvana is another important concept, one that Hinduism shares with Buddhism. This topic is discussed in the following section.

Buddhism

Buddhism springs from Hinduism, originating about 2,600 years ago. Buddhism has approximately 360 million followers, mostly in South and East Asia from India to Japan. There are, however, small Buddhist societies in Europe and America. Buddhism is, to some extent, a reformation of Hinduism. It did not abolish caste, but declared that Buddhists were released from caste restrictions. This openness to all classes and both sexes was one reason for Buddhism's growth. While accepting the philosophical insights of Hinduism, Buddhism tried to avoid its dogma and ceremony, stressing tolerance and spiritual equality.

At the heart of Buddhism are the Four Noble Truths:

1. The Noble Truth of Suffering states that suffering is omnipresent and part of the very nature of life.
2. The Noble Truth of the Cause of Suffering cites the cause of suffering to be desire, that is, desire for possessions and selfish enjoyment of any kind.
3. The Noble Truth of the Cessation of Suffering states that suffering ceases when desire ceases.
4. The Noble Truth of the Eightfold Path that leads to the Cessation of Suffering offers the means to achieve cessation of desire. This is also known as the Middle Way because it avoids the two extremes of self-indulgence and self-mortification.

The eightfold path includes (1) the right views, (2) the right desires, (3) the right speech, (4) the right conduct, (5) the right occupation, (6) the right effort, (7) the right awareness, and (8) the right contemplation. This path, though simple to state, is a demanding ethical system. Nirvana is the reward for those who are able to stay on the path throughout their lifetime or, more probably, lifetimes.

Nirvana is the ultimate goal of the Hindu and Buddhist. It represents the extinction of all cravings and the final release from suffering. To the extent that such an ideal reflects the thinking of the mass of the people, the society's values would be considered antithetical to such goals as acquisition, achievement, and affluence. This is an obvious constraint on business.

Islam

Islam dates from the seventh century AD. It has over 900 million adherents, mostly in Africa, Asia, and the Middle East. Most of the world of Islam is found across the northern half of Africa, in the Middle East, and throughout parts of Asia to the Philippines. Islam is usually associated with Arabs and the Middle East, but non-Arab Muslims outnumber Arab Muslims by almost three to one. The nations with the largest Muslim populations are all outside the Middle East. Indonesia, Pakistan, Bangladesh, and India all have over 100 million Muslims. Although there are two major groups in Islam (Sunni 85%, and Shi'ite 15%), they are similar enough on economic issues to permit identification of the following elements of interest to firms.

Muslim theology, *Tawhid*, defines all that one should believe; whereas the law, *Shari'a*, prescribes everything one should do. The Koran (*Qur'an*) is accepted as the ultimate guide. Anything not mentioned in the Koran is likely to be rejected by the faithful. Introducing new products and techniques can be difficult in such an environment. An important element of Muslim belief is that everything that happens, good or evil, proceeds directly from the Divine Will and is already irrevocably recorded on the Preserved Tablet. This belief tends to restrict attempts to bring about change in Muslim countries; to attempt change may be a rejection of what Allah has ordained. The name "Islam" is the infinitive of the Arabic verb to *submit*. "Muslim" is the present participle of the same verb; that is, a Muslim is one submitting to the will of Allah.

The Five Pillars of Islam

The Five Pillars of Islam, or the duties of a Muslim, include (1) the recital of the creed, (2) prayer, (3) fasting, (4) almsgiving, and (5) the pilgrimage. The creed is brief: there is no God but Allah, and Mohammed is his Prophet. The Muslim must pray five times daily at stated hours. During the month of Ramadan,

Muslims are required to fast from dawn to sunset—no food, no drinking, and no smoking. Because the Muslim year is lunar, Ramadan sometimes falls in mid-summer, when the long days and intense heat make abstinence a severe test. The fast is meant to develop self-control and sympathy for the poor. During Ramadan, work output falls off markedly, which is attributable as much to the Muslims' loss of sleep from the many late-night feasts and celebrations—as to the rigors of fasting. The average family actually spends more money on the food consumed at night during Ramadan than on the food consumed by day in the other months. Other spending rises also. Spending during Ramadan has been said to equal six months of normal spending, corresponding to the Christmas season elsewhere. Sales increases of 20 to 40 percent of furniture, cars, jewelry, and other large or expensive items are common. One firm stated that between 35 and 40 percent of all auto sales take place during Ramadan.

By almsgiving, the Muslim shares with the poor. It is an individual responsibility, and there are both required alms (*zakat*) and free-will gifts. The pilgrimage to Mecca is a well-known aspect of Islam. The thousands who gather in Mecca each year return home with a greater sense of the international solidarity of Islam. Spending for the pilgrimage is a special form of consumption directly associated with religious behavior.

There is a relationship between culture and law. Behavior deemed acceptable or not acceptable is often reflected in the laws of a nation or group of people. The tie between religion and law is perhaps most clear in Islam. With respect to business, Muslims are not allowed to consume pork or alcohol. Furthermore, people are not allowed to invest in firms whose primary business involves alcohol, defense, entertainment, gambling, or the manufacture of or processes using pork products. Under Shari'a law, investors are not allowed to hold any stake in conventional banks or insurance companies because these institutions are believed to engage in usurious practices that are illegal. Even the ability to own stock or shares in companies with large amounts of debt or that make annual interest payments is being called into question. While there is some tolerance for investing in these companies, devout Muslims point out that this is a breach of Shari'a rules against usury.

Japan: Shinto, Buddhism, and Confucianism

Japan is a homogeneous culture with a composite religious tradition. The original national religion is Shinto, "the way of the gods." In the seventh century, however, Japan came under the influence of China and imported an eclectic Buddhism mingled with Confucianism. In 604, Prince Shotoku issued a moral code based on the teachings of both Confucius and Gautama Buddha. Its 17 articles still form the basis of Japanese behavior. The adoption of the religions from China was only after the authorities decided they would not conflict with Shinto.

Traditional Shinto contains elements of ancestor and nature worship; state or modern Shinto added political and patriotic elements. Official estimates of 90 million Japanese Buddhists are somewhat misleading. An old refrain is that Japanese are born Shinto, get married as Christians, and die as Buddhists. Figures on followers of Buddhism in Japan vary widely, from 20 to 90 percent of the Japanese population. (The high figures are based on birth records and on Buddhism being the "preferred religion" in a response to research questions posed; the low figures incorporate the response of up to 75 percent of Japanese who claim to be nonreligious.)

Among the more important aspects of modern Shinto are (1) reverence for the divine origin of the Japanese people and (2) reverence for the Japanese nation and the imperial family as head of that nation. The term "modern Shinto" is used because when the imperial powers were restored in 1868, state Shinto became a patriotic cult, whereas sectarian Shinto was purely religious. Of course, sectarian Shinto, through ancestor worships, also affects Japanese attitudes. In many houses, there is a god-shelf (*kamidana*) on which the spirits of the family ancestors are thought to dwell and watch over the affairs of the family. Reverence is paid to them, and the sense of the ancestors' spirit is a bulwark of the family's authority over the individual.

The impact of modern Shinto on Japanese life is reflected in an aggressive patriotism. The mobilization of the Japanese of World War II and their behavior during the war are examples. One longtime observer said, "Nationalism is the Japanese religion." More recently, the economic performance of Japan is due, at least in part, to the patriotic attitude of those working in the economic enterprise. The family spirit is carried over to the firm, which has meant greater cooperation and productivity. Some Eastern religion seeks virtue through passivity. Shinto, by contrast, stresses the search for progress through creative activity. Japan's economic performance clearly seems to follow the Shinto path. The aggressive Japanese attitude is reflected in the company song of Kyocera, a Japanese firm.

> As the sun rises brilliantly in the sky, revealing the size of the mountains,
> The market, oh, this is our goal.
> With the highest degree of mission in our heart, we serve our industry,
> Meeting the strictest degree of customer requirement.
> We are the leader in this industry, and our true path
> Is ever so bright and satisfying.

Christianity

Christianity is a major religion worldwide, and little time will be spent describing its general teachings. The emphasis here is the impact of the different Christian religious groups (Roman Catholic and Protestant) on economic attitudes and behavior. Two studies have dealt with this subject: Max Weber's *The*

Protestant Ethic and the Spirit of Capitalism and R. H. Tawney's *Religion and the Rise of Capitalism*. The Eastern Orthodox churches are not discussed in this section, but their impact on economic attitudes is similar to that of Catholicism.

Roman Catholic Christianity traditionally has emphasized the Church and the sacraments as the principal elements of religion and the way to God. The Church and its priests are intermediaries between God and human beings; apart from the Church, there is no salvation. Another element is the distinction between the members of religious orders and the laity, with different standards of conduct applied to each. An implicit difference exists between the secular and the religious life.

The Protestant Reformation, especially Calvinism, made some critical changes in emphasis, but retained agreement with Catholicism on most traditional Christian doctrine. The Protestants, however, stressed that the Church, its sacraments, and its clergy were not essential to salvation: "Salvation is by faith alone." The result of this was a downgrading of the role of the Church and a consequent upgrading of the role of the individual. Salvation became more of an individual matter.

Another change by the reformers was the elimination of the distinction between secular and religious life. Luther said that all of life was a *Beruf*, a "calling," and even the performance of tasks considered secular was a religious obligation. Calvin carried this further by emphasizing the need to glorify God through ones calling. Whereas works were necessary to salvation in Catholicism, works were evidence of salvation in Calvinism.

Hard work was enjoined to glorify God, achievement was the evidence of hard work, and thrift was necessary because the produced wealth was not to be used selfishly. Accumulation of wealth, capital formation, and the desire for greater production became Christian duty. The Protestant Reformation thus led to greater emphasis on individualism and action (hard work), as contrasted with the more ritualistic and contemplative approach of Catholicism.

Although it is useful to recognize the separate thrust of Roman Catholic and Protestant Christianity, it is also important to note the various roles Christianity generally plays in different nations. Some nations reflect varying mixtures of Catholic and Protestant, and the resulting ethic may become a combination of both doctrines. Of course, within Christianity (as with Buddhism, Hinduism, and Islam), wide variations exist in the degree to which adherents follow the teachings. In all groups, segments range from fundamentalist to conservative to casual.

Religion and the Economy

In discussing various religions, some economic implications were suggested that will be elaborated on here. Religion has a major impact on attitudes toward economic matters. The following section, Attitudes and Values, will discuss the different attitudes religion may inspire. Besides attitudes, however, religion may affect the economy more directly, as in the following examples.

- Religious holidays vary greatly among countries—not only from Christian to Muslim but also from one Christian country to another. In general, Sundays are a religious holiday where Christianity is an important religion. In the Muslim world, however, the entire month of Ramadan is a religious holiday for practical purposes. A firm must see that local work schedules and other programs take into account local holidays, just as American firms plan for a big season at Christmas.

- Consumption patterns may be affected by religious requirements or taboos. Fish on Friday for Catholics used to be a classic example. Taboos against beef for Hindus or pork for Muslims and Jews are other examples. The Muslim prohibition against alcohol has been a boon to companies such as Coca-Cola. Heineken and other brewers sell a nonalcoholic beer in Saudi Arabia. On the other hand, dairy products find favor among Hindus, many of whom are vegetarians.

- The economic role of women varies from culture to culture, and religious beliefs are an important cause. Women may be restricted in their capacity as consumers, as workers, or as respondents in a marketing study. These differences may require major adjustments in the approach of a management conditioned in the U.S. market.

    Procter & Gamble's products are used mainly by women. When the company wanted to conduct a focus group in Saudi Arabia, however, it could not induce women to participate. Instead, it used the husbands and brothers of women for the focus group.

- The caste system restricts participation in the economy. A company may feel the effects not only in its staffing practices (especially its sales force) but also in its distribution and promotional programs because it must deal with the market segments set up by the caste system.

- The Hindu joint family has economic effects. Nepotism is characteristic of the family business. Staffing is based more on considerations of family rank than on any other criteria. Furthermore, consumer decision making and consumption in the joint family may differ from those in the U.S. family, requiring an adapted strategy. Pooled income in the joint family may lead to different purchase patterns.

- Religious institutions themselves may play a role in economic matters. The church, or any organized religious group, may block the introduction of new products or techniques if it sees the innovation as a threat. On the other hand, the same product or technique can be more effectively introduced if the religious organization sees it as a benefit. The United States has seen the growing role of religious groups. This is true in other countries too, as one can see by following the daily news and business press.

- Religious divisions in a country can pose problems for management. A firm may find that it is dealing with different markets. In Northern Ireland, there is strong Catholic-Protestant hostility. In India, Muslim-Hindu clashes led to the formation of the separate nation of Pakistan; but the animosity continues. In the Netherlands, major Catholic and Protestant groups have their own political parties and newspapers. Such religious divisions can cause difficulty in staffing an operation or in distributing and promoting a product. Religious differences may indicate buyer segments that require separate strategies.

Clearly, an international firm must be sensitive to religious differences in its foreign markets and be willing to make adaptations. To cite one example, a firm that is building a plant abroad might plan the date and method of opening and dedicating the building to reflect the local religious situation. In particular, a firm's advertising, packaging, and selling practices need to consider local religious sensitivities.

ATTITUDES AND VALUES

People's attitudes and values help determine what they think is right or appropriate, what is important, and what is desirable. The attitudes that relate to business will be presented. It is important to consider attitudes and values because, as Douglas North, the Nobel Prize–winning economist said, "People act on the basis of ideologies and religious views." People have attitudes and values about work, money, time, family, age, men, women, and a host of other topics that have an impact on business. The list is long; only those topics most important for business will be highlighted here.

Business Activities

Ever since Aristotle, selling activities have failed to gain high social approval. The degree of disapproval, however, varies from country to country. In countries where business is looked upon unfavorably, as a wicked or immoral profession, business activities are likely to be neglected and underdeveloped. Capable, talented people are not drawn into business. Often these activities are left to a special class or to expatriates. One is reminded of the medieval banking role filled by Jews or the merchant role of the Chinese in Southeast Asia. In any case, depending on a country's attitude toward business, an international firm may have problems with personnel, distribution channels, and other aspects of its marketing program.

Wealth, Material Gain, and Acquisition

The United States has been called the "affluent society," the "achieving society," and the "acquisitive society." Those somewhat synonymous expressions reflect motivating values in society. In the United States, wealth and acquisition are often considered signs of success and achievement and are given social approval. In a Buddhist or Hindu society, where nirvana or "wantlessness" is an ideal, people may not be so motivated to produce and consume. Businesses obviously prefer to operate in an acquisitive society. However, as a result of rising expectations around the world, national differences in attitudes toward acquisition seem to be lessening. For example, Buddhist Thailand is proving to be a profitable market for many consumer goods firms.

Work may be an end unto itself for some people, and one's position with a particular organization may be an important measure of the person's social status. For others, family, leisure time, and friends take precedence over money and position. German and French workers have gone on strike and even rioted over plans to extend their workweek beyond 35 hours, to cut paid vacation time, or to raise the age that one becomes qualified for retirement benefits.

Change

When a company enters a foreign market, it brings change by introducing new ways of doing things and new products. In general, North Americans accept change easily. The word "new" has a favorable connotation and facilitates change when used to describe techniques and products. Many societies are more tradition oriented, however, revering their ancestors and traditional ways of consuming.

Business as an agent of change has a different task in traditional societies. Rather than emphasizing what is new and different about a product, the business might relate the product to traditional values, perhaps noting that it is a better way of solving a consumer problem. In seeking acceptance of its new product, a firm might try to get at least a negative clearance—that is, no objection—from local religious leaders or other opinion leaders. Any product must first meet a market need. Beyond that, however, to be accepted the product must also fit in with the overall value system.

The Campbell Soup Company met this kind of obstacle when it introduced its canned soups into Italy. In conducting research, it received an overwhelmingly negative response to the question, "Would you marry a user of prepared soups?" Campbell had to adjust its questionnaire accordingly.

Risk Taking

Consumers take risks when they try a new product. Will the product do what they expect it to do? Will purchasing or using the product prejudice their standing or image with their peers? Intermediaries handling the untried product may also face risks beyond those associated with their regular line. In a conservative society, there is a greater reluctance to take such risks. Therefore a firm must seek to reduce the risk perceived by customers or distributors in trying a new product. In part, this can be accomplished through education; guarantees, consignment selling, and other techniques can also be used.

Risk avoidance is a major factor in the low number of online shoppers. While the number of users is growing exponentially, a recent survey found that one-third of Internet users did not shop online because they did not want to risk providing credit card information over the Internet. One-quarter of those surveyed believed it was safer to purchase at a retail shop. The number of Internet users who are also online shoppers is highest—between 15 and 25 percent—among developed nations, and lowest—below 5 percent—among developing nations. Recent research indicates that this differs from one culture to another, but this may also be a reflection of different use patterns; that is, some people use the Internet for entertainment or research, while others use it for shopping.

Consumer Behavior

The attitudes just discussed are relevant to understanding consumer behavior in the markets of the world. International managers must have such an understanding to develop effective programs. Because of the impossibility of gaining intimate knowledge of a great number of markets, they must rely not only on company research but also on help from others. Those who can assist managers in understanding local attitudes and behavior include personnel in the firm's subsidiary, the distributor, and the advertising agency. Although a firm is interested in changing attitudes, most often it has to adapt to them. As Confucius said, "It is easier to move mountains than to change the minds of men."

AESTHETICS

Aesthetics refers to the prevalent ideas in a culture concerning beauty and good tastes, as expressed in the arts—music, art, drama, and dance—and the appreciation of color and form. International differences abound in aesthetics, but they tend to be regional rather than national. For example, Kabuki theater is exclusively Japanese, but Western theater includes at least all of Western Europe in addition to the United States and Canada in its audience.

Musical tastes, too, tend to be regional rather than national. In the West, many countries enjoy the same classical and popular music. In fact, due to modern communications, popular music has become truly international. Nevertheless, obvious differences exist between Western music and music of the Middle East, Africa, or India. Likewise, the dance styles of African tribal groups or the Balinese are quite removed from Western dance styles. The beauty of India's Taj Mahal is different from that of Notre Dame in Paris or the Chrysler Building in New York City.

Design

The aesthetics of a culture probably do not have a major impact on economic activities. In aesthetics, however, lie some implications for international business. For example, in the design of its plant, product, or package, a firm should be sensitive to local aesthetic preferences. This may run counter to the desire for international uniformity, but the firm must be aware of the positive and negative aspects of its designs. Generally, Asians appreciate complex and decorative styles, particularly when it comes to gift wrapping, for instance.

A historical example of a lack of cultural sensitivity is illustrated by early Christian missionaries from Western nations who were often guilty of architectural "imperialism." The Christian churches built in many non-Western nations usually reflected Western rather than indigenous architectural ideas. This was not done with malicious intent, but because the missionaries were culture-bound in their aesthetics; that is, they had their own ideas about what a church should look like.

The U.S. government faces a similar problem in designing its embassies. The U.S. Embassy in India received praise both for its beauty as a building and for the way it blended with Indian architecture. The U.S. Embassy in London, however, has received more than its share of criticism, including comments about the size of the sculpted American eagle on top of the building. Some Britons also took exception to the architecture of the London Hilton. For a firm, the best policy is to design and decorate its buildings and commercial vehicles to reflect local aesthetic preferences. In its thousands of outlets abroad, McDonald's has learned to adapt its facilities to local tastes.

Color

The significance of different colors also varies from culture to culture. In the United States, for instance, people use colors to identify emotional reactions; people "see red," they are "green with envy," and they "feel blue." Black signifies mourning in Western countries, whereas white is often the color of mourning in Eastern nations. Green is popular in Muslim countries, while red and black have a negative connotation in several African countries. Red is an appealing and lucky color in China, blue sometimes suggests evil, and yellow is often associated with authority. Certain colors have particular meanings because of religious, patriotic, or aesthetic reasons. Businesspeople need to know the significance of colors in a culture when planning their company's products and the products' packaging. For any market, the choice of colors should be related to the aesthetic sense of the buyer's culture rather than that of the manager's culture. Generally, the colors of the country's flag are safe colors. Japan has a Study

Group for Colors in Public Places. It wages war on "color pollution," and its mission is "to seek out better uses for color, to raise the issue of colors."

Music

There are also cultural differences in music. An understanding of these differences is critical in creating advertising messages that use music. The music of non-literate cultures is generally functional, or has significance in the people's daily lives, whereas the music of literate cultures tends to be separate from people's other concerns. For example, a Western student has to learn to "understand" a Beethoven symphony, but aborigines assimilate musical culture as an integral part of their existence. Ethnomusicologist William Malm stated that understanding the symbolism in different kinds of music requires considerable cultural conditioning. Therefore homogeneity in music throughout the world cultures is not possible. There are exceptions, of course, but one implication for a firm is that wherever it utilizes music, it should use music of the local culture. Recognizing the importance of music in popular culture, companies such as Coca-Cola, PepsiCo, and Nike are frequent sponsors of events such as MTV Video Music Awards Latin America and WOMAD (Festival of World Music, Arts & Dance).

NOTE

1. "Calling across the Divide," *The Economist*, March 12, 2005, 11.

CHAPTER 14

GLOBAL VALUE-ADDED STRATEGIES

John Caslione

INTRODUCTION

In today's competitive marketplace, successful companies develop *value-added strategies* to build and sustain important customer-supplier relationships, relationships that rise above the traditional confines of both product and price. Both customer and supplier share a common vision: to engage in innovative strategies to enhance their respective long-term profitability in a spirit of mutual self-interest.

Too often, however, suppliers and customers alike have a tendency to become a bit greedy in their approach to each other, forgetting that the most successful business relationships are founded upon the concept that both parties find value in working together from the very beginning.

After years of feeling as though they have been giving away too much value to customers in the form of value-adding services, many suppliers are now adopting a misguided and short-term strategy in which they attempt to charge the customer for every service provided. This classic "cafeteria"-style pricing approach is nothing more than turning virtually everything that the supplier provides to a customer into a chargeable product or service.

This is not a strategy at all; it is just another desperate attempt by corporate finance departments to wrest every last dollar from their customers under the justification that all things of value provided to customers should result in direct and immediate revenue for the supplier.

A similar situation exists on the customer's side, but with a different directional flow. With the economic slowdown, it seems that customers are trying to take the quick and easy way to meet their company's challenged profit streams. They pressure their suppliers by extracting price reductions first, and then maybe, if the customer is sophisticated enough, by thinking about true cost reductions.

Both supplier and customer must temper their eagerness for quick, short-term gains and look to attack the true enemy for them both: their common operating expenses. Even with today's ultra-short-term focus on profits, both are significantly better off using their respective core competencies to lower each other's operating costs in a spirit of true alliance: a *strategic supplier alliance* initiated by the supplier.

LUCENT TECHNOLOGIES AND DIGITAL CHINA

Digital China, a spin-off of Legend Group Ltd. in 2000, was listed on the Hong Kong Stock Exchange in 2001. The company embraces innovation to provide first-tier products, solutions, and services for e-commerce infrastructure. Digital China is currently the largest IT products distributor and systems integrator in China.

Lucent Technologies, with its headquarters in Murray Hill, New Jersey, designs and delivers the systems, services, and software that drive next-generation communications networks. Backed by Bell Labs research and development, Lucent uses its strengths in mobility, optical, software, data and voice networking technologies, as well as services to create new revenue-generating opportunities for its customers while enabling them to quickly deploy and better manage their networks.

Lucent Technologies and Digital China formed the strategic supplier alliance in 2004. This is a win-win solution. The alliance allows Digital China to become the exclusive general distributor of Lucent's network management software to enterprises in mainland China. Lucent will be able to influence the network of resellers and agents across the United States to provide a broader range of software products and related services to Chinese service providers and enterprises. This will help the Chinese enterprises migrate toward next-generation networking technologies, while minimizing the overall network operations costs for everyone involved.

Digital China has already established a channel network consisting of more than 3,500 integrators, agents, and industrial customers, backed by its strong capabilities in technical support, after-sale maintenance, and customer training. Lucent offers network management software with cutting-edge technologies that best support Digital China's strategy in growing value-added businesses. By forming this strategic alliance, Digital China manages to deliver more products and value-added services to Chinese customers.

Suppliers that engage in real value-added strategy have the freedom to charge a premium for their products and services and refrain from reducing prices. These suppliers often charge a premium because the value they deliver to customers, in the form of increased bottom-line profits, routinely far exceeds the price of the charged premium.

DEVELOPING A GLOBAL CUSTOMER SERVICE STRATEGY

Enlightened customers engaging in such value-adding relationships are typically at the forefront of their industries. While these customers often pay a premium for the products and services their suppliers provide, the overall cost of doing business together may be among the lowest in their respective industries. The customers' selection of suppliers represents the best, most profitable business decisions that these customers can make for their businesses to build market share, increase revenues, and enhance profitability for today and also for the long term.

As both customer and supplier work together, their common vision enables each to rise above the primal desire to operate using traditional competitive product and pricing strategies. Instead, these companies strive to work together in a customer-supplier relationship dedicated to pursuing long-term high profitability for both, in a relationship called a strategic supplier alliance.

For example, a supplier of seals used in automatic transmissions knew that its customers, the major auto manufacturers, were incurring high warranty costs for failed transmissions under warranty. No transmission component supplier in the industry, including the auto manufacturers themselves, knew exactly why the transmissions failed all the time. Some failures were obvious as to the cause, while other failures were not so obvious. In the ambiguous situations, by default, the seal manufacturers were routinely blamed for the failure.

Tired of working in such a contentious environment, one highly motivated U.S.-based seal manufacturer created a customized database to collect data and information from one of their customer's three repositories of failed transmissions, where transmissions were dismantled and tested.

The supplier's goal was to uncover the reasons why faulty transmissions failed, and then to provide recommendations to the customer on how to reduce transmission failures and consequently reduce the high warranty costs. Specifically, the seal supplier used this database for its own organization to develop a special knowledge to know how and why transmissions failed all the time.

With this valuable knowledge and the ability to provide profit improvement recommendations to the customer, the seal manufacturer was able to directly reduce warranty costs by more than $50 million in the first year alone. This seal supplier provided all of this information at no additional charge to one of its carefully selected customers, one of the few customers dedicated to pursuing long-term strategic supplier relationships.

Not surprisingly, this automobile manufacturer promptly gave the seal supplier an exclusive supply contract on its next three transmission platforms for the next five years. Despite paying a slight premium for this supplier's seals, doing business with this particular supplier represented the best, most profitable business decision that the auto manufacturer could make in choosing its seal supplier. And, unlike most of its competitors in a price-driven industry, this auto manufacturer made its decision based upon lowest total cost and highest overall profitability rather than lowest product price.

WHAT IS "VALUE-ADDED"?

True value-added strategy goes above and beyond the product level to create a strategic relationship between the two companies. The product itself does not change, and in fact, it sometimes becomes almost incidental to the customer-supplier relationship.

Value-added strategies are based on the supplier's competencies and other areas of expertise as an organization. They are designed to provide high value to a selected customer's bottom line, versus merely seeking to "add value" to the individual products and services it sells. It is a supplier's organizational value rather than its product or service value that is at the core of value-added strategies.

From the customer's perspective, a value-added strategy enhances profitability. The supplier develops projects and programs that boost the customer's profits in one or more of three ways:

1. Enhancing customer's revenues

2. Reducing customer's current costs

3. Avoiding customer's future costs

Whether a supplier achieves one, two, or all three of these objectives, the result is that it improves the customer's bottom line. A value-added strategy focuses on achieving these objectives by utilizing core competencies or other areas of special expertise in the supplier's organization to materially benefit the customer's profitability.

VALUE-ADDED VERSUS ADDED-VALUE

A value-added strategy should not be confused with an added-value sales approach to marketing products and services. While many companies use the terms interchangeably, the difference between the two is significant. It is also essential that companies understand the difference between the two; otherwise value-added cannot be used effectively to develop marketing differentiation strategy.

With added-value, a company focuses on the same objective as in a value-added strategy, namely improving the customer's bottom line, but it does so by increasing the tangible benefits a customer receives from using the actual products and services the supplier sells. In other words, the supplier's product or service is still the source of the value delivered, such as increased customer revenues or reduced or avoided customer costs.

For example, if a supplier's product has lower installation costs and lower life-time maintenance costs, these are added-value product benefits, because the source of the value to the customer emanates from the product itself.

This approach does indeed add value, and it makes sense to position products and services sold that way. But customers typically do not perceive one company's product and service offerings to be highly differentiated from another's, especially when they look at the suppliers' product and service portfolios in their entirety.

Today, there increasingly exists product and service parity in customers' eyes. Even if a supplier has great technology or a tremendously valuable product, its biggest and best competitors probably have similar and comparable products. If they do not, it will not be very long before they do, wiping out any competitive advantage that the original supplier had.

Competitive parity of products typically exists between most suppliers' products and services today. Any customer value that may be derived from products is largely the same; the playing field is virtually level. This ultimately leads to more "commoditization" of product and service offerings in the marketplace, which in turn creates increased supplier frustration. They then dismiss the power of value-added strategies, largely because they are mistakenly engaging in added-value sales, which is product-based differentiation in its marketing differentiation strategy and not true value-added strategy.

In today's highly competitive and technology-driven environment, companies must begin to understand and finally accept that product-oriented strategies can no longer provide suppliers with any meaningful or sustainable differentiation from their competition beyond the short to medium term.

A value-added strategy helps overcome the issue of product parity by taking the customer-supplier relationship to a higher level. Value-added strategies connect the two companies at the organizational level, not the product level. Value-added is organizationally based value, creating a relationship between supplier and customer through the development of multiple cross-functional department relationships and through the integration of intercompany systems and processes.

If effectively applied in marketing strategy, the competitive advantages gained by a supplier are not easily replicated and can become a sustainable competitive advantage over several years.

In executing value-added strategy, company size does not matter as much as one might think. In the example of the seal manufacturer, its fiercest competitor, a global company with six times more in revenue, is unable to pursue a similar strategy because its management and company culture pursues a product-based differentiation strategy that strives to differentiate by offering a wide product line at discounted prices. At the time of this writing, the gap between the two seal suppliers has closed to less than four times in revenue due to the success of the value-added supplier's increased share of the market.

Because so few companies understand the value-added approach, let alone have the kind of company culture needed to implement it, significant opportunities to differentiate from the competition await suppliers willing to take the more difficult road by pursuing a value-added approach.

TOTAL VALUE PROPOSITION = VALUE-ADDED + ADDED-VALUE

Countless business books have been written about value-added and added-value, and most of these books offer different and conflicting definitions of the two. Still more talk about the "total value proposition" and usually fail to tie together a clear and concise definition that is both tangible and easy to explain. There should be little mystery or disagreement about what comprises a supplier's total value proposition if one provides clear definitions of value-added and added-value. Both enhance the customer's revenues, reduce current operating costs, and avoid future operating costs of the customer. They just approach it from two different and distinct directions.

Simply, a supplier's total value proposition is the sum total of the value its products (added-value) bring to the customer and the value that the supplier's organization brings (value-added) to this same customer; in other words, product value plus organizational value equals a supplier's total value proposition.

EXAMPLES OF VALUE-ADDED STRATEGIES

United Parcel Service, USA

At United Parcel Service, a core competency is their understanding and application of information and communications technology. It is unparalleled in the industry and could otherwise match up with even the most successful telecommunications supplier. This expertise came in very handy recently with one of UPS's largest global accounts.

UPS's global account manager (GAM), responsible for the global account of a major European electronics company, had uncovered that this customer was in the early planning stages of building a new, state-of-the-art manufacturing facility for one of its divisions. As part of this effort, this division was preparing to contract with a telecommunications consultancy in Europe to write the technical specifications for a tender (request for proposal). The tender, once developed, would then be let to one of the major telecommunications providers, e.g., Nortel, Lucent, etc.

Learning of this opportunity, the UPS GAM for the account offered to provide UPS's own telecommunications consultants to write the specifications for the tender at no additional charge to the company. After a bit of initial skepticism with such a generous offer, the customer eventually agreed.

UPS then dedicated four of its telecommunications consultants for a period of almost three months to complete the task, saving this particular customer division over $660,000 in avoided telecommunications consultancy costs.

What did UPS gain for all their effort? They more than doubled their account share within this customer division to more than 80 percent of business in that division that next year. Pursuing similar value-added strategies, they also went on to achieve sizeable increases in sales and account share within other divisions of this same global customer.

British Sugar Ltd., Europe

One of the ultimate commodity products in the world is sugar. Companies have tried unsuccessfully for decades to differentiate their sugar from that of their competitors. UK-based British Sugar Ltd. succeeded in differentiating sugar by not even trying. They ignored their product and focused upon other sources of value within their organization that they could provide.

British Sugar's value-added strategy was founded upon two key value-added contributions.

Leverage Consulting Expertise

The first strategic value-added contribution involved making use of the environmental consultancy expertise that they had developed over the years for internal use. Many of British Sugar's customers are in the food-processing industry and, like British Sugar, had an ongoing problem of treating environmental waste resulting from the processing of sugar as well as in the processing of foods.

As part of its strategy, British Sugar offered its environmental consultancy to a selected group of six strategically important customers at no additional charge. All six customers who received the offer accepted. Each was able to significantly reduce and avoid considerable costs in their businesses almost from the first day. Some customers no longer needed to pay outside consultants for these services, and some eventually eliminated the need to maintain an internal environmental consulting department altogether.

Sell Excess Capacity

The second involved selling excess capacity of electricity to this same select group of six customers. One of British Sugar's major cost drivers is electricity (a "20/80 cost"). Years earlier, when the UK was going through its own deregulation of the electric utility industry, as the United States is currently doing, British Sugar had acquired a power generation company for its own exclusive energy generation and consumption.

Over time, it found that it had more potential power than it could use in its own operations. Instead of selling it outright for a profit, executive management decided to offer its excess capacity at cost to this same group of six strategic customers, and not one pence (cent) more. The price offered to these customers, British Sugar's actual cost, was 70 percent below the lowest wholesale price in the industry. It was also estimated that this excess capacity of electricity would be enough to satisfy anywhere from 25 to 35 percent of the six customers' needs at their UK-based facilities.

When offered this opportunity to purchase electricity at a much-reduced price, all six customers were interested, especially after the very positive experience with British Sugar assuming the responsibility for environmental consultancy within their companies.

What was in this for British Sugar? Quite a lot. Not only did all six customers give either all or most of their business to British Sugar, but British Sugar was able to demand a premium price for the sugar they sold to these customers. Moreover, it gained a tremendous amount of control over its business within the customers' businesses.

For example, as a condition under UK law, in order for British Sugar to effectively "sell" electricity at its cost, it must have a British Sugar office inside every facility that consumes its electricity. This meant that, as part of the agreement with these customers, there needed to be a British Sugar office inside each of these customers' locations that consumed British Sugar's electricity.

In the world of strategic or global account management, such a cohabitation arrangement is invaluable for the supplier to increase its business in the customer account and to maintain control of its business in that account over the long term.

Some people believe that British Sugar should have made a small profit by charging a slightly higher price for its electricity. Would these same British Sugar customers still be interested in buying electricity if British Sugar offered it at 50 percent below the lowest wholesale price versus 70 percent?

Certainly they would, but two potentially dangerous things would likely happen if they did begin to sell their excess electricity:

First, if British Sugar charged any price above its actual costs, then under UK regulatory law it would have to begin to create a number of reports and filings and routinely submit these to the government. This would have created a lot of new internal expenses and a need to staff new departments.

Second, a more insidious problem, such an approach would defocus management from their core business—sugar—and on to an entirely new and different industry: electricity. Such a shift into a new complex industry in which they were novices meant that British Sugar really could not compete successfully long term unless it wanted to refocus its current driving forces from that of a manufacturer and marketer of sugar to a full-time generator and marketer of electricity. Attempting to do both would likely jeopardize the success of both, and British Sugar's executive management was unwilling to take such a dangerous step.

INTERNATIONAL TRADING COMPANIES

The international trading operating system in China is changing dramatically. International trading companies, which used to specialize in sales and marketing, now have started to develop their manufacturing branches in order to provide value-added services to its customers. These trading companies have managed to establish strategic relationships with their customers, obtaining accurate understandings of their needs. This is an effective strategy, because customers tend to pay more attention to the value-added services that the suppliers can bring to them.

Shartex International Trading Co., a Shanghai-based trading company, established its research and development (R&D) center, engaging in market trend projection, raw-material proportion, product design, and product sample development. This enables the company to improve the efficiency of product renovation, hence significantly reducing the time that customers usually spend examining the sample products.

Another international trading company, located in Beijing, specializes in hand-crafted products selected from a supplying base of over 10 manufacturing factories in Jiangsu and Zhejiang provinces. These 10 factories are responsible for manufacturing the products to meet the requirement and demand of the trading company, while the trading company is responsible for the sales of these products to its major customer, a large-scale retailer from South America. By simply contacting the trading company, customers are able to complete their purchasing tasks. The suppliers are able to expand their market share by providing these value-added services to the customers.

WHAT ABOUT VALUE-ADDED IN A SERVICES COMPANY?

About a year ago when I was conducting a value-added marketing and sales management workshop in Europe, a participant asked me how to apply value-added strategy in a services company and not just a product company. My answer was simple. I asked her to truly understand what services her company is currently providing at a specified price, and then determine which of these services should become value-added contributions, or services without charge.

This participant provided a great example. She was the senior marketing and sales director for the largest and most prestigious advertising and communications services agency in Germany. She shared with all of us in the workshop group her company's current marketing dilemma.

There were five major companies in Germany that they were unable to really break into to do a lot of business. The problem was always the same. In this industry, the marketing director was the equivalent of most companies' purchasing director, and the marketing director routinely prevented access by ad agencies and other suppliers to the company president. Although this ad agency was doing some business with these clients, it was a fraction of the potential that they could be doing.

In the seminar I asked if her company offered speech mentoring and speech writing as a service in her company. She immediately replied that they did and that although they were viewed as the best in Germany in providing this service, it was never a big revenue generator.

After hearing her answer, I offered her a challenge. I told her to send a letter to the presidents of five clients offering private, personalized speech mentoring at no cost to them under a special program with "exclusive clients."

I also instructed her to continue reinforcing this offer every few weeks for at least three months. Finally, I made her promise to notify me at the end of the three months and then after six months with a progress report.

At the end of the second month, she contacted me to tell me that three of the five presidents had accepted their offer and had begun their one-on-one, personalized speech-mentoring classes. She proceeded to tell me that within a matter of weeks, a great deal of rapport was developed between each client president and his or her personal speech coach.

Not long afterward, the marketing directors from each of these client companies had begun to invite this agency in to bid on more and more business. And even though this agency was usually higher priced than most of its competitors in the bidding process, the agency had begun to quickly increase its business in all three clients.

The agency always had this tool available to them. At the same time, they never recognized it for what it was, a powerful value-added contribution. Speech mentoring now was a valuable asset that could open doors otherwise inaccessible if they had kept it in their traditional portfolio of services for sale. The same is true for product companies with the services that they sell.

USING VALUE-ADDED STRATEGY IN A TARGETED MARKET SEGMENT

In the telecommunications industry throughout the 1990s, the long-distance providers began to encounter a problem called "churning," in which small-business and residential customers would change long-distance carriers, sometimes monthly, to take advantage of promotional discounts and other pricing incentives.

AT&T was one such company that was victimized by the widespread churning in the marketplace, until one day when one of its suppliers presented them with an innovative strategy to help regain customer loyalty and minimize churning.

AT&T SOHO Division

To market to and service small businesses with fewer than 100 employees, AT&T created a dedicated group called the Small Office/Home Office (SOHO) division. This department was charged with the responsibility to build the market share in this fast-growing customer segment that was very vulnerable to being "churned" by competitors. Needless to say, in this very price-conscious segment of the business, churning became almost "sport" for a many SOHO small-business customers.

A woman whose husband became a victim of a downsizing initiative of his company in the late 1990s relayed a story to me in one of my executive marketing seminars. Her husband had over 25 years of employment with his company and found it difficult to land a new job, so, like so many other middle-aged unemployed business executives, he became a consultant. Having recently seen their last of four children off to college, he converted one of their now vacant bedrooms in their home into his business office. He proceeded to begin his new and exciting career in consulting.

AT&T SOHO Division wanted this man's long-distance business, as did all of AT&T's competitors. Over time, it had become increasingly difficult to differentiate long-distance "dial tone" and, not surprisingly, the industry had become commoditized with price discounting running rampant.

As a result, there was little price difference between suppliers in this industry; the spread between the highest priced and the lowest priced competitors was typically less than 5 percent. This created especially tight operating margins when the average SOHO customer working out of his or her home spent less than $200 each month on his or her long-distance service.

As the story goes, one of AT&T's suppliers of office products proposed an innovative value-added strategy to AT&T in an effort to help it stem the increasing trend of churning. It seemingly caught the attention of the right AT&T executive and led to the development of a full-blown value-added strategy.

The recently unemployed company executive, now-turned-consultant, was offered a full package of inducements if he would sign a one-year service agreement with AT&T. The package included all of the following value-added contributions from AT&T at no additional charge:

- An offer to provide a customized office design to make the most efficient and effective utilization of space within the consultant's "office"

- The ability to purchase everything from computer and office furniture, office supplies, courier and shipping services, etc., at AT&T's steep volume price discounts

- The ability to take advantage of AT&T's discounted group health and life insurance, which would save the consultant several hundreds of dollars each month after his former employer's extended insurance coverage ran out

- A list of accountants and bookkeepers that specialize in working with small businesses in the consultant's local area

The consultant was provided several hundreds, or even thousands, of dollars each year in savings if he was willing to commit to AT&T for one year. This commitment would require him to pay, at most, a $10 price premium each month, calculated at a rate of 5 percent on $200 each month. When he analyzed the total value proposition that AT&T was providing him, it was an easy and quick decision for him. He signed up immediately and has stayed loyal to AT&T for more than three years now.

In this case study, AT&T's service became almost incidental and even unimportant to the relationship as it was tacitly acknowledged by AT&T that the product of long-distance service was a commodity and nearly impossible to differentiate from the competition.

AT&T approached the situation differently than its competitors. It made some minimal investments in developing this new value-added strategy, and then by engaging its own suppliers to help execute the plan, AT&T created such an attractive total value proposition that it began to reduce the problem of churning and once again regain substantial stability in its small-business customer base.

WHAT IS "VALUE-EXPECTED"?

In my executive management seminars, I am repeatedly asked if there is a logical and inevitable end to value-added contributions; i.e., at some point aren't all value-added contributions likely to be matched by competitors, thus becoming part of the product offering and eliminating any prior competitive advantage by a competitor? The answer is both yes and no.

Certainly, at the very foundation of free competition, if a competitor has a competitive advantage—especially a significant advantage, competitors in the industry will seek ways to minimize or eliminate that advantage. Sometimes when a value-added contribution becomes something that many competitors have matched, it does become part of the combined standard product offering. This is what is called value-expected. Technically it is still value-added, but because it no longer differentiates as it once did, the value-added contribution now becomes an expected value-added contribution, or just value-expected.

A good example of this is supplier-managed inventory (SMI) or vendor-managed inventory (VMI), wherein a supplier manages the inventory of its products on behalf of the customer. When it was first introduced in the late 1980s and into the early 1990s, it presented a significant competitive advantage for a number of suppliers in many industries. Beginning in the 1990s in many industries, it became a standard service offering, and soon it was considered as a basic component of a supplier's product offering. It became value-expected.

To minimize or delay a value-added contribution from becoming value-expected, two things can and should be considered.

There is a greater likelihood that a supplier can prolong its competitive advantage if it can proactively recommend value-added contributions before the customer even thinks about it. Too often, most suppliers are reactive in this endeavor, and if they do offer a value-added contribution to a customer, it is done for one of two reasons:

1. The first is that a competitor is already providing it to a customer and has gained a competitive advantage. The market's many reactive suppliers then want to minimize their competitor's advantage, thus creating a motivation to match the competitor's same value-added contribution.

2. The second is when the customer asks or demands that the supplier provide the additional service because it will represent a cost savings to the customer. The trouble with this scenario is that when a customer initiates a cost or revenue improvement initiative, a supplier-provided value-added contribution, the customer typically designs it so there is a high level of substitutability in the service requested; i.e., the customer can easily substitute one supplier's value-added contribution for another supplier's value-added contribution.

The key for a supplier is to propose value-added contributions to the marketplace that the customers have not yet even considered. In this way, suppliers can design and engineer their value-added contributions in ways to minimize the degree of substitutability that can exist in the contribution provided. In essence, suppliers can more readily maintain a balanced peer relationship with its customers.

The most effective way to design any value-added contribution to be as nonsubstitutable as possible by a customer is to make the contribution systemic and as integrated as possible between both the customer's and the supplier's many different functional departments and their business operations.

For example, a manufacturer of flour and other mixing and baking ingredients supplied a leading commercial bakery in North America. The flour supplier was noted for its world-class transportation logistics.

However, when the flour manufacturer's trucks unloaded its raw flour and other mixing ingredients at the customer's commercial baking facilities, some of these trucks "deadheaded" back to the supplier's production locations; that is, they traveled back empty. Not surprisingly, the commercial bakery's trucks also did a lot of deadheading back to their sites after they unloaded the finished baked goods at their customer's locations, the major supermarket chains.

The flour manufacturer proposed that a lot of operating costs between both companies could be driven out if the two companies were to merge their transportation logistics functions, and the bakery agreed. By combining the two transportation-scheduling functions, and by utilizing the supplier's expertise in transportation logistics planning, both companies saved millions of dollars each year in operating costs. Moreover, the supplier was able to maintain a high degree of control of its business within the customer's business because it *systematized* the value-added contribution and made it essential to the operation of both companies.

As compelling as it is, if the supplier were to stop here with only this single value-added contribution as part of its strategy, it would be only a matter of time, even if it were an extended period of time, before a competing flour producer would find a way to replicate and eliminate any competitive advantage in the market.

But what the incumbent supplier does have is access to this customer's people and information in key areas of this customer's business that its competitors do not have. With this proprietary access, the supplier has the ability to pursue additional proactive integrations of customer systems and processes.

In doing so and in pursuing a deliberate, cogent strategic supplier alliance strategy, the supplier can create a multitude of such linkages and entanglements, which can integrate the two companies so much that they create tremendously high barriers of entry to competitors. This prevents, or severely hampers, the competitors' ability to gain a foothold into this customer's business.

Likewise, such a series of entanglements will also be critical in creating the high barriers of exit necessary to make it costly and difficult for the customer to substitute this supplier for another.

VALUE-ADDED: KEY TO DEVELOPING ACCESS STRATEGY

Let's examine more closely some of the examples just presented. They underscore the fact that in most companies, the executive management does not know the difference between value-added and added-value. Moreover, they often fail to recognize the difference between what are products and services they should be selling and what is customer service that supports the presales and postsales servicing of the products and services sold.

Even more important, companies are unaware of the value-added contributions they currently or potentially can provide as key components of their total value proposition. These value-added contributions provided by companies facilitate the needed access to people and information within the customer's organization.

When the supplier believes that it has a service that may be of value to a customer, the temptation to put a price tag on it to develop new revenue streams becomes so great that most suppliers end up pricing everything they can. This is almost always a critical mistake.

Imagine three buckets. Also imagine a supplier that understands what should properly go into each of the three buckets. A supplier that understands this is a supplier that can build true strategic market differentiation strategy.

Obviously, the key is to know what rightly goes into each bucket and then how to use each in practical business strategy, particularly value-added contributions.

The fundamental and essential advantage of a value-added contribution is gaining access to people and information in the targeted customer's organization that would otherwise be unattainable by pursuing the traditional sales process. This exclusive access is critical to the successful execution of the supplier's marketing differentiation strategy.

Let's examine the three earlier case study examples.

UPS

In the shipping industry, the customer's traditional buying department typically chooses two suppliers, and then the actual end users of the service in each department of the account are able to use their shipper of choice on a case-by-case basis.

Imagine that UPS's telecommunications consultants have been given free rein to meet with every department manager, every project manager, every secretary, etc., within the account. Also imagine that this is being done as an effort to effectively design the voice/data/video specifications for the new telecommunications system, rather than as an effort to sell traditional UPS shipping services.

Over time, UPS telecommunications experts did this. They dug deep into every department within the European Economic Community (EEC), and along the way built a tremendous amount of rapport with virtually everyone in the EEC who could be a potential decision maker in each department.

It is no wonder that UPS became the shipper of choice in 8 out of 10 times that managers and secretaries had to select their preferred shipper.

British Sugar

Think about all of the customer's different departments and managers that the account team from British Sugar needed to work with to implement the two value-added contributions it offered. With the environmental consultancy at no additional charge, the list of managers in the targeted food-manufacturing company include the plant manager, quality control manager, operations manager, CFO, the legal department, etc. All of these departments are very influential within these organizations, and British Sugar interacted closely with a large number of them.

These managers have a tremendous amount of influence concerning the decision to use or not use British Sugar as a supplier. Furthermore, this is also the group of managers that will be in the best position to consider British Sugar's value-added contributions, and subsequently assess the true total value proposition that British Sugar will bring to their company.

Advertising Agency (Service Company)

As we learned in the example of the German advertising and marketing communications company, the marketing director was the key decision maker, and oftentimes a hindrance in the marketing and sales process. The marketing department routinely withheld access to the client company's president, making it virtually impossible for the ad agency's account managers to develop any real relationship with the client company's president.

Consider that, through this ad agency's value-added contribution, the company president is in a closed room with a speech mentor from the ad agency several times over a month or more. In these sessions, the president allows himself or herself to be exposed to criticisms in a very personal and sensitive area, that of his or her public speaking skills. In addition, the president realizes after a few sessions that there is noticeable improvement of his or her public speaking skills. Imagine the closeness of the relationship and the level of rapport that now exists between the client president and his or her speech mentor.

With such a positive halo effect spilling over to the ad agency overall, it is not surprising that the clients' marketing directors were strongly encouraged to do more business with this particular ad agency, even with their higher fees.

CONCLUSION

With a better understanding of the fundamental differences between value-added and added-value, a company can utilize value-added concepts in strategy development. Knowing how to do this will assist in avoiding the mistakes commonly made by so many companies, the most common one being the development of product-based marketing differentiation strategies that routinely create higher operating costs and encourage even greater price competition.

In fact, many such purported value-adding programs routinely become nothing more than mere "giveaway programs," or programs that provide ever-increasing benefits to customers, but do very little to actually generate any real reciprocal benefits for the supplier.

The flip side of this approach is to put a price tag on all value-added contributions, turning them into nothing more than added-value services to be sold within the supplier's portfolio of products and services. By doing this over the long term, suppliers inadvertently accelerate the commoditization of their product and service offerings, as well as stimulate even more aggressive price discounting in the marketplace.

One might say that if a "value-adding service" provided by a supplier is so valuable, then a customer should be willing to pay for it. Though this makes sense, it is not always the case. The willingness of a customer to pay is "sometimes yes" and "most often no." The question of whether or not to charge for value-adding services holds dire consequences for suppliers that get the answer wrong.

Most often, by charging for a value-added contribution, suppliers inadvertently enter into new and different industries that provide this contribution as one of their primary service offerings. When companies mistakenly begin to offer services for a price that are either tangential or complementary to their core business, they end up shifting their company's driving force and find they are unable to compete in new and different industries, for example, British Sugar and the electric utility industry. The results are usually disastrous, unless the company is willing to make a full commitment to the new industry they are entering, a commitment complete with a long-term plan to compete head-to-head with these new competitors in the new industry.

It is absolutely necessary to understand how to apply value-added contributions in strategy, by utilizing the strategic supplier alliance continuum to develop long-term, sustainable customer-supplier relationships.

It is only a matter of time before more companies acknowledge that they cannot compete on price- or product-based strategy. They must instead forge true value-adding relationships together. Value-added strategies will enable customer and supplier alike to a secure truly beneficial scenario every time.

CHAPTER **15**

GLOBAL CUSTOMER SERVICE

Calin Veghes

INTRODUCTION

The days are long gone when a company can rest on their past laurels with the relative assurance that their customers will not stray to "the other side." A lot of money and resources are spent each year to obtain faithful customers; it would be a shame to risk losing them to poor customer service. Inventory shortages, back orders, and long delivery times can quickly eat up profits with returns and canceled orders. This has been true for some time now, whether a company is only doing business domestically or starting to venture into the new global marketplace. The challenges are certainly compounded, sometimes exponentially, when dealing at the global level.

To maintain and cultivate relationships with existing customers or initiate business with new ones, companies are compelled to constantly and consistently provide the best products, at competitive prices that give the most value and at the highest levels of service possible. Only now, companies must find ways to do all of this on a global level.

As a result of this new decree from the global marketplace, companies need to focus more and more on providing the best service to their customers. But a problem arises, because every company, in every industry, wants to deliver quality customer service. Therefore the real issue before global business leaders is not "How do I offer and deliver stronger customer service?" Instead, the fundamental questions are, first, "How do I develop a global customer service strategy?" and second, "What must I actually do to deliver high-quality customer service globally?"

DEVELOPING A GLOBAL CUSTOMER SERVICE STRATEGY

For most companies doing global business, it is likely that the only thing their customers share is the fact that they buy the same products and services. Beyond basic product requirements, however, each global customer is as unique as the culture and nation from which it comes. In addition, global customers can differ in terms of product application, geographic area, market mix, and target markets.

A successful global customer service strategy must recognize customers' differences and then address these differences as fundamental parts of the global customer service strategy. This is best accomplished by:

- Customer-focused mind-set: learning what is most important to your customers
- Overdelivering: exceeding customer expectations
- Flexibility: the ability to respond quickly and appropriately
- Adaptability: growth requires continuous ability to embrace changes
- Delivering value: differentiating the company's offerings in a commoditized world
- Empathy: getting into the customer's thinking
- Spotting trends: listening for the future
- Reinforcing your message: reminding customers of how the company serves them

Customer-Focused Mind-Set: Learning What Is Most Important to Your Customers

Global customer service should be far more than a department title or a promotional slogan; it should be an integral part of the global strategic plan. Partnering with key suppliers to deliver recognized and measurable global customer service should be as much a part of the corporate culture as achieving sales goals, increasing inventory turns, or improving return on investment.

For the proper execution of a global customer strategy, a company must clearly understand the expectations and needs of its key customers. To best do this, many global firms learn as much as they can about the top 20 percent of their customers, who probably represent about 80 percent of their business according to Pareto's Rule of 80/20. Some of the ways they investigate include:

- Holding regular meetings with a key customer's functional management groups
- Meeting routinely with key distribution partners in each market where the company employs independent distributors or agents to market, sell, or service your company's products and services
- Conducting local market customer focus groups for the smaller customers (nonglobal account customers), consumers, etc.
- Engaging in discussions with end users of the company's products and services

- Observing firsthand selected customers' business and work processes and procedures in selected key markets (or all of their individual markets if necessary), especially as they relate to how customers use your products or services

- Documenting each key customer's or customer segments, industry segments, unique traits, and capabilities by individual market

- Sharing all relevant information with your company's own sales, marketing, manufacturing, and customer service personnel, which will help to enhance customer service globally and locally

Overdelivering: Exceeding Customer Expectations

Implementing successful global customer service requires carefully analyzing customers individually, the major customers' groups, and specific markets to find specific areas where a company can excel in terms of product and service offerings and the accompanying customer service to be provided, with the ultimate objective being to consistently exceed the customer's expectations. Some of the ways this can be accomplished include:

- Making it easy for customers to do business with the company

- Developing a website and pursuing e-commerce for product information, order entry, project status, etc.

- Demanding accurate and reliable shipping dates from vendors, and handling field installation and quality issues in a priority manner

- Keeping customers apprised of current codes and regulations, and sharing new product information from key suppliers

Flexibility: The Ability to Respond Quickly and Appropriately

The ability to be flexible and change quickly is fundamental to global business success. The great distances and dimensions that affect the normal conduct of global business demand that leaders maintain a high degree of flexibility. In addition to the routine customer service issues facing those who do business beyond their own domestic markets, things can get off track quickly and in a big way when a company elevates business to a multicontinental and global level, perhaps due to weather, material supply problems, or a myriad of other reasons. It can happen quite quickly and with little or no warning.

To constantly improve their level of global customer service, leaders align themselves with manufacturers and other suppliers who are also flexible. They also develop delivery programs unilaterally or with their suppliers that use their own warehouse facilities as a resource to always be best positioned to meet their global customers' service requirements.

Adaptability: Growth Requires Continuous Ability to Embrace Changes

In global markets, customer groups and market segments will most likely differ in terms of product requirements and service requirements from one market to another in each newly entered market. As with any new experience, bringing new product and service offerings will require certain amounts of adaptation to each local market's needs and wants, especially as experience in these markets grows and evolves.

Not only will your company's product and service offerings need to be adapted to each local market over time, so too will the customer service organization itself have to adapt to the changes in each market. Very often this will require that specific groups within the customer service organization assemble and become market or regional experts to ensure the proper level of localization and regionalization is brought to each market and region. These experts greatly assist in maintaining high-quality market and culturally sensitive customer service.

Unlike adapting to changes in a domestic market, global customer service organizations will need to either develop their own internal expertise or develop trusted alliances with local enterprises to serve as a channel of customer and consumer information and competitive product and service information. Such information is essential for the successful global company to identify trends in these faraway markets, which then enables the company to maintain and enhance the company's customer service, keeping it competitive.

Delivering Value: Differentiating the Company's Offerings in a Commoditized World

It is often said that "value is total benefits delivered minus price." If price is the only measurement for products and services, then there is usually no differentiating characteristic to the buyer in today's world of commoditized products and services. If there is no perceived value, product and service together becomes a commodity. Thus there is no measurable way to differentiate one supplier from another.

To assure value, global firms must partner to provide clear, consistent, and reliable product and service features that deliver measurable benefits to customers and end users. A few obvious (but often overlooked) traits of extraordinary customer service include quality products, complete and on-time deliveries, unexpected product and service features at no extra cost, professional and knowledgeable support staff, problem solving, and attention to detail.

Empathy: Getting into the Customer's Thinking

Global firms consider what they want from manufacturing partners; they certainly want more than a competitive price point. They want reliability, effective promotions, market intelligence, specification interpretation, loyalty, unique sales features, and polite and courteous personal attention. This list is basic, but it is not negotiable. All items must be present all the time to ensure satisfaction. A global customer service strategy makes sure that a firm is giving their customers the same consideration.

Spotting Trends: Listening for the Future

Global firms continually ask their customers what they want and what they expect. They try to spot trends before their competitors, and they carefully listen for subtle ways to improve their customer service. They also search for what their competitor is doing well, is not doing, or is doing poorly. Moreover, besides the salesperson selling the actual product or service, it is the customer service person who has ongoing contact and communication with customers and consumers using the product or service. In fact, even more than the salesperson, it is the customer service representative, whose primary responsibility is only servicing the customer, who is in the better position to probe customers and consumers in a nonthreatening manner, under the guise of servicing versus selling.

As the founder of Sony was once quoted as saying when he spotted a new emerging trend, "We do not create products, we create markets." His new company's initial success was launched with the development of the Sony Walkman to capitalize on the trends he saw with the emerging generation that embraced music as a new religion, i.e., the Woodstock Generation that needed to have music with them everywhere they went. So it is with a global company's customer service organization; they will need to work very closely with global marketing, sales, and product and service development groups to communicate the new trend information they receive from the customers. Additionally, the global customer service organization serves a vital role as a key conduit for these departments to initiate discussions with customers and consumers alike to elicit perceptions, opinions, experiences, and other needed information. With such invaluable information, the global company is in the best position to spot and confirm trends, and then to capitalize on these trends with new and enhanced product and service offerings.

Reinforcing Your Message: Reminding Customers of How the Company Serves Them

How customers view their suppliers may be directly related to how often they are reminded of how they are being supported. Global firms let their customers know what is done for them on a regular basis, in terms of both products delivered and customer service support.

KEY AREAS TO FOCUS UPON

To help you go further in delivering excellent customer service to customers globally, here are a few key areas upon which to focus.

Making Ordering Easy

Superior global customer service starts from the first customer contact; make it especially easy for your customers to order from you and order in many different ways to suit their own needs. This requires spending time adapting your company's ordering processes right down to the forms that you ask customers to fill out. A few key areas to pay close attention to are:

1. *Customer name and address*: Make sure you leave plenty of space for the name and address; foreign addresses tend to be a lot longer than U.S. addresses.

2. *Instructions*: If you are selling clothing or shoes, reduce the number of potential customer returns by providing easy access to easy-to-read size conversions. By adapting your product and service descriptions and order form into the local language and preferred color schemes, you will also reduce any possible confusion by the customer when they are ordering from you.

3. *Mailings*: If you are mailing anything directly to the customer, consider a multilingual format with ordering instructions in both English and all local languages. Also, be sure to specify that the customer should complete the information in printed Roman characters. If you do not, you may need to have your orders deciphered or translated. This will take a lot more time than you think, and the costs are high.

4. *Customer responses*: Provide your customers alternative and convenient ways to respond back to you, such as telephone, fax, mail, or Web. Most orders taken today in the United States still are done by telephone. This is not necessarily the case in other markets where the cost of a telephone call is much higher as compared to the United States, so most orders are placed via fax or through the mail. If you are selling business-to-business, you need to include an Internet option as well as a fax option. Despite the seemingly ubiquitous use of the Internet, many business-to-business orders are still received via fax.

Handling Customer Orders

If your company offers a telephone ordering option, carefully consider how your company will handle incoming calls from customers in foreign markets. How will your company route these calls to its domestic operation? Will your company set up facilities in Europe, in Asia, etc.? Differing cultures, multiple languages, time, and operating costs are key reasons why it often makes sense to set up an overseas call center. While many people living outside of North America comprehend and speak English to varying degrees, they typically feel more comfortable talking in their native language when placing orders and for requesting service.

An overseas customer call center may make financial sense, too. It is generally less costly to have a large volume of calls that originate in Europe also terminate in Europe at a European call center versus a U.S.-based call center. Also, if non-domestic calls are being routed to the U.S.-based call center, make sure your company considers time zone changes when it schedules its customer call center hours.

One aspect of handling customer orders to particularly consider is payment alternatives. Be sure your company understands the preferred methods of payment in each local market, and then offer a variety of market-appropriate payment options. The United States and Canada are still largely check-based economies, whereas most of the rest of the world (industrialized or developing markets) are transaction-based economies that use either direct debit or bank transfer. Also, cash on delivery, check, and payment by invoice may be other options to consider.

Unlike the United States and Canada, it would be a mistake to assume that customers will pay by credit card. In much of Europe and especially in Germany, the payment for most mail-order goods is done on open account; in other words, customers are billed only after the product is received and in good order.

Product Fulfillment

Product fulfillment depends on the products your company is shipping, your company's acceptable turnaround time, and its investment in its global markets, including its global customer service. If your company is in the early stages of developing its global business or if it has products with relatively low rates of return, it should generally consider using your current domestic fulfillment operation. If your company's strategy is committed to establishing a fully globalized business or it has products that have high rates of return, it may be better to set up foreign product fulfillment operations or hire a local market firm to handle local order fulfillment.

How your company ships products will impact delivery time. It will be a lot cheaper to ship products via ocean freight, but your company will definitely save more time by sending your products by airfreight.

Also, if you are shipping products as individual orders and the U.S. Postal Service (USPS) or your company's freight consolidator uses the USPS as its delivery agent, the order travels as mail from your company to the customer. This can be quite expensive. Alternatively, if the package is being shipped from the United States for delivery by a host market postal administration, the package travels to the destination country as cargo and then it becomes mail upon entering the postal system of the destination country, a process that is typically at lower cost to the shipping company, your company.

If your company is distributing from a nondomestic fulfillment location, products usually leave the United States in bulk. Then the products are usually delivered to your company's overseas operation or a contracted operation in the local market. The local fulfillment operation then separates the merchandise, and packages and addresses the orders. Packages then enter the local market postal distribution system via an optimized and cost-effective fulfillment scheme.

Customer Returns and Refunds

To provide superior customer service, companies should not allow currency fluctuations to impact a customer's refund. Customers around the world should be reimbursed at the same conversion rate as when the sale was processed. Companies and customers should not seek to make or lose money on returns or refunds.

Decisions to reimburse customers for postage spent to return an item usually depend on your company's profit margin on that product or that specific order or order type. If margins are substantial, companies may want to refund the customer for any shipping costs incurred to demonstrate its dedication to superior customer service and to motivate the customer for future purchases.

CREATING GLOBAL CUSTOMER SERVICE STANDARDS

When creating standards for global customer service, global firms make certain that they are measurable. For example, one objective may be 100 percent packing accuracy. Packing inspection of 100 percent packing inspection is not an objective. It is one possible solution. Packing inspection is only one task of many that could achieve the objective. Other tasks or alternatives may be more effective for accomplishing the objective.

How will you measure the objective on an ongoing basis? If you cannot measure an objective, you will never know whether it was achieved. For example, 100 percent shipping accuracy may be measured using statistical sampling after final packing but prior to shipment.

Establish Global Customer Service Rules and Constraints

Identify key restrictions (hard rules) and guidelines (soft rules) that will form the boundaries around the customer service strategy. These rules include company policies, expected return on investment, project organization, personnel availability, computer system development/support constraints, and internal operations procedures.

The rules represent key compromises between revenue producers (customer support, marketing, and sales personnel) with operations, engineering, MIS, and other project resources. Only upper management can change the rules and guidelines after the project starts. These rules are the foundation for effective communication and timely decision making.

Disassemble Each Objective into Unique Tasks

A task identifies what must be accomplished, not how. After analyzing the objectives, clearly identify what tasks are within the scope of the global customer service team and prioritize the tasks to optimize dependencies and return on investment. The task definition and sequence is very critical to the effectiveness of the program.

It is important to establish minimum customer service standards, make sure everyone understands them, and have a way to recognize superior performance. As procedures are developed, be sure that all three criteria are satisfied. Use creative problem-solving techniques to develop a list of feasible solutions for the task. Select a combination of possible solutions that will accomplish the objective with minimal ongoing effort.

MAINTAINING GLOBAL CUSTOMER SERVICE STANDARDS

Beyond developing a global customer service strategy, a global firm must maintain customer service standards for their employees, suppliers, and, ultimately, their customers. Unfortunately, some companies have been unwilling to enhance their customer service functions and create standards because they assumed it was not required, or the benefits did not appear tangible. Historically, it was wiser to wait until external circumstances (e.g., economic conditions, product trends) appeared imminent and then react. In today's global economy, however, such thinking is clearly contradictory to the proactive global customer service approach demanded if a company is to transform itself into a truly successful global company competing in the new global marketplace.

What Are the Standards We Are Maintaining?

Maintaining standards may involve the weekly or monthly analysis of the measurement of a company's global customer service standards. Such questions as "Can we offer additional services that the customer may not be aware we offer?"

or "What would it take to have the customer use only our services?" make this process more fluid and responsive to customer needs.

Handling Complaints

Companies must maintain standards for the handling of complaints. One study by the Technical Assistance Research Program Institute shows that 70 percent of unhappy global customers will not make another purchase from the offending firm. On the other hand, 95 percent of customers will return if their complaint is resolved quickly. It goes without saying that effective, speedy resolution of complaints keeps customers happy.

CONCLUSION

Successful global customer service does not just happen. It must be planned, implemented, monitored, and then continually refined. The creation of a global customer service strategy and the organization to deliver it successfully requires fine-tuning new management processes to bring about exceptional customer service on a global scale. Shifting an organization's central focus from primarily domestic customers to customers in markets in the four corners of the world means that extraordinary multicultural customer relations and service will need to become a natural operating procedure for the aspiring global customer service organization. When customers from markets around the world feel that they are the central and primary concern of a company, they buy more and repeatedly from that company regardless of where that company may be located, whether it is around the corner or around the world.

Making the shift from a domestically focused customer service approach to a global customer service approach requires a complete change of mind-set of how a company does business. Such new thinking will undoubtedly require customer service executives to concentrate on the critical success factors of people, process, technology, and environment, and all of these at a global level. Ultimately, a tight focus on these critical factors leads to the creation of an environment that supports the acquisition and maintenance of the right people, the right processes, and the right technology to compete on a global basis.

In the exploding borderless economy, a long-term dedication to not only developing a full global customer service strategy but also evolving such a strategy when implemented as a comprehensive approach to building the total global company will undoubtedly produce a true, sustainable competitive advantage.

INDEX

Note: Page numbers followed by f indicate figure.

About the Editor and Contributors

BRUCE D. KEILLOR is a professor of marketing and international business and director of the Williamson Center for International Business at Youngstown State University. He has published over 100 journal articles and is the author of *Winning in the Global Market: A Practical Guide to International Business Success* as well as general editor of the three-volume set *International Business in the 21st Century* and the four-volume set *Marketing in the 21st Century*. He also serves on the board of several U.S. firms. He received his MBA from Minnesota State University and his PhD from the University of Memphis.

ROBERT BLACK has over 30 years of experience as a corporate executive and is a registered professional engineer. A highly successful entrepreneur, he is the inventor and marketer of Clean Shower.

JOHN CASLIONE is the founder of GCS Business Capital. He serves as director and advisor for a number of companies in the United States, Asia, and Europe. He earned his MBA from the University of New York and his JD from the Illinois Institute of Technology.

KEN DICKEY is the cofounder of The Institute of Strategic Mapping. He has served as president/CEO of the multinational Cleveland Motion Controls. Prior to that he served in an executive capacity for Reliance/Rockwell Automation and Reliance Electrical Industrial Motors. He holds an Executive MBA from Case Western Reserve University.

JASON DILAURO served as vice president and senior financial advisor for Merrill Lynch.

WILLIAM J. HAUSER is an associate professor and the director of the Suarez Institute at the University of Akron. Before joining academia he served for over 20 years as an executive for Rubber Maid, Inc., Little Tykes, and Key Bank. He is ranked as one of the foremost experts in the fields of direct marketing and market analytics.

JON M. HAWES is a retired professor emeritus at the University of Akron. He is also the founding director of the Fisher Institute for Professional Selling at the University of Akron.

GRETCHEN M. KEILLOR is a partner with BBA Associates, a social media and marketing consulting firm. Her clients range from Fortune 500 firms to small local businesses. She specializes in developing integrated social media marketing strategies.

GARY A. KNIGHT is a professor at Florida State University. He has written over 100 articles and books and serves on numerous editorial boards. He obtained his MBA from the University of Washington and his PhD from Michigan State University and was an executive in industry before joining academia. He speaks fluent Japanese and French.

DANIEL J. LESLIE has been an active salesperson and sales manager for several Fortune 500 firms including Northwestern Mutual. He is a certified coach and specializes in sales force strategy.

DALE M. LEWISON is a retired professor of marketing at the University of Akron and founding director of the Taylor Institute for Direct Marketing at the University of Akron.

STEPHEN M. MILLETT is a futurist and leader of Technology Foresight at Social Technologies. He is coauthor of *A Manager's Guide to Technology Forecasting and Analysis Methods*. He has also authored several dozen professional articles dealing with forecasting and proactively managing the future.

LINDA M. ORR is a professor of marketing and the former director of the Fisher Institute for Professional Selling at the University of Akron. A recognized expert in professional selling and sales force management, she specializes in relationship-based selling and relational marketing. She received her PhD from the University of Mississippi.

NADJI TEHRANI is the founder, chairman, and CEO of Technology Marketing Corporation. Over the years he has served in an executive capacity in a variety of organizations around the world. He is acknowledged as one of the pioneers in the telemarketing industry and owns the copyright for the term "telemarketing."

VERN TERPSTRA is emeritus professor of international business at the University of Michigan. He has served as a visiting professor in Hong Kong, Indonesia, Taiwan, the Netherlands, and England.

CALIN VEGHES is senior lecturer, Department of Marketing, Faculty of Marketing, Academy of Economic Studies, Bucharest, Romania.